The Fundamentals of Emotive Behaviour Therapy

A Training Handbook

Second Edition

by

Windy Dryden
and
Rhena Branch

John Wiley & Sons, Ltd

Other Wiley Editorial Offices

John Wiley & Sons Inc., 111 River Street, Hoboken, NJ 07030, USA

Jossey-Bass, 989 Market Street, San Francisco, CA 94103-1741, USA

Wiley-VCH Verlag GmbH, Boschstr. 12, D-69469 Weinheim, Germany

John Wiley & Sons Australia Ltd, 42 McDougall Street, Milton, Queensland 4064, Australia

John Wiley & Sons (Asia) Pte Ltd, 2 Clementi Loop #02-01, Jin Xing Distripark, Singapore 129809

John Wiley & Sons Canada Ltd, 6045 Freemont Blvd, Mississauga, ONT, L5R 4J3, Canada

Wiley also publishes its books in a variety of electronic formats. Some content that appears in print
may not be available in electronic books.

Library of Congress Cataloging-in-Publication Data

Dryden, Windy.
    The fundamentals of rational emotive behaviour therapy : a training handbook / by Windy Dryden &
Rhena Branch. – 2nd ed.
        p. ; cm.
    Includes bibliographical references and index.
        ISBN 978-0-470-31932-1 (cloth : alk. paper) – ISBN 978-0-470-31931-4 (pbk. : alk. paper) 1.
Rational emotive behavior therapy–Handbooks, manuals, etc.
    I. Branch, Rhena. II. Title.
        [DNLM: 1. Psychotherapy, Rational-Emotive–methods. 2. Behavior Therapy–methods.
WM 420.5.P8 D799fa 2008]
    RC489.R3D7866 2008
    616.89'14–dc22
                                                2008002742

British Library Cataloguing in Publication Data

A catalogue record for this book is available from the British Library

ISBN 978-0-470-31932-1 (hbk) 978-0-470-31931-4 (pbk)

Typeset in 10/13pt Scala and Scala Sans by Thomson Digital, India
Printed and bound in Great Britain by CPI Antony Rowe, Chippenham, Wiltshire

Contents

About the authors

Windy Dryden is Professor of Psychotherapeutic Studies, Goldsmiths, University of London. He is a Fellow of the British Psychological Society and of the British Association of Counselling and Psychotherapy. He began his training in REBT in 1977 and became the first Briton to be accredited as an REBT therapist by the Albert Ellis Institute. In 1981, Windy spent a six-month sabbatical at the Center for Cognitive Therapy, University of Pennsylvania, one of the first British psychologists to do an extended training in Cognitive Therapy. He is a Fellow of the Albert Ellis Institute and a Founding Fellow of the Academy of Cognitive Therapy.

While his primary therapeutic orientation is REBT, Windy has been very much influenced by his cognitive therapy colleagues and by the working alliance theory of Ed Bordin. His research interests are in the historical and theoretical roots of REBT (with Arthur Still) and the phenomenology of hurt, the study of which is informed by REBT theory.

Windy is perhaps best known for his voluminous writings in REBT/CBT and the wider field of counselling and psychotherapy. To date he has authored or edited over 160 books, making him probably the most prolific book writer and editor currently alive in the field today. He has also edited 17 book series including the best selling 'Counselling in Action' series.

Windy was the founding editor of the *British Journal of Cognitive Psychotherapy* in 1982 which later merged with the *Cognitive Behaviorist* to become the *Journal of Cognitive Psychotherapy: An International Quarterly*. Windy was co-founding editor of this journal with E. Thomas Dowd. In 2003, Windy became the editor of the *Journal of Rational-Emotive and Cognitive-Behavior Therapy*.

Rhena Branch is an accredited CBT therapist. Rhena runs her own private practice in North London and also teaches on the Masters (MSc RECBT) at Goldsmith's University.

Introduction

Having given numerous introductory training courses in Rational Emotive Behaviour Therapy (REBT) in Britain and throughout the world, it seemed to me (WD) that it would be valuable to write a training handbook on the fundamentals of REBT in which we attempt to recreate the atmosphere of these training courses. In particular, because REBT is a simple approach that is difficult to practise well, we wanted to alert trainees to areas of difficulty that they are likely to experience while attempting to use the approach and show them how they can deal constructively with the problems that they will doubtless encounter along the way.

To do this, we have used constructed verbatim transcript material between trainees and ourselves as trainer. What this means is that to highlight trainee difficulty and trainer response, we have constructed dialogues that approximate those that have occurred between ourselves and our trainees over the years. None of these dialogues have actually taken place, however. As we do not record our training sessions, we do not have access to actual trainer–trainee dialogues that have occurred. Nevertheless, the constructed dialogues illustrate the typical errors that trainees make in the practice of REBT. In addition, we will make extensive use of actual and constructed dialogue between ourselves as therapist and our clients. Where the dialogue was real, we have obtained permission from clients to use our therapeutic work for educational purposes. In these cases, we have changed all names, some clients' gender and all identifying material.

Please note that on introductory training programmes in REBT, peer counselling is used extensively as a training vehicle. This means that trainees form a pair and take turns counselling one another on real emotional problems and concerns using REBT. In our experience this is a far more effective way of learning how to use REBT and what it feels like to be an REBT client than the use of role-plays. To preserve confidentiality, any dialogue that appears in this book between trainees in peer counselling has also been constructed. However, these dialogues are typical of the emotional problems that are raised in this part of the course by trainees in the client role. The performance of REBT trainees in these interchanges approximates the level of skill beginning trainees tend to demonstrate on introductory training courses.

It is important for us to stress that no book on Rational Emotive Behaviour Therapy, however practical, can be a substitute for proper training and supervision in the approach. Thus, this book is best used as an adjunct to these educational activities. We have provided information on where to get training and supervision in REBT in Appendix III, should you be interested in pursuing your interest in this therapeutic approach. Indeed, we hope that this handbook might encourage you to attend initial and more advanced training courses in REBT so that you can learn for yourself what it has to offer you and your clients.

As we said earlier, this training handbook deals with the fundamentals of REBT practice. As such, we have omitted issues of greater complexity, which may distract you from learning the basics. Let us briefly summarise what we will cover in this volume. In the first two chapters, we outline the basic theoretical and practical information that you need to begin to practise REBT. In the third chapter, we present material on how to teach your clients the 'ABCs' of REBT, whilst in the fourth chapter, we deal with the important issue of helping your clients to distinguish between healthy and unhealthy emotions. In Chapter 5, we stress that when you come to assess your clients' problems, at the outset it is important to be specific. In Chapters 6, 7 and 8, we show you how to assess 'C', 'A' and irrational beliefs respectively. Then, in Chapter 9, we discuss how you can assess your clients' meta-emotional problems and when to work with them in therapy. In Chapter 10, we go on to deal with the important issue of helping your clients to set goals, while in Chapter 11, we show you how to build on goal-setting by encouraging your clients to make a commitment to change. At the heart of REBT is the key task of disputing clients' irrational beliefs and we devote the next four chapters (Chapters 12–15) to disputing. Then, in Chapter 16, we discuss how to help clients construct rational alternatives to their irrational beliefs and how to question these constructed rational beliefs. In the next two chapters, we discuss how to negotiate homework assignments with your clients (Chapter 17) and how to review them (Chapter 18). We conclude the book (Chapter 19) by discussing how you can deal with your clients' misconceptions of REBT theory and practice.

Throughout this book we will address you directly as if you are on one of our training courses. Please note that we will alternate the gender of the client.

We hope that you find this training handbook of use and that it stimulates your interest to develop your skills in REBT.

Windy Dryden & Rhena Branch

London

December, 2007

What you need to know about the theory of rational emotive behaviour therapy to get started

Most books on counselling and psychotherapy begin by introducing you to the theory and practice of the approach in question. This is obviously a sensible way to start such a book because otherwise how are you to understand the practical techniques described by the author(s)? However, in our experience as readers of such books, we are often given more information than we need about an approach to begin to practise it, at least in the context of a training setting. As we explained in the introduction, our aim in this training handbook is to recreate the atmosphere of a beginning training seminar in REBT. In such seminars the emphasis is on the acquisition of practical skills and, consequently, theory is kept to a minimum. What we aim to do in such seminars and what we will do in this opening chapter is to introduce the information you will need to know about the theory of REBT so that you can begin to practise it in a training seminar setting. In the following chapter, we will cover what you need to know about the *practice* of REBT to get started.

Let us reiterate a point that we made in the introduction. When learning any approach to counselling and psychotherapy, you will need to be trained by a competent trainer in the approach you are learning and supervised in your work with clients by a competent supervisor in that approach. To do otherwise is bad and, some would say, unethical practice. Certainly, when learning to practise REBT you will need to be trained and supervised by people competent not only in the practice of REBT, but also in educating others how to use it (see Appendix III). A book such as this, then, is designed to supplement not to replace such training and supervision.

► The situational 'ABC' model of rational emotive behaviour therapy

Rational Emotive Behaviour Therapy is one of the cognitive-behavioural approaches to psychotherapy. This means that it pays particular attention to the role that cognitions and behaviour play in the development and maintenance of people's emotional problems. However, as we will presently show, REBT argues that at the core of emotional disturbance lies a set of irrational beliefs that people hold about themselves, other people and the world.

When assessing clients' psychological problems, REBT therapists employ a situational 'ABC' framework and we will now discuss each element of this framework in turn.

Situations

In this handbook, you will learn how to help your clients deal with their problems by working with specific examples of these problems. These specific examples occur in specific 'situations'. Such 'situations' are viewed in the 'situational ABC' model as *descriptions* of actual events about which you form inferences (see below). Briefly, inferences go beyond the data at hand and may be accurate or inaccurate.

'Situations' exist in time. Thus, they can describe past actual events (e.g. 'My boss asked me to see her at the end of the day'), present actual events (e.g. 'My boss is asking me to see her at the end of the day'). or future events (e.g. 'My boss will ask me to see her at the end of the day'). Note that we have not referred to such future events as future actual events since we do not know that such events will occur and this is why such future events may prove to be false. But if we look at such future 'situations', they are still descriptions of what may happen and do not add inferential meaning (see below).

'Situations' may refer to internal actual events (i.e. events that occur within ourselves, e.g. thoughts, feelings, bodily sensations, aches and pains, etc.) or to external actual events (i.e. events that occur outside ourselves, e.g. your boss asking to see you). Their defining characteristic is as before: they are descriptions of events and do not include inferential meaning.

'As'

'As' are usually aspects of situations which your client is potentially able to discern and attend to and which can trigger his beliefs at 'B'. Whilst your client is potentially able to focus on different 'As' at any moment, in an 'ABC' episode, what we call the 'critical A' represents that actual or psychological event in his life which activates, at that moment, the beliefs that he holds (at 'B') and which lead to his emotional and behavioural responses (at 'C'). The key ingredient of a 'critical A' is that it activates or triggers beliefs. A 'critical A' is usually an aspect of the situation that your client was in when he experienced an emotional response. The other 'As' that he could have focused on in that situation, but didn't may be regarded as 'non-critical As' in that they did not trigger his beliefs in the situation.

'Critical As' have a number of features that we will explain below.

'Critical As' can be actual events When actual events serve as belief-triggering 'As' they do not contain any inferences that your client adds to the event.

> While Susan was in therapy, her mother died. She felt very sad about this event and grieved appropriately. Using the 'ABC' framework to understand this we can say that the death of her mother represented an actual event at 'A' which activated a set of beliefs that underpinned Susan's grief.

'Critical As' can be inferred events

> When Wendy was in therapy, her mother died. Like Susan she felt very sad about this and as such we can say that the death was an actual 'critical A', which triggered her sadness-related beliefs. However, unlike Susan, Wendy also felt guilty in relation to her mother's death. How can we explain this?

According to REBT, people make interpretations and inferences about the events in their lives. We regard interpretations and inferences as hunches about reality that go beyond observable data which may be correct or incorrect, but need to be tested out. Whilst most REBT therapists regard interpretations and inferences to be synonymous, we make the following distinction between them. Interpretations are hunches about reality that go beyond observable data, but are not personally significant to the person making them. They are, thus, not implicated in the person's emotional experience. Inferences are also hunches about reality that go beyond the data at hand, but unlike interpretations they *are* personally significant to the person making them. They are, then, implicated in the person's emotional experience.

For example, imagine that I (RB) am standing with my face to a window and I ask you to describe what I am doing. If you say, 'You are looking out of the window', you are making an interpretation in that you are going beyond the data at hand (e.g. I could have my eyes closed) in an area that is probably insignificant to you (i.e. it probably doesn't matter to you whether I have my eyes open or not) and thus you will not have an emotional response while making the interpretation.

However, imagine that in response to my request for you to describe what I was doing in this example, you said, 'You are ridiculing me.' This, then, is an inference in that you are going beyond the data available to you in an area that is probably significant to you (i.e. it probably matters to you whether or not I am ridiculing you) and thus you will have an emotional response while making the inference. Whether this emotional response is healthy or not, however, depends on the type of belief you hold about the inferred ridicule.

Returning to the example of Wendy who felt guilty about the death of her mother, we hope you can now see that she is guilty not about the death itself, but about some inferred aspect of the death that is significant to her. In this case it emerged that Wendy felt guilty about hurting her mother's feelings when she was alive. This, then, is an inferred 'critical A' – it points to something beyond the data available to Wendy; it is personally significant to her and it triggered her guilt-producing belief.

'Critical As' can be external or internal   So far we have discussed 'critical As' that relate to events that have actually happened (e.g. the death of Susan's mother) or were deemed to have happened (e.g. Wendy's inference that she hurt her mother's feelings when she was alive). In REBT, these are known as external events in that they are external to the person concerned. Thus, the death of Susan's mother is an actual external 'critical A' and Wendy's statement that she hurt her mother's feelings is an inferred external 'critical A'.

However, 'critical As' can also refer to events that are <u>internal</u> to the person. Such events can actually occur or their existence can be inferred.

An example of an actual internal event is when Bill experiences a pain in his throat. An example of an inferred internal event is when Bill thinks that this pain means that he has throat cancer. When Bill is anxious in this situation, the inferred internal event ('I have cancer') is more likely to trigger his irrational belief than the actual internal event ('I have a pain in my throat'). As such the inferred internal 'A' is critical and the actual internal 'A' is non-critical.

As well as bodily sensations, internal 'As' can refer to such phenomena as a person's thoughts, images, fantasies, emotions and memories.

It is important to remember that, as with external 'As', internal 'As' have their emotional impact by triggering beliefs at 'B'. When they do they are regarded as critical and when they do not they are regarded as non-critical.

'Critical As' can refer to past, present and future events   Just as 'As' can be actual or inferred and external or internal, they can also refer to past, present or future events. Before we discuss the time-dimensional nature of 'As', remember that the 'critical A' in an 'ABC' episode, by definition, is that part of the person's total perceptual field which triggers his belief at 'B'.

When your client's 'A' in an 'ABC' episode is a past actual event, then she does not bring any inferential meaning to this event. Thus, if her father died when she was a teenager, this very event can serve as a 'critical A'. However, more frequently, particularly in therapy, you will find that your clients will bring inferential meaning to past events. Thus, your client may infer that her father's death meant that she was deprived in some way or she may infer that his passing away was a punishment for some misdeed that she was responsible for as a child. It is important to remember that it is the inferences your client makes now about a past event that triggers her beliefs at 'B'. Such inferences may relate to the past, present and future.

> An example of a future-related inference that your client might make about an actual past event is as follows:
>
> > Because my father died when I was a teenager, I will continually look for a father figure to replace him.

We have already discussed present 'As'. However, we do want to stress that your clients can make past-, present- or future-related inferences about present events.

> For example, if one of your clients has disturbed feelings about his son coming home late (present actual 'A'), he may make the following time-related inferences about this event that trigger his disturbance-provoking beliefs:
>
> 1. Past-related inference: 'He reminds me of the rough kids at school who used to bully me when I was a teenager.'
> 2. Present-related inference: 'He is breaking our agreement.'
> 3. Future-related inference: 'If he does this now he will turn into a criminal.'

The importance of assuming temporarily that the 'critical A' is true As we will show in greater detail in Chapter 7, in order to assess a client's beliefs accurately you will need to do two things. First, you will need to help your client to identify the 'critical A' which triggered these beliefs. Because there are many potential 'As' that are in your client's perceptual field, it takes a lot of care and skill to do this accurately. To distinguish between the 'A' that triggered the client's beliefs and the other 'A's' in his perceptual field, we have adopted the convention where the former is called the 'critical A' and the latter, 'non-critical As'. Second, it is important that you encourage your client to assume temporarily that the 'critical A' is true when it is an inferred 'A'. The reason for doing this is to help your client to identify the beliefs that the 'critical A' triggered. You may well be tempted to help your client to challenge the inferred 'critical A' if it is obviously distorted, but it is important for you to resist this temptation if you are to proceed to assess B accurately.

This is such an important point that we wish to emphasise it.

> Assume temporarily that your client's 'critical A' is true when it is an inferred 'A'

'Bs'

A major difference between REBT and other approaches to cognitive-behaviour therapy is in the emphasis REBT gives to beliefs. In REBT, beliefs are at the core of clients' emotions and significant behaviours. Such beliefs are the only cognitions that constitute the 'B' in the 'ABC' framework in REBT. Thus, whilst other approaches which use an 'ABC' framework lump all cognitive activity under 'B', REBT reserves B for beliefs and places inferences, for example, under 'A'. It does so because it recognises that it is possible to hold two different types of beliefs at 'B' about the same inferred 'As'. It is the type of belief that determines the nature of the person's emotional response at 'C'.

Let us stress this point because it is very important that you fully grasp it.

> In REBT, beliefs are the only cognitions that constitute 'B' in the 'ABC' framework

Rational beliefs REBT keenly distinguishes between rational and irrational beliefs. In this section, we will discuss rational beliefs. When applied to beliefs, the term 'rational' has five defining characteristics as shown in Figure 1.1.

<u>Rational beliefs are:</u>

Flexible or non-extreme

Consistent with reality

Logical

Largely functional in their emotional, behavioural and cognitive consequences

Largely helpful to the individual in pursuing his basic goals and purposes

Figure 1.1 Defining characteristics of rational beliefs

People do not only proceed in life by making descriptions of what they perceive, nor do they just make interpretations and inferences of their perceptions. Rather, we engage in the fundamentally important activity of holding beliefs about what we perceive and infer. REBT theory posits that people have four types of rational beliefs as shown in Figure 1.2.

Non-dogmatic preferences

Non-awfulising beliefs

High frustration tolerance (HFT) beliefs

Self-acceptance/Other-acceptance/Life-acceptance beliefs

Figure 1.2 Four types of rational beliefs

Non-dogmatic preferences   As humans we often express our flexible beliefs in the form of preferences, wishes, desires, wants, etc. According to REBT, our non-dogmatic preferences are at the core of psychological health.

> Non-dogmatic preferences are often expressed thus:
>
> 'I want to do well in my forthcoming test ('asserted preference' component), but I do not have to do so ('negated demand' component).'

If only the first part of this rational belief was expressed which we call the 'asserted preference' component – 'I want to do well in my forthcoming test' then your client could, implicitly, change this to a demand, which as we shall see, REBT theory considers an irrational belief – 'I want to do well in my forthcoming test... (and therefore I have to do so)'. So, it is important to help your client express fully his non-dogmatic preference and this involves helping him to include *both* the 'asserted preference' component (i.e. 'I want to do well in my forthcoming test') *and* the 'negated demand' component (i.e. 'but I do not have to do so').

> In short, we have:
>
> Non-dogmatic preference = 'Asserted preference' component + 'Negated demand' component

This non-dogmatic preference belief is rational for the following reasons:

- It is flexible in that your client allows for the fact that he might not do well.

- It is consistent with reality in that (a) your client really does want to do well in the forthcoming test and (b) there is no law of the universe dictating that he has to do well.

- It is logical in that both the 'asserted preference' component and the 'negated demand' component are not rigid and thus the latter follows from the former.

- It will help your client to have immediate functional emotions, behaviours and cognitions and help him pursue his longer-term goals. Thus, the rational belief will motivate him to focus on what he is doing as opposed to how well he is doing it.

According to Albert Ellis, the originator of REBT, a non-dogmatic preference is a primary rational belief and three other rational beliefs are derived from it. These beliefs are non-awfulising beliefs, high frustration tolerance beliefs and self-, other- and life-acceptance beliefs and we will deal with each in turn. In doing so, we will emphasise and illustrate the importance of negating the irrational belief component in formulating a rational belief in each of these derivatives.

Non-awfulising beliefs When your client does not get his non-dogmatic preference met, then it is rational for him to conclude that it is bad, but not awful that he has failed to get what he wanted. The more important his non-dogmatic preference, then the more unfortunate is his failure to get it. Evaluations of badness can be placed on a continuum from 0 %–99.99 % badness. However, it is not possible to get to 100 % badness. The words of the mother of pop singer Smokey Robinson capture this concept quite nicely: 'From the day you are born till you ride in the hearse, there's nothing so bad that it couldn't be worse.' This should not be thought of as minimising the badness of a very negative event, rather to show that 'nothing is truly awful in the universe'.

> Taking our example of the client whose primary rational belief is: 'I want to do well in my forthcoming test, but I do not have to do so', his full non-awfulising belief is:
>
> 'It will be bad if I fail to do well in my forthcoming test ('asserted badness' component), but it is not awful if I don't do well ('negated awfulising' component).'

If only the first part of this rational belief was expressed which we call the 'asserted badness' component – 'It will be bad if I fail to do well in my forthcoming test' then your client could, implicitly, change this to an awfulising belief, which as we shall see, REBT theory considers an irrational belief – 'It will be bad if I fail to do well in my forthcoming test... (and therefore it will be awful if I don't do well).' So, it is important to help your client express fully his non-awfulising belief and this involves helping him to include <u>both</u> the 'asserted badness' component (i.e. 'It will be bad if I fail to do well in my forthcoming test') *and* the 'negated awfulising' component (i.e. 'but it is not awful if I don't do well').

> In short, we have:
>
> Non-awfulising belief = 'Asserted badness' component + 'Negated awfulising' component

This non-awfulising belief is rational for the following reasons:

- It is non-extreme in that your client allows for the fact that there are things that can be worse than not doing well on the test.
- It is consistent with reality in that your client really can prove that it would be bad for him not to do well and that it isn't awful.

- It is logical in that both the 'asserted badness' component and the 'negated awfulising' component are non-extreme and thus the latter follows logically from the former.

- It will help your client to have immediate functional emotions, behaviours and cognitions and help him pursue his longer-term goals. Thus, the non-awfulising belief will again motivate him to focus on what he is doing as opposed to how well he is doing it.

High frustration tolerance beliefs   When your client does not get his non-dogmatic preference met, then it is rational for him to conclude that while this is difficult to bear, it is not *intolerable* to do so and it is worth tolerating. Adhering to a philosophy of high frustration tolerance (HFT) enables your client to put up with the frustration of having his goals blocked and in doing so he is more likely to deal with or circumvent these obstacles so that he can get back on track. REBT holds that the importance of developing a philosophy of HFT is that it helps people to pursue their goals, not because tolerating frustration is in itself good for people.

Applying this to our example, when your client believes: 'I want to do well in my forthcoming test, but I do not have to do so', his HFT belief will be:

'If I don't do well in my forthcoming test, that will be difficult to bear ('asserted struggle' component), but I can stand it. It will not be intolerable ('negated unbearability' component) and it is worth it for me to tolerate it ('worth tolerating' component).'

If only the first part of this rational belief was expressed which we call the 'asserted struggle' component – 'If I don't do well in my forthcoming test, that will be difficult to bear' then your client could, implicitly, change this to a low frustration tolerance (LFT) belief, which as we shall see, REBT theory considers an irrational belief – 'If I don't do well in my forthcoming test, that will be difficult to bear … (and therefore I can't stand it if I don't do well)'. So, it is important to help your client express fully his HFT belief and this involves helping him to include all three components: the 'asserted struggle' component ('If I don't do well in my forthcoming test, that will be difficult to bear'); the 'negated unbearability' component ('but I can stand it. It will not be intolerable' and the 'worth tolerating' component ('and it is worth it for me to tolerate it'). The latter component, which we think of as the motivational component is particularly important as it gives the client reasons to tolerate the adversity.

In short, we have:

High frustration tolerance belief = 'Asserted struggle' component + 'Negated unbearability' component + 'Worth tolerating' component

This high frustration tolerance belief is rational for the following reasons:

- It is non-extreme in that the person allows for the fact that not doing well is tolerable as opposed to the extreme position that it is unbearable.

- It is consistent with reality in that the person (i) recognises the struggle involved in putting up with the adversity, (ii) acknowledges the truth that he really can bear that which is difficult to tolerate and (iii) can see the truth that it is in his interests to put up with the adversity.

- It is logical in that the 'asserted struggle' component and the 'negated unbearability' component are both non-extreme and thus the latter follows logically from the former.

- It will help him to have immediate functional emotions, behaviour and thoughts and help him pursue his longer-term goals. Thus, it will help him to do well in the sense that it will lead him to focus on what he needs to do to avoid the 'difficult to tolerate' situation of not doing well rather than on the 'intolerable' aspects of doing poorly.

Self-, other- and life-acceptance beliefs   In this section, we will focus on self-acceptance beliefs. However, the same substantive points apply to other-acceptance beliefs and life-acceptance beliefs. When your client does not get his non-dogmatic preference met and this failure can be attributed to himself, for example, then it is rational for him not to like his behaviour, but to accept himself as a fallible human being who has acted poorly. Adopting a philosophy of self-acceptance, for example, will encourage your client to focus on what needs to be done to correct his own behaviour.

> In our example, if your client who believes: 'I want to do well in my forthcoming test, but I do not have to do so', fails to do well on this test because of his own failings, then his self-accepting belief will be:
>
> 'I don't like the fact that I messed up on the test ('negatively evaluated aspect' component), but I am not unworthy for my poor performance ('negated global negative evaluation' component). Rather I am a fallible human being too complex to be rated on the basis of my test performance ('asserted complexity/unrateability/fallibility' component).'

If only the first two parts of this rational belief were expressed which we call the 'negatively evaluated aspect' component – 'I don't like the fact that I messed up on the test' and the 'negated global negative evaluation' component – 'but I am not unworthy for my poor performance' then the person could, implicitly, change this to a self-depreciating statement, which (as we shall see) REBT theory considers an irrational belief – 'I don't like the fact that I messed up on the test, but I am not unworthy for my poor performance (but I would be worthier if I did well than if I did poorly).' So, it is important to help your client express fully his self-acceptance belief and this involves helping him to include all three components: the 'negatively evaluated aspect' component ('I don't like the fact that I messed up on the test'); the 'negated global negative evaluation' component ('but I am not unworthy for my poor performance') and the 'asserted complexity/unrateability/fallibility' component ('Rather I am a fallible human being too complex to be rated on the basis of my test performance').

In short, we have:

Acceptance belief = 'Negatively evaluated aspect' component + 'Negated global negative evaluation' component + 'Asserted complex fallibility' component.

This self-acceptance belief is rational for the following reasons:

- It is non-extreme in that the person sees that he is able to perform well and also poorly.

- It is consistent with reality in that whilst he can prove that he did not do well on the test (remember that at this point we have assumed temporarily that his inferred A is true), he can also prove that he is a fallible human being and that he is not unworthy as a person.

- It is logical in that the person is not making the part-whole error. He is clear in asserting that the whole of himself is not defined by a part of himself.

- It will lead to immediate functional emotions, behaviours and thoughts and help him pursue his longer-term goals. For example, it will help him to do well in the future in the sense that he will be motivated to learn from his previous errors and translate this learning to plan what he needs to do to improve his performance on the next test rather than dwell unfruitfully on his past poor performance.

Once again let us state that the same points can be made for other-acceptance beliefs and life-acceptance beliefs.

Irrational beliefs As we mentioned above, REBT keenly distinguishes between rational and irrational beliefs. Having discussed rational beliefs, we will now turn our attention to irrational beliefs which are, according to REBT theory, the core of psychological problems. When applied to beliefs, the term 'irrational' has five defining characteristics as shown in Figure 1.3.

Irrational beliefs are:

Rigid or extreme

Inconsistent with reality

Illogical

Largely dysfunctional in their emotional, behavioural and cognitive consequences

Largely detrimental to the individual in pursuing his basic goals and purposes

Figure 1.3   Defining characteristics of irrational beliefs

We explained earlier in this chapter that people can have four types of rational beliefs. According to REBT theory, people easily transmute or change these rational beliefs into four types of irrational beliefs (see Figure 1.4).

Demands

Awfulising beliefs

Low frustration tolerance beliefs

Self-depreciation/Other-depreciation/Life-depreciation beliefs

Figure 1.4   Four types of irrational beliefs

Demands   As humans we often express our rigid beliefs in the form of musts, absolute shoulds, have to's, got to's, etc. According to REBT, our dogmatic musts or demands are at the core of psychological disturbance.

> Taking the example which we introduced above, the demand is expressed thus: 'I must do well in my forthcoming test'.

Dogmatic demands are often based on asserted preferences. According to Dryden (1999a), it is difficult for human beings only to think rationally when their desires are strong. Thus, in our example, if your client's asserted preference is strong it is easy for him to change it into a must: 'Because I really want to do well in my forthcoming test, therefore I absolutely have to do so.' As you can see this belief has two components: an 'asserted preference' component (i.e. 'I really want to do well in my forthcoming test') and an 'asserted demand' component ('... therefore I absolutely have to do so'). In practice, in a demand, the asserted preference component is rarely articulated and therefore is held to be implicit. Thus, demands are most often only shown with the 'asserted demand' component shown ('e.g. 'I must do well in my forthcoming test'). We will show both cases below.

> In short we have:
>
> Demand = 'Asserted demand' component
>
> Demand = 'Asserted preference' component + 'Asserted demand' component

This demand is irrational for the following reasons:

- It is rigid in that your client does not allow for the fact that he might not do well.

- It is inconsistent with reality in that if there was a law of the universe that decreed that your client must do well in his forthcoming test, then there could be no possibility that he would not perform well in it. Obviously, no such law exists.

- It is illogical in that there is no logical connection between his 'asserted preference' component which is not rigid and his 'asserted demand' component which is rigid. In logic, something rigid cannot logically follow from something that is not rigid.

- It will lead to immediate dysfunctional emotions, behaviours and thoughts and interfere with him pursuing his longer-term goals. It will interfere with him doing well in the sense that the belief will draw him to focus on how poorly he is doing rather than on what he is doing.

A note on language. The demands targeted for change in REBT are absolute unconditional 'musts' as described above. Your clients will often express their demands using terms such as 'must', 'should', 'got to', 'have to' and so on. As an REBT therapist it is important to be able to distinguish between unconditional demands that underpin emotional disturbance and conditional 'musts', and 'shoulds' which do not. In the course of normal conversation your client is likely to use non-absolute 'shoulds' regularly. At this point in your training it is a good idea to familiarize yourself with the different ways of using words like 'should' so you can better assess your client's irrational beliefs. Encouraging your client to place the pertinent descriptor before the word 'should' or 'must' can help you both to make a clear distinction between absolute and non-absolute 'shoulds'. Below is a list of different ways of using the word 'should'.

- *Recommendatory should*: This 'should' specifies a recommendation for self or other: 'You should read this book' translates to 'I recommend that you read this book' or 'I really should go to bed early tonight' means 'It's in my best interest to go to bed early tonight.'

- *Predictive should:* This use of 'should' indicates predictions about the future: 'I should be on time for my flight' is interpreted as 'I predict that I will be on time for my flight.'

- *Ideal should:* This 'should' describes ideal conditions. For example: 'People should not litter' expresses the viewpoint 'ideally people should not litter'. Another way of phrasing this 'should' is to say 'In an ideal world *x, y and z* conditions would exist.'

- *Empirical should:* This 'should' points to the existence of reality. It encapsulates the idea that when all conditions are in place for a given event to occur then that event *should* occur. For example: 'Because the car is old and in ill repair it *should* have broken down' or 'Because of laws of gravity you *should* have fallen when you stepped off the ladder.'

- *Preferential should:* This 'should' indicates a desire or preference for a given condition to exist: 'My husband preferably should remember our anniversary' for example, carries an implicit additional meaning 'it would be good if he remembered but he does not have to.'

- *Conditional should/must:* This 'should' denotes that in order for one condition to exist another primary condition must be met. Examples include: 'I *should* eat healthily in order to become slimmer' and 'I *must* pass the interview in order to be accepted onto the course.'

- *Absolute should:* This term obviously refers to disturbance-creating demands at B in the ABC model of REBT. 'I *absolutely should* visit my aunt in hospital' and 'I absolutely *must* tend to my aunt at all times and under any conditions' are examples of absolute 'shoulds.'

Given the fact that the word 'should' has many meanings in English, we recommend that you use the qualifier 'absolute' when using the disturbance-creating should with your clients.

According to Albert Ellis, a demand is the primary irrational belief and three other irrational beliefs are derived from it. These beliefs are awfulising beliefs, low frustration tolerance (LFT) beliefs and self-, other- and life- depreciation beliefs. We will deal with each in turn.

Awfulising beliefs   When your client does not get what he believes he must get, then he will tend to conclude that it is awful that he has failed to get what he considers essential. Awfulising, according to REBT theory, can be placed on a continuum from 101 % – infinity and means worse than it absolutely should be.

Taking your client whose primary irrational belief is: 'Because I really want to do well in my forthcoming test, therefore I absolutely have to do so', his full awfulising belief is:

'Not only will it be bad if I fail to do well in my forthcoming test ('asserted badness' component), it would be awful if I fail ('asserted awfulising' component).'

More frequently, this is abbreviated as:

'It would be awful if I fail to do well in my forthcoming test.'

In practice, in an awfulising belief, the asserted badness component is rarely articulated and therefore is held to be implicit. Thus, awfulising beliefs are most often only shown with the 'asserted demand' component shown ('e.g. 'It would be awful if I do not do well in my forthcoming test'). We will show both cases below.

In short we have:

Awfulising belief = 'Asserted awfulising' component

Awfulising belief = 'Asserted badness' component + 'Asserted awfulising' component

The awfulising belief (i.e. 'It would be awful if I fail to do well in my forthcoming test') is irrational for the following reasons:

- It is extreme in that your client does not allow for the fact that there are things that can be worse than not doing well on the test.

- It is inconsistent with reality in that your client really cannot prove that it would be awful if he does not do well. Whilst there is evidence that it would be bad for him not to do well, there is no evidence that it would be more than 100 % bad.

- It is illogical in the sense that the idea that it would be awful if he does not do well ('asserted awfulising' component) does not logically follow from the idea that it would be bad if this occurred ('asserted badness' component). The former is extreme and does not follow logically from the latter which is non-extreme.

- It will lead to immediate dysfunctional emotions, behaviours and thoughts and interfere with him pursuing his longer-term goals. It will not help him to do well in that it will discourage him from focusing on what he needs to do in order to perform well on the test; rather it will draw him to focus on how poorly he is doing while he is doing it.

Low frustration tolerance beliefs When your client does not get what he believes he must get, then he will tend to conclude that this situation is intolerable and that he can't stand it. In REBT theory 'I can't stand it' either means that the person will disintegrate or that he will never experience any happiness again if the 'dreaded' event occurs. Adhering to a philosophy of low frustration tolerance (LFT) discourages your client from putting up with the frustration of having his goals blocked and thus he will tend to back away from dealing with these obstacles.

Applying this to our example when your client believes: 'Because I really want to do well in my forthcoming test, therefore I absolutely have to do so', his LFT belief will be:

'Because it would be difficult for me to tolerate not doing well on my forthcoming test ('asserted struggle' component) it would be intolerable if I fail ('asserted unbearability' component).'

More frequently this is abbreviated as:

'If I don't do well in my forthcoming test, it will be intolerable.'

In practice, in an LFT belief, the 'asserted struggle' component is rarely articulated and therefore is held to be implicit. Thus, LFT beliefs are most often only shown with the 'asserted unbearability' component shown ('e.g. 'It would be intolerable if I do not do well in my forthcoming test'). We will show both cases below.

In short we have:

LFT belief = 'Asserted unbearability' component

LFT belief = 'Asserted struggle' component + 'Asserted unbearability' component

---

This LFT belief (i.e. 'If I don't do well in my forthcoming test, it would be intolerable') is irrational for the following reasons:

- It is extreme in that your client does not allow for the fact that not doing well is tolerable.

- It is inconsistent with reality in that if there was a law of the universe which stated that your client couldn't bear not doing well, then he couldn't bear it no matter what attitude he held. This means that he would literally disintegrate or would never experience any happiness again if he failed to do well in the test. Hardly likely!

- It is illogical in that the idea that not doing well on a test is unbearable ('asserted unbearability' component) does not logically follow from the idea that it is difficult to tolerate ('asserted struggle' component). The former is extreme and does not logically follow from the latter which is non-extreme.

- It will lead to immediate dysfunctional emotions, behaviours and thoughts and interfere with him pursuing his longer-term goals. It will interfere with him doing well in the sense that it will lead him to focus on the 'intolerable' aspects of doing poorly rather than on what he needs to do to circumvent the obstacles in his way.

For a detailed discussion of different categories of LFT see Chapter 5 of Neenan and Dryden (1999).

Self-, other- and life-depreciation beliefs In this section, we will focus on self-depreciation beliefs. However, the same substantive points apply to other-depreciation beliefs and life-depreciation beliefs. When your client does not get what he believes he must get and attributes this failure to himself, then he will tend to dislike himself as well as his own poor behaviour. Adopting a philosophy of self-depreciation, for example, will discourage your client from focusing on what needs to be done to correct his own behaviour.

In our example, if your client who believes: 'Because I really want to do well in my forthcoming test, therefore I absolutely have to do so', fails to do well because of his own failings, then his self-depreciation belief will be:

'Because I failed to do well on the test and that is bad ('negatively evaluated aspect' component), therefore I am a failure ('asserted global negative evaluation' component).'

Or more frequently: 'I am a failure for not doing well on the test' (see below).

In practice, in a self-depreciation belief, the 'negatively evaluated aspect' component is rarely articulated and therefore is held to be implicit. Thus, self-depreciation beliefs are most often only shown with the 'asserted global negative evaluation' component shown (e.g. 'I am a failure for not doing well on the test'). We will show both cases below.

In short we have:

Self-depreciation belief = 'Asserted global negative evaluation' component

Self-depreciation belief = 'Negatively evaluated aspect' component + 'Asserted global negative evaluation' component

---

The self-depreciation belief (i.e. 'I would be a failure if I fail to do well on the forthcoming test') is irrational for the following reasons:

- It is extreme in that the person only sees himself as a reflection of his behaviour, rather than a complex person with many different facets.
- It is inconsistent with reality in that whilst he can prove that he did not do well on the test, (remember that at this point we have assumed temporarily that his inferred A is true), he cannot prove that he is a failure. Indeed if he was a failure then he could only and ever fail in life. Again this is hardly likely!
- It is illogical in that the person's conclusion that he is a failure does not logically follow from the observation that he did poorly on the test. He is making a part-whole error of logic.
- It will lead to immediate dysfunctional emotions, behaviours and thoughts and interfere with him pursuing his longer-term goals. It will interfere with him doing well in the sense that the belief will motivate him to focus on his negatively evaluated self rather than on helping him to deal with his negatively evaluated behaviour.

Similar points can be made about other- and life-depreciation beliefs.

'Cs'

In REBT theory 'C' stands for consequences of holding beliefs about 'critical As'. These consequences can be emotional, behavioural and thinking in nature. We will deal with each set of consequences in turn.

Emotional consequences of beliefs   The REBT theory of emotions is distinctive both in the field of psychotherapy and even within the tradition of cognitive behaviour therapy (CBT). It is a qualitative theory of emotions rather than a quantitative theory in that it distinguishes between healthy and unhealthy negative emotions. For example, anxiety (healthy emotion) is deemed to be qualitatively different from concern (unhealthy emotion) rather than quantitatively different. We will discuss this issue more fully in Chapter 4.

Healthy and unhealthy negative emotions   As we will discuss in detail in Chapter 4, REBT theory holds that your clients experience *healthy* negative emotions when their preferences are not met. These negative emotions (which are listed in Figure 1.5) are healthy because they encourage your clients to change what can be changed or make a constructive adjustment when the situations that they face cannot be changed.

Alternatively, your clients experience *unhealthy* negative emotions when they get what they *demand* they must not get or when they do not get what they *demand* they must get. These negative emotions (which are also listed in Figure 1.5)

Healthy negative emotions	Unhealthy negative emotions
Concern	Anxiety
Sadness	Depression
Remorse	Guilt
Sorrow	Hurt
Disappointment	Shame
Healthy anger	Unhealthy anger
Healthy jealousy	Unhealthy jealousy
Healthy envy	Unhealthy envy

Figure 1.5 Types of healthy and unhealthy negative emotions

are unhealthy in that they tend to discourage your clients from changing what can be changed and from adjusting constructively when they cannot change the situations that they encounter. In short, healthy negative emotions stem from rational beliefs about negative 'critical As', whilst unhealthy negative emotions stem from irrational beliefs about negative 'critical As'.

As I (WD) have explained elsewhere (Dryden, 1991), it is important for you to understand that your clients may use emotion words very differently from the way they are used in REBT theory. As such, you will need to explain very carefully the distinctions between healthy and unhealthy negative emotions and adopt a shared vocabulary when working with your clients. We will discuss this issue fully in Chapter 4.

Mixed emotions As we will discuss in Chapter 5, when you and your client select a problem to work on, this problem is called a target problem. While assessing a target problem, you will ask for a concrete example of its occurrence. You need to realise at this point that it is likely that your client will have a mixture of emotions about the situation in which her problem occurred, rather than having a single, unalloyed emotion.

For example, let's suppose that Betty, your client, has difficulty expressing her negative feelings to her friends when she considers that they take advantage of her. Thus, Betty keeps her feelings to herself with the result that her friends continue to use her. When you come to assess a specific example of this problem you may well find that Betty experiences a mixture of the following emotions: anger, hurt, anxiety and shame. Now, it is important to appreciate that each of these emotions is about a different 'critical A', which as you know may be an actual event or, more frequently, an inferred event. Thus, Betty may be:

- unhealthily angry when focusing on the selfish aspects of her friends' behaviour
- hurt when focusing on the uncaring aspects of their behaviour

- anxious when thinking about the possible rejection that might follow any assertion and

- ashamed when focusing on her own weakness for not having the courage to speak up.

We argue that if you want to deal with all these issues, then it is helpful to do an 'ABC' analysis for each of the four unhealthy emotions that your client experienced. If you try to do one 'ABC' for the entire experience, you will become confused and so, undoubtedly, will your client.

Meta-emotions   As human beings, your clients have the ability to reflect on their experiences and think about their thoughts, feelings and behaviours. Thus, a client's emotion can serve as a 'critical A' in an 'ABC' episode in which her beliefs determine what subsequent emotions she will have about her prior emotion. We call these emotions about emotions, 'meta-emotions'. As is the case with negative emotions, negative meta-emotions can be healthy or unhealthy. Thus, as Figure 1.6 shows, your clients may have healthy negative meta-emotions about both healthy and unhealthy negative emotions and they may also experience unhealthy negative meta-emotions about both healthy and unhealthy negative emotions. The term we use to describe the latter situation, where clients have emotional problems about their emotional problems is 'meta-emotional problems'. As you will see in Chapter 9, the identification and analysis of meta-emotional problems plays a particularly important role in the overall REBT assessment process.

	Healthy negative emotion	Unhealthy negative emotion
Healthy negative meta-emotion	Disappointment about being healthily angry	Disappointment about being unhealthily angry
Unhealthy negative meta-emotion	Shame about being healthily angry	Shame about being unhealthily angry

Figure 1.6   Negative emotion and meta-emotion matrix

Behavioural consequences of beliefs   REBT theory distinguishes between an overt action and an action tendency. Whenever your client holds a belief then he has a tendency to act in a certain way. Whether or not your client actualises that tendency and goes on to execute a behaviour consistent with it depends mainly on whether or not he makes a conscious decision to go against the tendency. One major task that you have as an REBT therapist is to help your client to see the purpose of going against the action tendencies that are based on irrational beliefs and to develop alternative behaviours that are consistent with action tendencies based on the corresponding rational beliefs. Before you can do this you need to help your client to identify and dispute his irrational beliefs and to develop and strengthen his alternative rational beliefs. We will discuss more fully in Chapter 4, the action tendencies associated with each of the major healthy and unhealthy negative emotions listed in Figure 1.5 above.

For now, we just want to stress that according to REBT theory, constructive behaviours and action tendencies stem from rational beliefs about 'critical As' and unconstructive behaviours and action tendencies stem from irrational beliefs about 'critical As'

Thinking consequences of beliefs   You will recall that earlier we discussed the differences between actual events and inferred events. We argued that although inferences are cognitions, they are best considered as 'As' in that when critical, they trigger your client's beliefs at 'B'. In this straightforward case the A triggers the 'B'. We can denote this by the following formula:

'Critical A' → 'B'.

However, the beliefs that your client holds can influence the subsequent inferences that he makes at 'C'. Remember that 'C' can stand for thinking consequences of beliefs as well as emotional and behavioural consequences of beliefs. In this more complicated case, we can denote this influence by the following formula:

'B' → 'CInf'

Let us illustrate the influence of beliefs on subsequent inferences at 'C' in two ways. The first concerns a series of experiments that I (WD) conducted with my colleagues in the late 1980s. In one of these studies (Dryden, Ferguson & Clark, 1989), we asked one group of subjects to imagine that they held a rational belief about giving a class presentation and another group to imagine that they held an irrational belief about the class presentation. Then we asked them to make a number of judgements on a series of inferential measures related to giving a class presentation, while maintaining the belief that they were asked to hold. We found that the type of beliefs subjects held had a profound influence on the inferences that they subsequently made. In general, subjects holding the irrational belief made more negatively distorted inferences about their performance in the class presentation and about other people's reactions to it than did subjects who held the rational belief.

The second illustration of the effect of beliefs on subsequent inferences at 'C' is a clinical one. Sarah, a 34-year-old woman, came into therapy because she was depressed about her facial appearance. At the beginning of therapy she held the following irrational belief: 'I must be more attractive than I am and I am worthless because I am less attractive than I must be.' At this point she thought that everybody that she met would consider her ugly and that no man would want to go out with her. You will note that these latter statements are her inferences about the reactions of people in general and men in particular and that these inferences are the thinking consequences of her irrational beliefs. During therapy I (WD) worked predominantly at the belief level and at no time did I target her distorted inferences for change. As a result of my interventions, Sarah came to hold the following rational belief:

> I would like to be more attractive than I am, but there is no reason why I must be. I don't like the fact that I am less attractive than I would like to be, but I can accept myself as a fallible, complex human being with this lack. I am not worthless and my looks are just one part of me, not the total whole.

As a result of this belief change, Sarah reduced markedly her inferences that others would consider her ugly and that men would not want to go out with her. In fact, soon her after therapy ended she started dating a man whom she later married. This clinical vignette shows quite clearly, we believe, the influence of beliefs on inferences.

'ABCs' interact in complex ways: the principle of psychological interactionism

So far in this chapter, we have discussed the 'ABCs' of REBT as if they were separate processes, distinct from one another. However, while in therapy it is important to deal with the 'ABCs' as if they were separate components – because otherwise your clients will end up confused – in reality, REBT theory has, right from the outset, advocated the principle of psychological interactionism. This principle states that the events that we choose to focus on, our interpretations and inferences, the beliefs that we hold and the emotions, behaviours and thoughts that stem from these beliefs are all interrelated and reciprocally influence one another often in complex ways. It is beyond the scope of this book for us to discuss fully and in detail these complex interactions. Those of you who are interested to learn more about the principle of psychological interactionism should consult Ellis (1994) and Dryden (2000).

Having introduced you to the theoretical fundamentals of REBT in this chapter, in the next we will cover what you need to know about the practice of REBT to begin to practise it in a training seminar setting.

CHAPTER TWO

What you need to know about the practice of rational emotive behaviour therapy to get started

In this chapter, we will outline aspects of the practice of REBT that you need to know before beginning to practise it. In particular, we will discuss (i) the REBT perspective on the so-called 'core conditions'; (ii) the active-directive therapeutic style adopted by REBT therapists and the skills involved in the implementation of this style; (iii) the goals of REBT; and (iv) the tasks that both therapist and client need to accomplish in the REBT therapy process. The purpose of this chapter is to provide you with an overview of the practice of REBT so that you can make sense of the skills-based chapters that follow.

The 'core conditions'

In the late 1950s Carl Rogers (1957) wrote a highly influential paper on what has come to be known as the 'core conditions'. These represent the qualities which therapists need to communicate to clients who in turn need to experience their presence for their therapeutic effect to be realised. Before we present the REBT perspective on these 'core conditions', we want to address one point that Rogers made with which REBT therapists fundamentally disagree. Rogers argued that the 'core conditions' that he posited were necessary and sufficient for therapeutic change to occur. In contrast REBT theory claims that certain therapist qualities are desirable conditions for therapeutic change to occur, but that these qualities are neither necessary nor sufficient conditions for the occurrence of client change. REBT holds the view that therapeutic change can take place in the absence of such therapist qualities, although such change is more likely to occur when these 'core conditions' are present. What are the 'core conditions' in REBT?

Empathy

REBT therapists agree with our person-centred colleagues in regarding empathy as an important therapist quality. However, we distinguish between two different types of empathy. First, there is affective empathy whereby you communicate to your clients that you understand how they feel. Here, you need to clarify for yourself and for your clients whether they have experienced healthy or unhealthy negative emotions (see Chapters 1 and 4). This is an important pre-condition for the second type of empathy delineated in REBT, i.e. philosophic empathy. In this type of empathy, you communicate to your clients that you understand the rational or irrational beliefs that underpin their emotional experience. When you are accurate in communicating such philosophic empathy, your clients will often exclaim that they truly 'feel' understood.

Unlike our person-centred colleagues, however, REBT therapists do not see either type of empathy as curative. Rather, we consider that both types of empathy serve to strengthen the therapeutic bond between you and your clients and that philosophic empathy, in particular, has an educational effect in that it helps your clients to understand the link between their emotions and the beliefs that underpin them.

Unconditional acceptance

The second 'core condition' put forward by Rogers has been variously called unconditional positive regard, prizing, non-possessive warmth and respect. From an REBT perspective these terms are problematic in that they imply that you are giving your clients a global positive evaluation. As such, as an REBT therapist you will prefer to offer your client unconditional acceptance. This term means that you regard your client as a fallible human being, too complex to merit any kind of global evaluation, who has many different aspects, positive, negative and neutral.

In an interview with me (Dryden, 1985), Ellis cautioned REBT therapists against being overly warm with their clients. He feared that undue therapist warmth would sidetrack the therapeutic process, lead the client to become involved with the therapist at the expense of involving himself in self-change methods outside the consulting room, inhibit the therapist from confronting the client and reinforce the client's need for approval. Interestingly, in a research study (DiGiuseppe et al., 1993), Ellis was rated low on warmth by his clients, a finding consistent with his ideas on the dubious therapeutic value of this variable.

Genuineness

The third 'core condition' advocated by Rogers again has been described differently in the field. It has been called genuineness, congruence and openness. From an REBT perspective genuineness means that as therapist you do not hide behind a facade and answer your clients' questions honestly, even those directed to your personal life, as long as you do not consider that your client will disturb himself about what you may say. With this caveat, you will, for example, honestly point out to a client why you consider some of his behaviour self-defeating or anti-social.

In order to do this therapeutically, you need to show the client that you accept him unconditionally and your client needs to experience the presence of your acceptance.

Humour

Rogers did not write about therapist humour, but we consider this to be a desirable therapist quality in REBT. Ellis has argued that one way of looking at psychological disturbance is that it involves taking oneself, other people and life conditions, not just seriously, but too seriously (Dryden, 1990). As such, if you can help your client not to take anything too seriously, then this is considered therapeutic in REBT. It is important that you do not poke fun at the client himself; but, given this, then the judicious use of humour through the use of jokes, witticisms and even rational humorous songs (see Dryden, 1999a) can provoke constructive belief change in those clients who will accept such unorthodox behaviour in therapists.

▶ Therapeutic style

Although it is possible to practise REBT in a variety of different styles, the style adopted by most REBT therapists and that advocated by Albert Ellis is active-directive in nature. In our experience as trainers of REBT therapists, it is this aspect of the therapy with which most trainees struggle. This is especially the case with trainees who have had prior training in person-centred therapy or psychodynamic therapy. Therapists from these approaches have been schooled in the philosophy that it is therapeutic to give clients as much time and 'space' as they need and that the therapist should not interrupt or direct the flow of the client's exploration or experiencing.

In contrast, REBT therapists believe that it is beneficial for you to provide a structure to therapy and to be active in directing your clients' attention to salient points that will help them to understand their problems more clearly and that will enable them to do something productive to help themselves. Let us make an important point at this juncture. REBT represents *one* perspective and not *the* perspective in psychotherapy. It is our practice to explain this to our clients and to mention that there do exist other approaches to psychotherapy that may be equally or more useful to them. We then explain that we will be using the REBT structure for understanding and dealing with their psychological problems and encourage them to sample this to determine whether or not it could be helpful to them. We have found that this approach has been more successful in engaging clients in REBT than a messianic approach which lauds REBT as the only worthwhile approach to therapy and denigrates other therapeutic approaches.

Having thus explained to our clients that we will be using a structured approach to therapy, we then get down straight away to demonstrate this approach in action.

Whilst REBT is structured, it is important to stress, however, that this therapeutic structure should preferably be used flexibly by you as an REBT therapist. At times, the structure is loose, particularly when you give some of your clients an extended opportunity to talk about their concerns in their own way, while at other times you will employ a tight structure, as when you teach the 'ABCs' of REBT (see Chapter 3).

Therapist directiveness in REBT

Let us deal more explicitly with the issue of REBT's active-directive therapeutic style. If we break down this style into its constituent parts, we have therapist directiveness and therapist activity. Taking directiveness first, it is important for you to understand the issues towards which you as REBT therapist will direct your own and, more particularly, your clients' attention. As REBT is an emotional problem-solving approach to psychotherapy, at the outset you will direct your clients to their emotional problems and help them to describe these problems as concretely as possible. Then, you will ask clients directly to select a problem that they want to tackle first (this is called a target problem in REBT) and they are asked, again directly, to provide a specific example of this target problem which is then assessed using the 'ABC' framework discussed in Chapter 1 and to be expanded on in Chapters 6–9.

During this assessment, you are highly directive. You direct the assessment process because you know what you are looking for, whilst your clients do not. Your job, at this point, is to encourage your clients to provide you with the kind of information that will enable you to help them. We will deal with the practical skills needed to carry out an effective 'ABC' assessment in Chapters 6–9. For the present, let us outline the direction that such an assessment tends to take. In general, when your client starts to describe a specific example of her target problem, you, as 'REBT therapist' should ideally direct her attention to her feelings and help her to identify whether she has experienced a healthy negative emotion or an unhealthy negative emotion. If her negative emotion is unhealthy then you should* direct her attention to the 'critical A', which, as you will recall, is the aspect of the 'A' that she is most disturbed about. Once you have identified this, you should direct the discussion to your client's constructive goals for change.

Here, you should explain to your client that given the existence of the 'critical A', it would be in her best interests to aim for a healthy, albeit negative emotional response to this 'A'. Doing so will, in fact, make it more likely that she will be able to change this 'A' if it can be shown to exist or to correct any inferential distortions that she has been making in viewing the 'A' than if she retains an unhealthy negative emotional response to the 'critical A'.

Once you have elicited your client's goals for change, you should direct your attention to an assessment of the irrational beliefs that underpin your client's

---

* Please note that when we use the word 'should' in this context in the book we are you using it to denote what we advise you to do. So, it is an advisory 'should' not an absolute 'should'.

unhealthy negative emotion at 'C'. Once these have been identified, you should direct your client to the irrational belief–emotion link and ensures that she understands what is known colloquially as the 'iB'–'C' connection. This is an important stage in the therapeutic process in that it not only forms a bridge between assessment and intervention, it also provides a rationale for the disputing that follows.

As we will show later, while disputing your client's irrational beliefs, you, as therapist, direct her to three kinds of arguments: empirical, logical and pragmatic. In empirical disputing of irrational beliefs, you ask your client to find empirical evidence to support these beliefs. In logical disputing of irrational beliefs, you ask your client for logical justification for these beliefs and in pragmatic disputing of irrational beliefs you ask her to reflect on the immediate and longer-term consequences of holding these beliefs. If you are successful at this stage, you will have helped your client to see two things. First, she will understand that her irrational beliefs are: (i) inconsistent with reality; (ii) illogical and (iii) unconstructive (in that they lead to dysfunctional emotive, behavioural and cognitive consequences as well as being largely disruptive to her basic goals and purposes). Second, she will understand that her alternative rational beliefs are: (i) consistent with reality, (ii) logical and (iii) constructive (in that they lead to functional emotive, behavioural and cognitive consequences as well as being largely enhancing of her basic goals and purposes).

Your client's insight into the above is likely to be 'intellectual' at this point, which means that she may understand the points that you have helped her to see and agree with them, but her strength of conviction in these points will be low, i.e. she will not have so-called emotional insight. As such, you will need to help her to see what she needs to do to gain emotional insight into her rational beliefs. Again, if you do your job well at this point, your client will see that weakening her conviction in her irrational beliefs and strengthening her conviction in her rational beliefs so that the latter significantly influence how she feels and acts takes a lot of what Ellis calls 'work and practice'. Much of this work is undertaken by your client in the form of homework assignments which you negotiate with her and which you check in the following session (see Chapters 17 and 18).

We hope you can see from this brief overview of doing REBT with a single client problem the extent of therapist directiveness in this approach to psychotherapy. Effective REBT therapists not only vary the amount of structure in therapy sessions, but are also flexible concerning how much direction to provide at any point in the therapeutic process (see Dryden, 1994a, for a fuller discussion of this latter point).

Therapist activity

We have considered the directive constituent of your active-directive style as an REBT therapist, but what comprises the active component of this style of doing therapy?

Advancing hypotheses   As Ray DiGiuseppe (1991) has shown, REBT therapists follow the hypothetical-deductive approach to knowledge and this is especially true when assessing clients' problems. This involves using a body of knowledge to form hypotheses about, amongst others, (i) what your client may be feeling based on the inferences he makes about the world and (ii) what his beliefs may be, based on these inferences and the feelings they he has about these inferred 'As'. Rather than collect a great deal of information before advancing these hypotheses we recommend that you apply your knowledge of REBT theory to the discrete information provided by your client. Thus, if your client tells you about his feeling then you can generate a hypothesis about his inferred 'A' and if he tells you about his feeling <u>and</u> his 'critical A' you can generate a hypothesis about his beliefs. You should particularly use hypothesis testing when your clients do not respond to open-ended enquiry regarding the information we are seeking. Here are some examples of theory-driven questions when testing your hypotheses:

■ Could it be that you were feeling hurt when your partner ignored you and thus in your eyes showed that he did not care about you? (hypothesis about a feeling based on a disclosure of an inferred 'A').

■ When you were feeling hurt when your partner, in your view, demonstrated that he didn't care that much about you, I wonder if you were telling yourself something like: 'He must care about me. If he does not, it proves that I'm not worth caring about?' (hypothesis about an irrational belief based on a 'critical A' and a feeling).

When advancing such hypotheses, it is very important for you to do two things. First, make it clear to your client that you are testing a hunch (i.e. hypothesis) and that you could be wrong. Emphasise to your client that it is very helpful for him to give you honest feedback about your hunch and that he can help you in the assessment process by correcting or refining your hunches. In this way your client becomes an active participant in the assessment process and not a passive recipient of your clinical wisdom (or otherwise!). Second, pay particular attention to the way in which your client responds to your hypothesis. There is a world of difference between a client saying to you: 'That's exactly right. How did you know?' and 'Well, er...I guess...I suppose you could be right.' In the latter case, it is advisable for you to say something like: 'You seem quite hesitant. That tells me that my hunch is off target. Can you help me to correct it?'

Asking questions   Many people who are trained in person-centred therapy and other so-called non-directive approaches to therapy and then seek training in Rational Emotive Behaviour Therapy are shocked to discover the extent to which REBT therapists employ questions. Whilst they were initially trained to use questions sparingly, if at all, they are now asked to make liberal use of questions.

What are your purposes in asking questions as an REBT therapist? In addition to the questions that are a central part of hypothesis testing discussed above, you ask questions for the following reasons.

First, you should ask questions to gather general information about the client and his life situation.

Second, you should ask questions to obtain specific information in the assessment phase of therapy. These questions are directed towards the salient aspect of the 'ABC' framework that you are currently assessing (see Chapters 6 and 9).

Third, you should ask questions as part of the disputing phase of therapy, i.e. to help you to challenge your clients' irrational beliefs. As we will discuss in greater detail later in the book, we recommend that you ask questions that are directed towards the empirical status, the logical status and the pragmatic status of both your clients' irrational beliefs and alternative rational beliefs.

Fourth, we recommend that you ask Socratic questions to encourage client understanding of rational principles. While educating his pupils, Socrates would ask them questions to involve them actively in the educational process. Rather than tell them the answers, Socrates asked questions to encourage them to think for themselves as he gently guided them towards the answers. Thus, whenever you can, use the same type of orienting questions. Thus, for example, if you want your client to understand why self-rating is a pernicious concept, rather than tell her why this is so, ask questions designed to encourage her to think actively about this issue. In response to her incorrect answers, you should ask further questions based on her replies to guide her towards the correct answer. In reality, you will find that you will use a combination of Socratic questioning and brief didactic explanations (see below) to get your teaching points across because few of your clients will readily respond to the sole use of Socratic questioning.

Finally, we recommend that you ask questions to ensure that your client has understood any teaching points that you have made using didactic explanations (see below). REBT can be viewed as an educational approach to therapy. As such, its impact lies not in the information imparted, but in the information received and digested. Given this fact, it is important that you gauge whether or not your client comprehends and agrees with the point you are making. First, ask your client to put into his own words his understanding of the point that you have made. Once you are satisfied that your client has understood the point in question, ask your client for his views on that point.

You should note two things about the use of questions in REBT. First, avoid asking too many questions, particularly when these are directed at the same target. For example, when seeking information about your client's irrational beliefs, ask one question at a time. Second, when you ask a question that is directed at a particular target, e.g. the client's feelings, monitor closely the client's response to determine whether or not he has answered the question satisfactorily. If not, and the information is important, then ask the question again, using a different form of words if necessary.

Providing didactic explanations   The second major class of therapist activity involves the use of didactic explanations. As we have already mentioned, REBT can be viewed as an educational approach to therapy. As such, one way of presenting educational points is for you to provide explanations of these points in a didactic manner. You can generally make didactic explanations when your client has not understood a teaching point that you have tried to convey by the use of Socratic questioning (see above). Such explanations involve the deliberate imparting of information concerning, for example:

1. The 'ABCs' of REBT.

2. How REBT theory may help your client to understand his problems.

3. What is likely to happen in REBT.

4. How you construe your role (as therapist) in the therapeutic process and what tasks you need to carry out during therapy.

5. How you construe your client's role in the therapeutic process and what tasks she needs to carry out during therapy.

6. The importance of homework.

This illustrative list shows the range of issues that you need to be prepared to explain to your clients. A full list would be much longer. Given this range of issues, it is important for you to have a lot of information at your fingertips and be able to explain a lot of concepts in ways that are meaningful to different clients. We will briefly consider the variety of teaching methods you should be ready to employ as an REBT therapist in the next section. Before we do so, let us discuss a number of points that you need to bear in mind while using didactic explanations.

1. It is important for you to explain relevant information clearly and succinctly. Avoid long-winded, rambling expositions.

2. Explain only one concept at a time.

3. As discussed in the section on questioning, check out your client's grasp of the point you are making by encouraging him to put his understanding into his own words. This is a particularly important point. It is all too easy for you to think that your client has understood rational principles because he indicates understanding non-verbally. This is no substitute for your client putting his understanding into his own words. You should encourage him to do this whenever possible.

4. Elicit your client's view on the material you have presented, correct any misconceptions he may have and engage him in a dialogue on any matters arising.

Using other methods in teaching rational principles In addition to Socratic questioning and didactic explanations, you can employ a variety of other active methods to teach your clients rational principles. As our goal here is to give you a 'feel' of the active constituent of the active-directive therapeutic style, we will briefly mention some of these methods rather than give you a comprehensive list.

- *Use of visual aids*. Here you can use posters and flipcharts to present rational principles in visual form.

- *Self-disclosure*. Here you tell your client how you have used REBT to overcome your emotional problems. You can tailor such self-disclosure to highlight different rational principles with different clients.

- *Hypothetical teaching examples*. Here you can use hypothetical examples to teach your clients salient aspects of REBT. The 'money model' example of teaching the 'ABCs' of REBT presented in Chapter 3 is a good illustration of this.

- *Stories, aphorisms and metaphors*. You can employ these methods to teach a rational principle when you think that your client needs a vivid and memorable illustration of the principle.

- *Flamboyant therapist actions*. These are active examples of the use of humour in REBT. For instance, you may bark like a dog to demonstrate the point that you are not a fool even though you act foolishly at times.

▶ The goals of REBT

In the late 1960s, Alvin Mahrer (1967) edited a book entitled *The Goals of Psychotherapy*. In his summary chapter, Mahrer reviewed the ideas of his contributors and argued that the goals of psychotherapy can fall into one of two major categories: (1) relief of psychological problems and (2) promotion of psychological health. REBT therapists would basically concur with this view and extend it. First, you need to help your clients over their psychological disturbances, then you need to help them to address their life dissatisfactions and finally you can help them to become more psychologically healthy and strive towards self-actualisation.

This is fine as an ideal, but the actual world of the consulting room can be very different. As such, as we will show you, as an REBT therapist you often have to make compromises with your preferred goals (Dryden, 1991).

Philosophic change

Ideally, as an REBT therapist, your preferred goal is to help your clients to achieve philosophic change which means that they relinquish their irrational beliefs and adopt rational beliefs. Your clients may achieve philosophic change in specific situations, in one or more broad areas of their lives or more generally. According to REBT theory, the more your clients acquire and implement a general rational philosophy, the more psychologically healthy they are deemed to be. From our experience we make the following predictions:

- Only a minority of your clients will achieve general philosophic change.

- A larger number of them will achieve philosophic change in one or more broad areas of life.

- Most of your clients who achieve philosophic change will do so in specific situations.

When your clients do achieve a philosophic change, their inferences tend to be accurate representations of reality and they tend to behave constructively. The point we want to make here is that if your client achieves a philosophic change, this does not mean that she will only change her beliefs. Rather, making a philosophic change helps her to make other constructive changes in the 'ABC' framework.

Please note that not all of your clients will be willing or able to change their irrational beliefs and when this is the case then you need to make compromises with your preferred goals and help your clients in other ways. There are three kinds of change other than philosophic change that you can try to effect when promoting philosophic change. We will now discuss each in turn.

Inferential change

If you cannot help your clients to achieve philosophic change, you can attempt to help them to achieve inferential change. An example of a therapist helping a client to effect inferential change without accompanying philosophic change occurred when a colleague of mine (WD) failed to help his client think rationally about her husband's presumed uncaring behaviour, but succeeded in helping her to correct her faulty inference that he did not care for her. As such, if your client makes an inferential change she will identify and correct distorted inferences and will view situations more accurately. As with philosophic change, your clients may achieve inferential change in specific situations, in one or more broad areas of life or more generally. Given the REBT view that inferential distortions stem largely from underlying irrational beliefs, inferential change is deemed to be unstable as your clients are more likely to form distorted inferences about themselves, other people and the world if their irrational beliefs remain unchecked than if they hold rational beliefs.

Behavioural change

Sometimes when you fail to help your client achieve a philosophic change, you can assist him by encouraging him to change his behaviour. Thus, if your client is anxious about being rejected by women, you may help him to minimise rejection by teaching him to improve his social skills. If successful, this may be very therapeutic for your client. However, even sophisticated social skills do not guarantee that your client will never be rejected and thus he remains vulnerable to anxiety in this area because his underlying irrational beliefs remain.

Changing actual 'Critical As' and situations

Sometimes when some of your clients are unable or unwilling to think rationally about negative life events, change their inferences about these events or change their behaviour in the hope of modifying these events, then you may best help them by encouraging them to leave the relevant situation. In REBT, this is known as changing the 'A'. However, we have extended this to include changing actual 'critical As' and the situations in which they occur. Whilst such environmental change is fine in the overall context of other psychological changes that your clients may make (especially philosophic change), on its own it leaves your clients particularly vulnerable. Because they have not effected any philosophic change, such clients take their tendency to disturb themselves from situation to situation. Also, if solely relied upon, opting for environmental change teaches your clients that the only way that they can help themselves is by changing or leaving aversive situations. They will therefore not be motivated to attempt other, more psychologically-based changes.

Different types of change within a case

It is important to stress that a given client may make different types of change on different issues. In the following example please note the point that we have previously made: namely, when a client makes a philosophic change she will also make other relevant kinds of changes. However, when that client makes an inferential, behavioural or environmental change, she does not often change her irrational belief.

> For example, one of my (WD) clients, Belinda, came to therapy with the following problems: approval anxiety, coping with pressure from her mother, dealing with her boyfriend's lateness and a fear of spiders. At the end of therapy Belinda had made a philosophic change on the broad issue of approval anxiety, a philosophic change on the specific problem of dealing with her mother's pressure, an inferential change on the specific problem of her boyfriend's lack of punctuality and an environmental change of A on the specific issue of spiders (i.e. she moved house).

Clients' goals for change

So far, we have dealt with the goals that you have for your clients as an REBT therapist. We made the point that while you have preferred goals for client change which you are explicit about, you need to be flexible and be prepared to compromise and accept less preferred goals when it becomes clear that it is very unlikely that your client will achieve philosophic change.

It is also crucial to note that your clients come to therapy with ideas about what they want to achieve from the therapeutic process. They may state these goals explicitly or these may be implicit in what they say. Sometimes your client's true goals may be contrary to his stated goals and can only be inferred from his behaviour later in therapy. The point we want to stress here is that your clients' goals may well be at variance with your goals as therapist and this may be a source of conflict in the therapeutic process. One way to minimise such conflict is for you to encourage your client to make a problem list (which is updated throughout therapy) and to set goals for each problem. We will discuss this issue later in this book. For now we want to reiterate that you can be most helpful to your clients by encouraging them to set goals which are based on philosophic change. However, as noted above, this is not always possible.

▶ Tasks in REBT

When we write of therapeutic tasks we mean specific or general activity that a person carries out in psychotherapy. As Bordin (1979) noted in a seminal paper on the therapeutic alliance, both therapists and clients have tasks to accomplish in therapy. Some of these tasks are common across therapies, whilst others are specific to a given approach. In this and the following section, we will focus mainly on the tasks that are characteristic of REBT, but in doing so we will consider tasks that are also general in nature. As such, we will not consider specific techniques here because we want to give an overall picture of task-related activity in REBT.

Your tasks as an REBT therapist

In this section, we will mainly concentrate on those of your tasks that are characteristic of REBT and in the following section we will consider your client's tasks in this approach to therapy. Figure 2.1 summarises your major tasks as an REBT therapist across the therapeutic process.

The beginning phase   Your initial task as an REBT therapist is to establish a therapeutic alliance with your client. At this stage, this primarily involves you:

- encouraging your client to talk about her concerns;
- communicating affective empathy;
- helping your client to develop a problem list; and
- outlining REBT and how it may apply to the problems on this list.

Once your client has indicated that REBT could be useful to her, then you can begin to outline what your tasks are in therapy and what you expect of your client. Whilst you need to stress to your client that she needs to be active in the therapeutic process, you should do this without presenting an overwhelming picture of what she needs to do. We will presently discuss your client's tasks in REBT.

The beginning phase

> Establish a therapeutic alliance
>
> Socialise your client into REBT
>
> Begin to assess and intervene on target problem
>
> Teach the 'ABCs of REBT
>
> Deal with your client's doubts

The middle phase

> Follow through on target problem
>
> Encourage your client to engage in relevant tasks
>
> Work on your client's other problems
>
> Identify and challenge your client's core irrational beliefs
>
> Deal with obstacles to change
>
> Encourage your client to maintain and enhance gains
>
> Undertake relapse prevention and deal with vulnerability factors
>
> Encourage your client to become his own counsellor

The ending phase

> Decide on when and how to end
>
> Encourage your client to summarise what has been learned
>
> Attribute improvement to client's efforts
>
> Deal with obstacles to ending
>
> Agree on criteria for follow-ups and for resuming therapy

Figure 2.1 Your tasks as an REBT therapist

At this point you encourage your client to choose a problem on which to work (known as a target problem), you initiate an 'ABC' assessment of this problem and begin to intervene to help your client to overcome the problem. At a salient point in this assessment process, you will endeavour to teach your client the 'ABCs' of REBT. There are a number of ways of doing this and we will illustrate some of these in Chapter 3. Because REBT has a definite standpoint on people's problems and its practitioners are prepared to be explicit about this standpoint and the approach to therapy that follows from it, it is likely that your client may have certain doubts or questions about REBT. You should thus be aware of the possible existence of such doubts and questions and be prepared to help your client to express these. Indeed, you should indicate that you welcome questions and the expression of doubts and demonstrate an open, non-defensive approach to them so that your client can see that her doubts will be taken seriously. Once your client has, for example, expressed a reservation about some aspect of the therapy so far, respond respectfully to this communication, but correct any misconceptions that may underpin her reservation. You should do this with tact and show her that you accept her as a person even though you are correcting her misconception of REBT.

The middle phase　As you and your client get to grips with the latter's target problem, you both begin to move into the middle phase of therapy. It is here that the disputing process that may have been initiated in the beginning phase takes hold and here that you call upon your client to undertake a number of tasks which are designed to help him (i) to develop his own disputing skills and (ii) to go from an intellectual understanding of rational principles to being able to act on them and for them to make a difference to the way he feels.

As you and your client make progress on his target problem, you help him to apply his learning to other similar problems. In addition, you both do work on the client's other problems. As you both gain a detailed understanding of the client's problems and the irrational beliefs that underpin these problems, you are in a position to identify and work on the client's core irrational beliefs. These are usually few in number and account for the existence of the problems on his problem list. As such they are expressed in general terms (e.g. 'I must have the love of significant people in my life').

It is in the middle phase of therapy that most of the obstacles to client change occur. Whilst a detailed consideration of such obstacles is beyond the scope of this introductory text, it is important to bear in mind that an investigation of these obstacles is best done when you accept yourself and your client as fallible human beings who have tendencies to block the development of therapeutic progress. In brief, obstacles to client change can be attributed to client factors, therapist factors, the interaction between these two sets of factors or environmental factors (see Dryden, 2001; Dryden & Trower, 1989; and Ellis, 2002, for a more detailed discussion of obstacles to client change and how to deal with them).

As your client makes progress, you encourage him to maintain and enhance his gains. At this point, when he is feeling better, your client may be tempted to stop working on himself. However, this would be a mistake because there is a distinction between 'feeling better' and 'getting better'. The former involves a cessation of symptoms whilst the latter involves a philosophic change either at a specific level or more generally. In order to help your client achieve a philosophic change that is robust, you need to encourage him to continue to maintain his therapeutic gains in the first instance and later to extend these gains to other areas of his life that may not have featured in the therapeutic dialogue.

As part of the process of maintaining and extending therapeutic progress, you need to raise the issue of relapse prevention. In particular, this involves the identification of vulnerability factors, i.e. 'As' which if encountered would trigger the client's core and other irrational beliefs. You may not have discussed these 'critical As' with your client in therapy or, if you have, you may have done so only cursorily. Now is the time for you both to do thoroughgoing work on these issues.

Throughout the process of REBT, you will be looking for ways of encouraging your client to take responsibility for his self-change. Realistically, this particularly comes to the fore during the latter stages of therapy. Here, when your client discusses his problems, you encourage him to take the lead in assessing his underlying beliefs and in coming up with suggestions for how he might challenge and change these beliefs. At this point, you act more as a consultant prompting your client to use skills that he has been taught previously, but which he may not think of applying to his own problems, hoping perhaps that you will continue to take the lead as you did in the beginning and early-middle phases of therapy. You will show your client that he has the necessary tools to take the major responsibility for ongoing therapeutic change and that this will be his major task in the time that you have left together. It is often at this point that the issue of ending therapy is first raised and discussed.

The ending phase   Your first task in the ending phase of REBT is to agree with your client the best way to end therapy. There are a number of ways of bringing therapy to a suitable conclusion. The approach that we favour is to increase gradually the time between sessions so that clients can progressively rely on their own resources as they work towards becoming their own therapists.

Whenever I (WD) carry out an initial assessment session with new clients who have had previous experience of being in therapy, I ask what they have learned from that experience. I am frequently struck by how little they claim to have learned. Whether this means that they have, in fact, learned little or that they cannot articulate their learning is not clear. If the latter, one remedy is for you to encourage your clients to summarise what they have learned. Being able to articulate what they have learned makes it more likely that your clients will retain and apply it after therapy has ended. Consequently, encouraging your clients to summarise and keep a written record of what they have learned from therapy is one of your key tasks as an REBT therapist in the end phase of therapy.

As you review your client's progress and help her to summarise her learning, it is important that you encourage her to attribute her progress to her own efforts. The way I (WD) tend to do this is take some credit for helping my client to understand her problems and for showing her what she can do about them, but to encourage her to take credit for putting this learning into practice in her own life. If your clients attribute their progress mainly to your efforts, thus minimising their own efforts, they will be less likely to work to maintain and enhance their gains than if they take full responsibility for their contribution to their own progress.

Although REBT therapists do not strive to form and maintain close relationships with their clients, the latter do tend to perceive their therapists to be empathic, respectful and genuine (DiGiuseppe et al., 1993). As such, your relationships with your clients may well be significant to them and its end may well constitute a 'critical A' for them. Thus, you should elicit your client's feelings about the end of his therapeutic relationship with you and uncover, challenge and help your clients change her irrational beliefs if her feelings are negative and unhealthy and constitute obstacles to a productive end to therapy.

As an REBT therapist, we advise you not to take an absolutistic view on the ending of therapy. Be prepared to resume therapy with your client should the latter be in need of further therapeutic assistance. Our practice is to encourage our clients to use their REBT self-help skills when they encounter the recurrence of old problems or the appearance of new problems. We encourage them to deal with such problems even though they may have to struggle to do so, but tell them to contact us for booster sessions if their struggles fail. What we want to avoid is clients contacting us for extra sessions as soon as they encounter problems before even attempting to use their self-help skills to overcome these problems. What we advocate, then, is that you set agreed criteria with your clients concerning the resumption of therapy. It is also important that you and your client agree on the timing and purpose of relevant follow-up sessions.

Review Figure 2.1 which outlines your tasks as a therapist in the three phases of REBT treatment. Use your own words to devise your own 'aide memoire' that you can use while you are conducting therapy with your client. Having a readily available 'crib sheet' of the tasks involved in each phase of treatment can help you to remain structured and focused, particularly at times when you are feeling a little lost in a therapy session.

Below is an example of one REBT trainee's 'aide memoire'. This example is intended to show you how one trainee re-worked Figure 2.1. Do not unthinkingly duplicate it. It is important that you make your own aide memoire, using the language that best helps you to understand and remember your therapeutic tasks throughout the beginning, middle and end phases of treatment.

The Beginning Phase of REBT Treatment

- Develop a working relationship with the client.

- Explain the 'nuts and bolts' of REBT practice to the client.

- Start assessing and tackling a target problem.

- Use the 'money model' or 'brief comparison method' to teach the 'ABCs' of REBT.

- Ask the client if he has any doubts or questions thus far and work to resolve these issues.

The Middle Phase of REBT Treatment

- Continue tackling the target problem via disputing 'iBs' and formulating alternative 'rBs'.

- Collaboratively devise homework tasks to help strengthen the client's 'rBs'.

- Help the client to apply his REBT learning to other problems.

- Dispute core 'iBs'.

- Work through any obstacles to continued therapeutic progress.

- Urge the client to continue working on positive changes made thus far.

- Collaboratively devise a relapse prevention plan.

- Let the client do the bulk of the work in session so he learns to be his own therapist.

The End Phase of REBT Treatment

- Agree with the client when and how to terminate therapy.

- Help the client to 're-cap' on what he has learned through treatment.

- Give the client the credit for his improvement.

- Discuss any fears about or blocks to ending treatment.

- Discuss 'top-up' sessions and in what instances to consider resuming therapy.

Your client's tasks

As Bordin (1979) has pointed out, clients have tasks to carry out in psychotherapy. Shortly, we shall discuss the specific tasks that your clients are called upon to implement in REBT, but first we shall say a few general words about tasks, from the client's point of view. You need to help your clients in a number of ways in this respect.

1. *Help your clients understand the tasks they are called upon to carry out in REBT.* If they do not understand what these tasks are, they can hardly be expected to execute them.

2. *Help your clients see the relevance of carrying out their tasks and in particular, the link between these tasks and their goals for change.* If your clients do not understand the goal-directed nature of their tasks, they may well be reluctant to carry them out.

3. *Help your clients understand the tasks you as their REBT therapist will be carrying out and help them see the relationship between the execution of your tasks and their goals.* Again, unless your clients see this task-goal connection, they may well be puzzled and uncomfortable about your behaviour as an REBT therapist.

4. *Help your clients to understand the relationship between their tasks and your tasks as REBT therapist.* Therapy is more likely to go smoothly when your clients

see that their tasks complement those that you are carrying out than when they lack such understanding. Figure 2.2 reviews the client tasks that we will consider in this chapter.

Specify problems

Be open to the therapist's REBT framework

Apply the specific principle of emotional responsibility

Apply the principle of therapeutic responsibility

Disclose doubts, difficulties and blocks to change

Figure 2.2 The client's tasks in REBT

Specify problems The first client task that we will discuss concerns ability and preparedness to be specific about problems. REBT is a problem-solving approach to psychotherapy and as such you will need to ask your client to focus on his problems and discuss them in a specific manner, giving typical, explicit examples of these problems to enable you to carry out a proper 'ABC' assessment. If your client cannot be specific about his problems, he will probably derive less benefit from REBT than if he can talk specifically about his concerns. In addition, if your client is not specific about his problems you will have greater difficulty in carrying out your tasks than if he is specific about them. These tasks are themselves specific in nature and if you are to perform them effectively, you need specific information from your client.

Be open to the REBT framework The second client task that we will discuss involves his willingness to listen to your explanations of his problems and to be open-minded about the REBT viewpoint on the nature of his problems, how he perpetuates these problems and what he needs to do to overcome these problems. If your client's view of his problems is markedly at variance with the REBT perspective, and he is not willing to entertain an alternative perspective, then therapy will quickly stall. Now we are not suggesting that your client should accept uncritically the REBT perspective on his problems. Indeed, Ellis (2002) has argued that suggestibility and gullibility are hallmarks of emotional disturbance. We are saying, however, that your client needs to be open-minded enough to consider the merit of your ideas and is sceptical (in the healthy sense) about these ideas. You can help your client to think for himself about these matters by encouraging him to express his doubts and concerns about REBT principles so that you can have an open dialogue on these ideas where you correct your client's misconceptions in a respectful manner. If you are dogmatic about REBT theory, you not only serve as a poor role model of flexibility, you are also likely to create a situation where polarisation of viewpoints occurs with the result that your client defends his irrational position and cannot thereby benefit from therapy.

Apply the specific principle of emotional responsibility   The third client task that we wish to address involves your client applying the specific principle of emotional responsibility. We distinguish between the general and specific principles of emotional responsibility and discuss this further later in this text. The specific principle of emotional responsibility states that your client largely makes himself disturbed by the irrational beliefs that he holds about the adversities in his life. When your client applies this principle he actively looks for these irrational beliefs whenever he experiences an unhealthy negative emotion and he counters any tendency that he may have to blame other people and situations for causing his emotions. Whilst this principle places the responsibility for his psychological problems fairly and squarely on your client, it does not preclude him from acknowledging that negative events contribute to his problems. It is important to note that responsibility is a different concept from blame and as such the specific principle of emotional responsibility does not advocate your client blaming himself for making himself disturbed.

Apply the principle of therapeutic responsibility   The fourth client task that we will consider involves your client applying the principle of therapeutic responsibility. This principle logically follows on from the specific principle of emotional responsibility. It involves your client acknowledging that in order to overcome his emotional problems he needs to put into practice the REBT theory of therapeutic change (in this case, philosophic change) which we discuss more fully in the second part of this book. Albert Ellis and I (WD) have summarised this in our book, *The Practice of Rational Emotive Behavior Therapy* (Ellis & Dryden, 1997). We say there that to effect a philosophic change your clients are advised to:

1. First, realise that they create, to a large degree, their own psychological disturbances and that whilst environmental conditions can contribute to their problems they are in general of secondary consideration in the change process.

2. Fully recognise that they do have the ability to significantly change these disturbances.

3. Understand that emotional and behavioural disturbances stem largely from rigid and extreme beliefs.

4. Detect their irrational beliefs and discriminate these from their rational alternatives.

5. Dispute their irrational beliefs using the logical-empirical methods of science.

6. Work toward the internalisation of their new rational beliefs by employing cognitive, emotive, and behavioural methods of change.

7. Continue this process of challenging irrational beliefs and using multimodal methods of change.

Disclose doubts, difficulties and blocks to change   The final client task that we will consider involves your client disclosing to you her doubts about REBT principles, the difficulties that she experiences in implementing REBT and any blocks to psychological change that she encounters. If your client keeps these doubts, difficulties or blocks to herself or worse, if she dissimulates by actively stating that she agrees with REBT principles, that she is able to implement its techniques without difficulty and that she encounters no blocks to change, then she will derive little benefit from therapy. Now, whether she discloses her doubts etc. will depend, in part, upon you providing the kind of therapeutic climate that encourages such disclosure. However, assuming that you succeed in providing this climate and ask your client for this information, then she has the responsibility to provide it.

> Practise eliciting and resolving blocks to psychological change, problems implementing REBT and specific doubts about REBT principles through role-play exercises with a fellow trainee. Agree on a scenario but ensure that your role-play partner neither makes it too easy or too difficult for you to elicit or resolve their concerns. In real therapy situations your clients will often find it difficult to articulate their problems, doubts or reservations with REBT principles and application. Encourage your role-play client to select a specific issue that is blocking their therapeutic progress without disclosing it to you prior to the exercise. Doing this will more accurately replicate real client-therapist interaction and give you a more valuable practice experience. Record your work in this exercise and play it to your REBT trainer for feedback.

We have now presented the basic information about the theory and practice of REBT that you need to know to begin to use this approach to therapy. In the next chapter, we will discuss how to teach clients the 'ABCs' of REBT.

CHAPTER THREE

Teaching the 'ABCs' of REBT

As we have stressed so far in this book, the 'ABC' framework is at the heart of the REBT theory of psychological disturbance. It provides both you and your client with a way of assessing the client's problems. As an accurate assessment of the client's problems is a prerequisite for effective intervention, the ability to teach the 'ABCs' of REBT clearly and succinctly to clients is an important skill in which all aspiring REBT therapists need to develop competence. There are a number of ways in which you can teach your clients the 'ABCs' and in this chapter, I (WD) will demonstrate a few of these methods.

▶ The money model

The money model is a fairly elaborate method in which you help your client to see the primary role of demands and the secondary role of awfulising beliefs in psychological disturbance and the corresponding roles that non-dogmatic preferences and non-awfulising beliefs play in protecting people from such disturbance. It is a method originally devised by Albert Ellis and employed by him frequently in his clinical work. As such, it is an important method to learn and use when appropriate.

Let me (WD) go through the money model by providing a typical example of how I demonstrate it with a trainee (in this case, Robin) on a first-level training course in REBT. In this role play, I ask Robin to play the role of a client, while I play the role of REBT therapist.

Windy: OK, Robin. I'd like to teach you a model which explains the factors that account for people's emotional problems. Now this is not the only explanation in the field of counselling, but it is the one that I use in my work. Are you interested in learning about this explanation?

Robin: Yes, I am.

Windy: Good. Now there are four parts to this model. Here's part one. I want you to imagine that you have £10 in your pocket and that you believe the following: 'I would prefer to have a minimum of £11 on me at all times, but it's not essential that I do so. It would be bad to have less than my preferred £11, but it would not be the end of the world.' Now, if you really believed this, how would you feel about only having £10 when you want, but don't demand a minimum of £11?

Robin: I'd feel concerned.

Windy: Right. Or you'd feel annoyed or disappointed. But you wouldn't kill yourself.

Robin: Certainly not.

Windy: Right. Now, here's part two of the model. This time you hold a different belief. You believe the following: 'I absolutely must have a minimum of £11 on me at all times. I must! I must! I must! And it would be the end of the world if I had less.' Now, with this belief you look in your pocket and again find that you only have £10. Now, how would you feel this time about having £10 when you demand that you must have a minimum of £11?

Robin: I'd feel quite panicky.

Windy: That's exactly right. Now, note something really important. Faced with the same situation, different beliefs lead to different feelings. Now, the third part of the model. This time you still have the same belief as you did in the last scenario, namely: 'I absolutely must have a minimum of £11 on me at all times. I must! I must! I must! And it would be the end of the world if I had less.' This time, however, in checking the contents of your pocket you discover two pound coins nestling under the £10 note. How would you feel about now having £12 when you believe that you have to have a minimum of £11 at all times?

Robin: ... I'd feel very relieved.

Windy: Right. Now, here is the fourth and final part of the model. With that same £12 in your pocket and that same belief, namely: 'I absolutely must have a minimum of £11 on me at all times. I must! I must! I must! And it would be the end of the world if I had less', one thing would occur to you that would lead you to be panicky again. What do you think that might be?

Robin: Let me think... I believe that I must have a minimum of £11 at all times, I've got more than the minimum and yet I'm anxious. Oh I see I'm now saying 'I must have a minimum of £13.'

Windy: No. You are sticking with the same belief as before namely: 'I must have a minimum of £11 on me at all times. I NOW have £12...'

Robin: Oh! I see... I NOW have the £12. Right, so I'm scared I might lose £2.

Windy: Or you might spend £2 or you might get mugged. Right. Now the point of this model is this. All humans, black or white, rich or poor, male or female make themselves disturbed when they don't get what they believe they must get. And they are also vulnerable to making themselves disturbed when they do get what they believe they must get, because they could always lose it. But when humans stick rigorously (but not rigidly) to their non-dogmatic preferences and don't change these into musts then they will feel healthily concerned when they don't have what they prefer and will be able to take constructive action under these conditions to attempt to prevent something undesirable happening in the future. Now in our work together we will pay close attention to the differences between absolute musts and non-dogmatic preferences. Is that clear?

Robin: Yes.

Windy: Well, I'm not sure I've made my point clearly enough. Can you put it into your own words . . . ?

Let us now briefly summarise the steps here. As we do so, go back to the dialogue and see if you can follow the steps.

Step 1. Ask the client if he is interested in an explanation of emotional problems.

Step 2. Present part 1 of the model. Stress that the client has less money than he prefers and provide the associated non-awfulising belief (rational belief). Enquire about his feeling. If he does not give you a healthy negative emotion, explain why this would be his emotional response.

Step 3. Present part 2 of the model. Stress that the client has less money than he demands and provide the associated awfulising belief (irrational belief). Enquire about his feeling.

Step 4. Emphasise that different beliefs about the same situation lead to different feelings.

Step 5. Present part 3 of the model. Stress that the client has more money than he demands again giving the associated awfulising belief (irrational belief). Enquire about his feeling. If he does not give you a plausible response explain why his response is incorrect and prompt until his response is correct.

Step 6. Present part 4 of the model. Stress that he still has more money than he demands giving once again the associated awfulising belief (irrational belief), but ask him to imagine that he has a thought that leads him to feel disturbed again. Enquire about the nature of this thought. Encourage him to identify possible thoughts by himself, but give suggestions if he is stuck.

Step 7. Summarise all the information emphasising the importance of distinguishing between rational and irrational beliefs and showing their differential effects.

Correct your client's errors

One of the important points to note when you present the full money model to your clients is that you will have to both correct the errors that they make in responding to your questions and explain the nature of these errors. For example, when you present the first part of the model (i.e. the client is asked a rational belief) your client may say that he would experience an unhealthy negative emotion rather than a healthy negative emotion. Unless you correct this error and explain why it is an error then your client may take away erroneous information. Here is an example of what I mean.

Windy: There are four parts to this model. Here's part one. I want you to imagine that you have £10 in your pocket and that you believe the following: 'I would prefer to have a minimum of £11 on me at all times, but it's not essential that I do so. It would be bad to have less than my preferred £11, but it would not be the end of the world.' Now, if you really believed this, how would you feel about only having £10 when you want, but don't demand, £11?

Sarah: I'd be very anxious.

Windy: I don't think you would. Don't forget that your belief is that it would be undesirable not having the £11, not that it is an absolute, dire necessity to have that sum. Also you don't believe it would be the end of the world if you did not have the £11, rather that it would be unfortunate not to have this amount. Think carefully about this. Now how do you think you would feel?

Sarah: Oh, I see. I'd be concerned.

Common trainee errors in teaching the money model

When you present the money model correctly, it is a potent way of teaching the 'ABC' model. However, it is difficult to master and trainees do experience difficulty in learning it. When you first practise the money model, you may make a number of errors. In discussing such following errors, we will use illustrative dialogue from training situations.

Failure to distinguish fully between non-dogmatic preferences and demands A very common error that you may make is not keenly discriminating between a non-dogmatic preference and a demand. Typically, when this happens you do not make explicit both parts of the non-dogmatic preference as shown in the dialogue below.

Mary (in the role of counsellor): ... Now there are four parts to this model. Here's part one. I want you to imagine that you have £10 in your pocket and that you believe the following: 'I would prefer to have a minimum of £11 on me at all times.' Now, if you really believed this, how would you feel about only having £10 when you want a minimum of £11?

Windy (as trainer): Well. It was good that you began by stressing that there are four parts to the model and you started the model correctly with a rational belief. However, it is important that you present the client with the full version of the rational belief which is in two parts. The first part of the rational belief involves asserting the person's preference which is, as you said correctly: 'I would prefer to have a minimum of £11 on me at all times.'

However, REBT theory that people can easily change their preferences to demands and the major way of guarding against this when teaching the money example is to negate the person's demand as well as asserting his preference. You do this by saying: 'I would prefer to have a minimum of £11 on me at all times, but it's not essential that I do so.'

You will recall that REBT theory states that preferences are primary rational beliefs and three other rational beliefs are derived from these preferences, namely: non-awfulising, high frustration tolerance and self-/other-/life-acceptance. To reinforce the rational belief here, I recommend that you add the non-awfulising derivative. When you do this, it is once again to assert the rational belief and negate the irrational belief. Thus the full rational, non-awfulising derivative is: 'It would be bad to have less than my preferred £11, but it would not be the end of the world.'

If we put together the primary rational belief (i.e. the non-dogmatic preference) and its non-awfulising derivative remembering to assert the rational beliefs and negate the irrational beliefs we have: 'I would prefer to have a minimum of £11 on me at all times, but it's not essential that I do so. It would be bad to have less than my preferred £11, but it would not be the end of the world.'

Failure to clarify vague emotional statements, thus not distinguishing between healthy and unhealthy negative emotions As an REBT therapist you place great emphasis on encouraging your clients to be clear rather than vague about their emotions. Thus, if your client describes a vague emotion in the money model, you need to help him clarify its precise nature.

Windy: OK, Mary. Why not back up and then continue?

Mary: Now there are four parts to this model. Here's part one. I want you to imagine that you have £10 in your pocket and that you believe the following: 'I would prefer to have a minimum of £11 on me at all times, but it's not essential that I do so. It would be bad to have less than my preferred £11, but it would not be the end of the world.' Now, if you really believed this, how would you feel about only having £10 when you want, but don't demand a minimum of £11?

Arthur (in the role of client): Upset.

Mary: Right. Now here's part two of the model.

Windy: OK. Let's stop there. A very important part of REBT theory states that when a person faces a negative A, like having £1 less than her goal, her unhealthy negative emotions about this A stem largely from irrational beliefs, whilst her healthy negative emotions stem largely from rational beliefs. In order to clearly teach the client the difference between rational and irrational beliefs in the money model, it is very important that you help her to differentiate clearly her healthy from her unhealthy negative emotions. One way of doing this is to be precise about emotional terms. Now, when your client used the word 'upset' just then, we do not know whether this refers to a healthy negative emotion like concern, disappointment and annoyance or to an unhealthy negative emotion like anxiety, feelings of self-pity or anger. If you accept the word 'upset' uncritically here, then you are making life more difficult for yourself later in the model when you come to show the important role that irrational beliefs have in underpinning disturbed emotions. If by the word 'upset' here your client means a disturbed negative emotion then he will later be confused. He'll say something to himself like: 'Wait a minute. The therapist is now showing me that irrational beliefs underpin disturbed negative emotions. But she also accepted my point that my 'upset' feelings— which I also see as disturbed – stem from rational beliefs. I'm very confused.'

So instead of accepting the term 'upset' uncritically, you need to clarify what your client means by it and proceed accordingly. Let me demonstrate how to do this. In doing so I want Arthur in the first instance to construe 'upset' as a healthy negative emotion and in the second instance as an unhealthy negative emotion and I'll show you what to do in each case.

Here is how I modelled skilful therapist behaviour for Mary in both instances.

Instance 1: When 'upset' is a healthy negative emotion

> Windy: So you say that you would feel upset if you have £10 when you want, but don't demand a minimum of £11. I'm not quite sure what you mean by 'upset'. Do you mean upset in a healthy concerned way, for example, or upset in an unhealthy anxious way?
>
> Arthur: Put that way, I'd be concerned rather than anxious.

Instance 2: When 'upset' is an unhealthy negative emotion

> Windy: So you say that you would feel upset if you have £10 when you want, but don't demand a minimum of £11. I'm not quite sure what you mean by 'upset'. Do you mean upset in a healthy concerned way, for example, or upset in an unhealthy anxious way?
>
> Arthur: Put that way, I'd be anxious rather than concerned.
>
> Windy: Now I may be wrong here, but I don't think you would. Don't forget you believe that whilst you would like to have a minimum of £11 at all times, it is not essential. Can you see the difference between believing that having £11 at all times is desirable, but not essential and believing that having £11 at all times is absolutely essential?
>
> Arthur: Yes. In the first case, I believe that it is necessary for me to have £11 and in the second case, I believe that it would be nice to have it, but that it is not a necessity.
>
> Windy: That's right. Now which belief would lead to unanxious concern and which to anxious overconcern?
>
> Arthur: I see what you mean. I'd feel concerned about not having the £10 if I believed that having the £11 at all times is desirable, but not necessary.

Failure to emphasise the irrationality of the client's irrational belief in part two of the model When going over part two of the model, it is important to emphasise the irrationality of your client's irrational belief. If this is not done, your client may not understand its full implications. Let's go back to Mary and Arthur.

Mary: Right. Now, here's part two of the model. This time you hold a different belief. You believe the following: 'I must have a minimum of £11 on me at all times.' With this belief you look in your pocket and again find that you only have £10. Now, how would you feel this time about having £10?

Windy: Let's stop there, Mary. Now, at this point, it's really important to emphasise the irrationality of the irrational beliefs you are asking Arthur to hold in his mind. Just mentioning the must with little or no emphasis is usually insufficient. Listen carefully to what I usually say and see if you can see the difference between this and what you said.

'OK, Arthur, here's part two of the model. This time you hold a different belief. You believe the following: 'I absolutely must have a minimum of £11 on me at all times. I must! I must! I must! And it would be the end of the world if I had less.' Now, with this belief you look in your pocket and again find that you only have £10. Now, how would you feel this time about having £10 when you demand that you must have a minimum of £11?

Mary: Well first, you used the phrase 'absolute must' where I just used the word 'must'. Second, you repeated the phrase 'I must' three times with a considerable degree of emphasis. Then you provided an awfulising belief...(pause)....

Windy: Why do you think I did that?

Mary: I'm not sure.

Windy: I did that to emphasise the irrationality of the irrational belief.

Mary: I see. Then you asked Arthur how he would feel about having £10 when he demanded that he must have a minimum of £11? So once again you emphasised the irrational belief when I did not.

Failure to summarise accurately all the points in the money model One of the most difficult parts of the money model is the summary. To summarise all the points effectively, you need to have a full understanding of these points and the sequence in which they need to be presented. Let's consider Mary's summary.

Mary: Now the point of this model is this. All humans, black or white, rich or poor, male or female are upset (i) when they don't get what they demand. And they are also vulnerable to becoming upset (i) when they do get what they demand because they could always lose it. But when people stick with their desires (ii) they won't get upset (i) (iii).

Windy: That was a pretty good first attempt, Mary. You were able to show Arthur some key parts of the model such as the difference between musts and non-dogmatic desires. There are three points that you need to consider in order to improve this summary. [The following numbers correspond to the bracketed numbers shown in Mary's summary.]

(i) First, you used the word 'upset' throughout. This is problematic for two reasons. First, as discussed before 'upset' is a vague word and therefore you are helping the client neither to be precise about his own emotions nor to differentiate between healthy and unhealthy negative emotions. Second, in using 'upset' throughout the summary, you have unwittingly taught your client that emotional upset stems from both rational beliefs and irrational beliefs. This is obviously going to be confusing for him. So, what could you do differently next time?

Mary: I'll be precise in my use of emotional language and use words that clearly reflect healthy negative emotions like concern and words that clearly reflect unhealthy negative emotions such as anxiety.

Windy: Excellent. My second piece of feedback is as follows.

(ii) At the end you said, 'But when people stick with their desires they won't get upset'. Compare this with what I generally say at this point: 'But when humans stick rigorously (but not rigidly) to their non-dogmatic preferences and don't change these into musts then they will feel healthily concerned'. Can you see the difference between these two statements?

Mary: Well, I stated only part of the rational belief, whilst you stressed the full belief and that in holding this belief people won't implicitly change their desires to rigid demands. Also you stressed that people can rigorously hold a rational belief without it being rigid. I didn't mention that. Finally, whilst I used the vague term 'upset' you were explicit in stressing that a specific healthy negative emotion stems from a rational belief.

Windy: Again that is a full and excellent answer. Now, here is my third and final piece of feedback.

(iii) At the very end you mention, albeit vaguely, that a negative emotional state stems from a rational belief, whereas I also stress that holding a rational belief also leads to people being able to take constructive action to attempt to prevent something undesirable happening in the future.

The summary is difficult to master, so let me break it down point by point.

Point 1. Irrational beliefs underpin disturbance when the 'A' is negative.

'All humans, black or white, rich or poor, male or female make themselves disturbed when they don't get what they believe they must get...'

Point 2. Irrational beliefs leave people vulnerable to disturbance when the 'A' is positive because the 'A' could become negative in the future.

'...And they are also vulnerable to making themselves disturbed when they do get what they believe they must get, because they could always lose it...'

Point 3. Rational beliefs underpin healthy negative emotions and constructive behaviour when the 'A' is negative.

'...But when humans stick rigorously (but not rigidly) to their non-dogmatic preferences and don't change these into musts then they will feel healthily concerned when they don't have what they prefer and will be able to take constructive action under these conditions and to prevent something undesirable happening in the future...'

▶ Summary

In order to master this important method of teaching the 'ABCs' of REBT, let us suggest the following steps.

1. Rewrite our version on **pp. 45–47**, using your own words, ensuring that you don't change any of the meaning or any of the teaching steps.
2. Learn it off by heart, being careful to focus on the meaning of your words. Don't do this parrot fashion, though.
3. Test yourself by putting the model on a digital voice recorder. Play both yourself and a very cooperative client. If you get stuck, consult your written script. Do this until you can teach the model smoothly without self-prompting.
4. Pair up with a fellow trainee and teach him or her the model, ensuring that your colleague plays a cooperative client.
5. Repeat step 4, but this time encourage the client to make minor errors of understanding in the client role. Correct these errors until the 'client' understands the model fully.

6. Repeat step 4, but this time encourage the client to make major errors of understanding in the client role. Again, correct these errors until the 'client' understands the model fully.

7. Teach the model to several people who are unfamiliar with REBT.

8. Bring any problems in teaching the model to your REBT trainer or supervisor.

▶ The *lateness example*

While the money model is a comprehensive approach to teaching the 'ABCs' of REBT, not all clients relate to it or understand it. The lateness example is an alternative to the money model. It is comprised of the same seven steps and four parts as the money model. It is important that you remember to teach your client the learning points in the same order. Below is a script of the lateness example. The wording of the script is altered slightly from that of the money model above. This is done to illustrate how you can put these methods of teaching the 'ABCs' into your own language provided you keep the meaning in tact and retain the teaching sequence.

Rhena: OK Paul, I'd like to teach you a model which explains the factors that account for people's emotional problems. There are other explanations in the field of counselling but this is the one I use in my work. Are you willing to hear about this explanation?

Paul: Yes.

Rhena: OK. There are four parts to this model. Now here's part one. I'd like you to imagine that you are 10 minutes late for an appointment and that you believe the following, 'I prefer to be on time for all my appointments, but it's not essential that I am on time. It's bad to be late, but it's not the end of the world.' So, if you really believed this, how do you imagine you would feel about being 10 minutes late for your appointment bearing in mind that you want, but don't demand, that you arrive on time?

Paul: I guess I'd be concerned.

Rhena: Right. Or perhaps you'd feel annoyed or disappointed, but the point is you wouldn't kill yourself over it, right?

Paul: No, certainly not.

Rhena: Now here's part two of the model. This time you hold a different belief. Now you believe 'I absolutely must, under all conditions, be on time for appointments! I must, must, MUST arrive on time and it would be the end of the world if I was late!' Now, whilst holding this belief you look at your watch and realise that you are in fact 10 minutes late. How would you feel about being 10 minutes late when you are demanding that you must always arrive at appointments on time?

Paul: I'd feel panicky.

Rhena: That's exactly right. Now, I'd like you to take note of a very important point, in the same situation different beliefs lead to different types of feelings. Let's move on to part 3 of the model. This time you hold the same belief as you did in the last scenario, 'I absolutely must be on time for all my appointments, I must, must, MUST! It would be the end of the world if I was late!' This time though, you glance up at a clock in the street and realise that your watch is 20 minutes fast. So in fact you are actually 10 minutes early for your appointment. How do you imagine you would feel about being 10 minutes early when you believe that you absolutely have to be, absolutely must be on time for your appointment?

Paul: Uh…I'd be relieved.

Rhena: That's right you would feel relieved. Now consider the fourth and final part of the model. Realising that you're 10 minutes early for your appointment and still holding the same belief namely 'I must be on time for all my appointments, I must, must, MUST! To be late would be the end of the world!' Despite being 10 minutes early, something will occur to you that will cause you to feel panicky again. Can you think what that might be?

Paul: That I'll be delayed somehow and still end up arriving late.

Rhena: Precisely. Or that the street clock was wrong or perhaps you got the appointment time wrong and you are in fact late rather than 10 minutes early. Right. Now the point this model makes is that all humans – be they male or female, rich or poor, of any age or race – make themselves emotionally disturbed when they don't get what they truly believe they must get. Even when they do get or achieve what they believe they absolutely must, they are still vulnerable to further disturbance in the future. Why? Because it is always possible that they will lose it. But when humans hold non-absolute or non-dogmatic preferences and resist converting them into demands such as 'I must!', they experience healthy negative emotions like concern when they don't get or achieve what they prefer. They are also able to take constructive action when their preferences are not met and are able to work toward preventing something undesirable happening in the future. So in our work together we're going to focus closely on the differences between demands such as 'musts' and non-dogmatic preferences like 'I want' or 'I'd prefer'. Does that make sense to you?

Paul: Yeah, it does.

Rhena: Good. These are some pretty complex principles I've been showing you. Can you tell me what you've understood from the model, in your own words, so I can check that I've made the points clearly?

Having already addressed correcting client errors and common trainee therapist errors with respect to the money model, these points will not be reiterated here.

▶ Simpler ways of teaching the 'ABCs'

Despite your best efforts, some of your clients will not be able to readily digest the information included in the lateness example and the money model. As such, it is useful to have at your fingertips one or two simpler ways of teaching the 'ABCs.'

The brief money model

When taught accurately and clearly, the full money model is a powerful way of teaching the 'ABCs' of REBT. However, you need to shorten it for those of your clients who you think would not be able to understand the full money model. This involves presenting the first two parts of the model (as broken down in steps 1 to 4 on **pp. 47**). These first two parts show that irrational beliefs (demands and awfulising beliefs) underpin unhealthy negative emotions and rational beliefs (non-dogmatic preferences and non-awfulising beliefs) underpin healthy negative emotions. You can also just present these two parts when you are pressed for time or when you want to present the bare bones of the REBT model. Let us present those two parts again here.

Windy: OK, Robin. I'd like to teach you a model which explains the factors that account for people's emotional problems. Now this is not the only explanation in the field of counselling, but it is the one that I use in my work. Are you interested in learning about this explanation?

Robin: Yes, I am.

Windy: Good. Now there are two parts to this model. Here's part one. I want you to imagine that you have £10 in your pocket and that you believe the following: 'I would prefer to have a minimum of £11 on me at all times, but it's not essential that I do so. It would be bad to have less than my preferred £11, but it would not be the end of the world.' Now, if you really believed this, how would you feel about only having £10 when you want, but don't demand a minimum of £11?

Robin: I'd feel concerned.

Windy: Right. Or you'd feel annoyed or disappointed. But you wouldn't kill yourself.

Robin: Certainly not.

Windy: Right. Now, here's part two of the model. This time you hold a different belief. You believe the following: 'I absolutely must have a minimum of £11 on me at all times. I must! I must! I must! And it would be the end of the world if I had less.' Now, with this belief you look in your pocket and again find that you only have £10. Now, how would you feel this time about having £10 when you demand that you must have a minimum of £11?

Robin: I'd feel quite panicky.

Windy: That's exactly right. Now, note something really important. Faced with the same situation, different beliefs lead to different feelings. Your demand and awfulising belief lead you to feel unhealthily panicky and your non-dogmatic preference and non-awfulising belief lead you to feel healthily concerned.

Brief comparison between a demand and a non-dogmatic preference

In this approach, you briefly help your client to see that when you hold a demand about a negative 'critical A' you experience an unhealthy negative emotion and when you hold a non-dogmatic preference about the same 'A' you experience a healthy negative emotion.

Windy: So do you know what determines the way we feel?

Peter: I'm not sure.

Windy: Here's the way I see it. Imagine that two men are rejected by the woman they love. One feels depressed, can't adjust to the loss and with-draws from life, while the other feels sad, mourns the loss appropriately and gets on with his life. Now, I'm going to outline two beliefs and you tell me which man holds which belief. OK?

Peter: OK.

Windy: One man believed: 'She absolutely should not have rejected me' while the other one believed: 'I really wish she hadn't rejected me, but such rejection is part of life and I'm not immune from it.' Now which man held which belief?

Peter: The man who felt depressed and withdrew from life held the first belief and the one who felt sad held the second.

Windy: That's right. This shows two things. First, our feelings are deter-mined not by what happens to us, but by our beliefs about what happens to us. Second, an unhealthy emotional response is based on a rigid belief system, while a healthy emotional response is based on a flexible belief system.

You can use this brief method to compare a non-awfulising belief with an awfulising belief, an HFT belief with an LFT belief and an acceptance belief with a depreciation belief.

Let me end this chapter, by showing how I (WD) could have used the brief comparison method to teach Peter the difference between a self-acceptance belief and a self-depreciation belief.

Brief comparison between a self-depreciation belief and a self-acceptance belief

In this approach, you briefly help the client to see that when you hold a self-depreciation belief about a negative 'critical A' you experience an unhealthy neg-ative emotion and when you hold a self-acceptance belief about the same 'A' you experience a healthy negative emotion.

Windy: So do you know what determines the way we feel?

Peter: I'm not sure.

Windy: Here's the way I see it. Imagine that two men are rejected by the woman they love. One feels depressed, can't adjust to the loss and withdraws from life, while the other feels sad, mourns the loss appropriately and gets on with his life. Now, I'm going to outline two beliefs and you tell me which man holds which belief. OK?

Peter: OK.

Windy: One man believed: 'This rejection proves that I am a worthless loser' while the other one believed: 'This rejection is painful, but is not a reflection of my worth as a person. I am the same person whether I am accepted or rejected.' Now which man held which belief?

Peter: The man who felt depressed and withdrew from life held the first belief and the one who felt sad held the second.

Windy: That's right. This shows two things. First, our feelings are determined not by what happens to us, but by our beliefs about what happens to us. Second, an unhealthy emotional response is based on a self-rejecting belief system, while a healthy emotional response is based on a self-accepting belief system. So it wasn't being rejected that led to the first man's depression; rather, it was his rejection of himself.

In role-play, practise teaching your partner the difference between the two types of beliefs using the brief comparison method. Keep your focus on one belief pairing at a time. Repeat the role-play in order to gain practice using this method to teach the difference between (i) a demand and a non-dogmatic preference, (ii) an awfulising belief and an anti-awfulising belief, (iii) an LFT belief and an HFT belief and (iv) a self-depreciation belief and a self-acceptance belief.

When using the brief comparison method try to generate alternative hypothetical situations in addition to the rejection example shown here. It can be useful to have several examples at your disposal so you can choose one that you think is likely to resonate with your client.

Record the role-play and ask your REBT trainer for feedback.

In teaching clients the 'ABCs' of REBT it is important to distinguish clearly between healthy and unhealthy negative emotions. In the following chapter, we will discuss more fully how to make this distinction with clients.

CHAPTER FOUR

Distinguishing between healthy and unhealthy negative emotions

I (WD) first trained in REBT (or RET as it was known in those days) in 1977. At that time the distinction between healthy and unhealthy negative emotions was present in REBT theory, but was not particularly emphasised. Since that time we have come to realise the central place this distinction occupies in the theory and practice of REBT and how important it is to teach it to clients early in the therapeutic process. In this chapter, we will provide a diagrammatic summary of the eight major unhealthy negative emotions and their healthy counterparts (see Figure 4.1). In doing so, we will review the inferences, beliefs, cognitive consequences and action tendencies that are associated with each healthy and unhealthy pairing. It is crucial that you understand the factors that help differentiate between healthy and unhealthy negative emotions before explaining these distinctions to your clients. After providing the diagrammatic summary and reviewing briefly each component we will demonstrate how to introduce some of these distinctions to clients by using illustrative therapist–client dialogue. Finally, we will suggest an exercise that you can do in small training groups to become personally and professionally more familiar about the distinctions between healthy and unhealthy negative emotions. This exercise will also help you to practise assessing the emotional problems of your fellow trainees before you do so with your clients. But first, let us say a word about terminology.

▶ Terminology ('healthy-unhealthy' vs. 'appropriate-inappropriate' negative emotions)

You will have noted that we use the words 'healthy' and 'unhealthy' to distinguish between two types of negative emotions. Albert Ellis once used the terms 'appropriate' and 'inappropriate' in making this distinction and you will find numerous references to these terms in all but his latest writings where he now uses 'healthy' and 'unhealthy'. Gilmore (1986) was one of the first to consider the use of the terms 'appropriate' negative emotions and 'inappropriate' negative emotions problematic. He did so because it is not clear, especially to clients and beginning

Emotion	Healthy or unhealthy	Inference[1] in relation to personal domain[2]	Type of belief	Cognitive consequences	Action tendencies
Anxiety[3] (ego or discomfort)	Unhealthy	• Threat or danger	Irrational	• Overestimates probability of threat occurring • Underestimates ability to cope with the threat • Creates an even more negative threat in one's mind • Has more task-irrelevant thoughts than in concern	• To withdraw physically from the threat • To withdraw mentally from the threat • To ward off the threat (eg. by superstitious behaviour) • To tranquilise feelings • To seek reassurance
Concern	Healthy	• Threat or danger	Rational	• Is realistic about probability of threat occurring • Views the threat realistically • Realistic appraisal of ability to cope with the threat • Does not create an even more negative threat in one's mind • Has more task-relevant thoughts than in anxiety	• To face up to threat • To deal with the threat constructively • To take constructive action to reduce/minimise the risk or danger
Depression[4] (ego or discomfort)	Unhealthy	• Loss (with implications for future) • Failure	Irrational	• Sees only negative aspects of the loss or failure • Thinks of other losses and failures that one has experienced • Thinks one is unable to help self (helplessness) • Only sees pain and blackness in the future (hopelessness)	• To withdraw from reinforcements • To withdraw into oneself • To create an environment consistent with feelings • To attempt to terminate feelings of depression in self-destructive ways
Sadness	Healthy	• Loss (with implications for future) • Failure	Rational	• Able to recognise both negative and positive aspects of the loss or failure • Able to help self • Able to look to the future with hope	• To express feelings about the loss or failure and talk about these to significant others • To seek out reinforcements after a period of mourning
Unhealthy anger	Unhealthy	• Frustration • Goal obstruction • Self or other transgresses personal rule • Threat to self-esteem	Irrational	• Overestimates the extent to which the other person acted deliberately • Sees malicious intent in the motives of others • Self seen as definitely right; other(s) seen as definitely wrong • Unable to see the other person's point of view • Plots to exact revenge	• To attack the other physically • To attack the other verbally • To attack the other passive-aggressively • To displace the attack on to another person, animal or object • To withdraw aggressively • To recruit allies against the other

Figure 4.1 A diagrammatic summary of healthy and unhealthy negative emotions

Emotion	Healthy or unhealthy	Inference in relation to personal domain	Type of belief	Cognitive consequences	Action tendencies
Healthy anger	Healthy	• Frustration • Goal obstruction • Self or other transgresses personal rule • Threat to self-esteem	Rational	• Does not overestimate the extent to which the other person acted deliberately • Does not see malicious intent in the motives of the other(s) • Does not see self as definitely right and the other(s) as definitely wrong • Able to see the other's point of view • Does not plot to exact revenge	• To assert self with the other • To request, but not demand, behavioural change from the other • To non-aggressively leave an unsatisfactory situation after taking steps to deal with it
Guilt	Unhealthy	• Violation of moral code (sin of commission) • Failure to live up to moral code (sin of omission) • Hurts the feelings of a significant other	Irrational	• Assumes that one has definitely committed the sin • Assumes more personal responsibility than the situation warrants • Assigns far less responsibility to others than is warranted • Does not think of mitigating factors • Does not put behaviour into overall context • Thinks that one will receive retribution	• To escape from the unhealthy pain of guilt in self-defeating ways • To beg forgiveness from the person wronged • To promise unrealistically that she will not 'sin' again • To punish self physically or by deprivation • To disclaim responsibility for wrongdoing • To reject offers of forgiveness
Remorse	Healthy	• Violation of moral code (sin of commission) • Failure to live up to moral code (sin of omission) • Hurts the feelings of a significant other	Rational	• Considers behaviour in context and with understanding in making a final judgement concerning whether one has 'sinned' • Assumes appropriate level of personal responsibility • Assigns appropriate level of responsibility to others • Takes into account mitigating factors • Puts behaviour into overall context • Does not think one will receive retribution	• To face up to the healthy pain that accompanies the realisation that one has sinned • To ask, but not beg, for forgiveness • To understand reasons for wrongdoing and act on one's understanding • To atone for the sin by taking a penalty • To make appropriate amends • No tendency to make excuses for one's behaviour or enact other defensive behaviour • To accept offers of forgiveness
Shame	Unhealthy	• Something shameful has been revealed about self (or group with whom one identifies) by self or others • Acting in a way that falls very short of one's ideal • Others will look down on or shun self (or group with whom one identifies)	Irrational	• Overestimates the 'shamefulness' of the information revealed • Overestimates the likelihood that the judging group will notice or be interested in the information • Overestimates the degree of disapproval self (or reference group) will receive • Overestimates the length of time any disapproval will last	• To remove self from the 'gaze' of others • To isolate self from others • To save face by attacking other(s) who have 'shamed' self • To defend threatened self-esteem in self-defeating ways • To ignore attempts by others to restore social equilibrium

Figure 4.1 (Continued)

DISTINGUISHING BETWEEN HEALTHY AND UNHEALTHY NEGATIVE EMOTIONS

Emotion	Healthy or unhealthy	Inference in relation to personal domain	Type of belief	Cognitive consequences	Action tendencies
Disappointment	Healthy	• Something shameful has been revealed about self (or group with whom one identifies) by self or others • Acting in a way that falls very short of one's ideal • Others will look down on or shun self (or group with whom one identifies)	Rational	• Sees information revealed in a compassionate self-accepting context • Is realistic about the likelihood that the judging group will notice or be interested in the information • Is realistic about the degree of disapproval self (or reference group) will receive • Is realistic about the length of time any disapproval will last	• To continue to participate actively in social interaction • To respond to attempts of others to restore social equilibrium
Hurt	Unhealthy	• Other treats self badly (self undeserving)	Irrational	• Overestimates the unfairness of the other person's behaviour • Other perceived as showing lack of care or as indifferent • Self seen as alone, uncared for or misunderstood • Tends to think of past 'hurts' • Expects other to make the first move toward repairing relationship	• To shut down communication channel with the other • To sulk and make obvious one is hurt without disclosing details of the matter • To indirectly criticise or punish the other for the offence
Sorrow	Healthy	• Other treats self badly (self undeserving)	Rational	• Is realistic about the degree of unfairness in the other person's behaviour • Other perceived as acting badly rather than as uncaring or indifferent • Self not seen as alone, uncared for or misunderstood • Less likely to think of past hurts than when hurt • Doesn't think that the other has to make the first move	• To communicate one's feelings to the other directly • To influence the other person to act in a fairer manner
Unhealthy jealousy	Unhealthy	• Threat to relationship with partner from another person	Irrational	• Tends to see threats to one's relationship when none really exists • Thinks the loss of one's relationship is imminent • Misconstrues one's partner's ordinary conversations as having romantic or sexual connotations • Constructs visual images of partner's infidelity • If partner admits to finding another attractive, believes that the other is seen as more attractive than self and that one's partner will leave self for this other person	• To seek constant reassurance that one is loved • To monitor the actions and feelings of one's partner • To search for evidence that one's partner is involved with someone else • To attempt to restrict the movements or activities of one's partner • To set tests which partner has to pass • To retaliate for partner's presumed infidelity • To sulk

Emotion	Healthy or unhealthy	Inference in relation to personal domain	Type of belief	Cognitive consequences	Action tendencies
Healthy jealousy	Healthy	• Threat to relationship with partner from another person	Rational	• Tends not to see threats to one's relationship when none exists • Does not misconstrue ordinary conversations between partner and other men/women • Does not construct visual images of partner's infidelity • Accepts that partner will find others attractive but does not see this as a threat	• To allow partner to express love without seeking reassurance • To allow partner freedom without monitoring his/her feelings, actions and whereabouts • To allow him/her to show natural interest in members of the opposite sex without setting tests
Unhealthy envy	Unhealthy	• Another person possesses and enjoys something desirable that the person does not have	Irrational	• Tends to denigrate the value of the desired possession and/or the person who possesses it • Tries to convince self that one is happy with one's possessions (although one is not) • Thinks about how to acquire the desired possession regardless of its usefulness • Thinks about how to deprive the other person of the desired possession • Thinks about how to spoil or destroy the others desired possession	• To disparage verbally the person who has the desired possession • To disparage verbally the desired possession • To take away the desired possession from the other (either so that one will have it or the other is deprived of it) • To spoil or destroy the desired possession so that the other person does not have it
Healthy envy	Healthy	• Another person possesses and enjoys something desirable that the person does not have	Rational	• Honestly admits to oneself that one desires the desired possession • Does not try to convince self that one is happy with one's possessions when one is not • Thinks about how to obtain the desired possession because one desires it for healthy reasons • Can allow the person to have and enjoy the desired possession without denigrating the person or the possession	• To strive to obtain the desired possession if it is truly what one wants

Figure 4.1 *(Continued)*

Notes

[1] *Inference = Personally significant hunch that goes beyond observable reality and which gives meaning to it; may be accurate or inaccurate.*

[2] *Personal domain = The objects – tangible and intangible – in which a person has an involvement (Beck, 1976). REBT theory distinguishes between ego and comfort aspects of the personal domain, although those aspects frequently interact.*

[3] *REBT theory distinguishes between ego anxiety and discomfort anxiety.*

[4] *Depression in this context refers to non-clinical depression.*

REBT trainees, to what the terms refer. It could be said that they refer to emotional responses to activating events at 'A'. However, this view that events can determine the appropriateness of an emotion implies a kind of 'A causes C' thinking that runs counter to REBT theory. On the other hand, the terms 'appropriate' and 'inappropriate' can be construed as referring to the beliefs on which these emotions are based. In this case 'appropriate' negative emotions are deemed to stem from 'appropriate' (i.e. rational) beliefs and 'inappropriate' negative emotions from 'inappropriate' (i.e. irrational). However, the terms 'appropriate' and 'inappropriate' beliefs do not appear in the REBT literature and if terms were needed to stress the link between emotions and beliefs in this way, 'rational' negative emotions and 'irrational' negative emotions would make this connection clearer. Indeed, for a time, I (WD) experimented with the use of just these terms.

In addition, there is a problem with using the terms 'appropriate' and 'inappropriate' when pointing to the relationship between emotions and beliefs. It could be argued that given the REBT view that emotions stem largely (but not exclusively) from beliefs, an 'appropriate' negative emotion is one that is appropriate to the belief that the person holds irrespective of whether this belief is rational or irrational. Thus, an inappropriate negative emotion in REBT theory is really an appropriate negative emotion in that it is an appropriate response to an irrational belief.

To avoid these problems with the terms 'appropriate' and 'inappropriate' negative emotions, we suggest using terms such as 'healthy' and 'unhealthy' or 'constructive' and 'unconstructive' negative emotions. These terms make it clear that 'healthy' negative emotions stem from rational beliefs and have functional consequences and that 'unhealthy' negative emotions stem from irrational beliefs and have dysfunctional consequences. As such they aid both trainee and client learning.

▶ Healthy and unhealthy negative emotions: a diagrammatic summary

Figure 4.1 presents a comprehensive diagrammatic summary of the major distinctions between healthy and unhealthy negative emotions. Looking at the columns from left to right, the first column provides the name of each emotion. You will note that there are eight pairs of unhealthy and healthy negative emotions, with the unhealthy negative emotion listed first. Please note that we have used the names of emotions as we currently use them in REBT theory. Different REBT therapists may use different words to describe the same emotions. For example, some use the term 'annoyance' for healthy anger, Also, as we will presently discuss, clients bring to therapy their own emotional terminology and may well not understand the REBT distinctions just by being introduced to the REBT emotional terminology. Your tasks at this point are to discover your client's emotional terminology, to explain the REBT version and to negotiate a shared language which reflects the distinctions between healthy and unhealthy negative emotions as they are made in REBT theory. This does not necessarily involve using REBT terminology. I (WD) jokingly explain to trainees that it is acceptable to use the words 'fish' and 'chips' to distinguish between what REBT theory calls 'anxiety' and 'concern' as long as you and your client understand that 'fish' has the inferences, irrational beliefs, cognitive consequences and action tendencies that are associated with what REBT calls 'anxiety' and that the term 'chips' has the inferences, irrational beliefs, cognitive consequences and action tendencies associated with what REBT theory calls 'concern'.

The second column from the left in Figure 4.1 shows whether the emotion listed in the first column is an unhealthy or a healthy negative emotion. The main way to distinguish between a healthy and an unhealthy negative emotion is to look at their effects. According to REBT theory unhealthy negative emotions about negative 'critical As' are unhealthy in the sense that they do not help your clients to change these negative 'As' if indeed they can be changed, nor do they encourage them to make a constructive adjustment if these 'As' cannot be changed. Healthy negative emotions do encourage productive attempts to change negative 'critical As' and do facilitate constructive adjustment to 'As' that cannot be changed. Also healthy negative emotions aid your clients in their pursuit of their basic goals and purposes, whilst unhealthy negative emotions impede people in this pursuit.

The third column gives the major inferences related to each healthy-unhealthy emotional pairing. To help you to understand inferences fully in the context of your client's emotional experiences, we need to introduce you to the concept of the 'personal domain'. This concept was first introduced in the mid-1970s by Aaron T. Beck (1976) and refers to the objects – both tangible and intangible – in which a person has an involvement. REBT theory distinguishes between ego and comfort-related aspects of the personal domain, although it does emphasise that these aspects frequently interact.

Inferences are personally significant hunches about reality that give meaning to it. Inferences go beyond the data at hand and need to be tested out by your client. They may be accurate or inaccurate. If you consider the 'inference' column in Figure 4.1, you will note that within each pairing, a healthy negative emotion and its unhealthy counterpart share the same inference. This makes the REBT position on emotions very clear, i.e. inferences contribute to, but do not determine emotions. Put slightly differently, whilst inferences are important in determining the flavour of a negative emotion, they do not determine the health of that emotion. For that we need to turn to the fourth column which outlines the type of belief associated with each pair of healthy-unhealthy negative emotions.

We have already reviewed these beliefs in Chapter 1 and will say more about assessing them in Chapter 8. Here we just want to underscore the central part that beliefs play in determining emotions and to state once again that healthy negative emotions about negative 'critical As' stem largely from rational beliefs and unhealthy negative emotions about these 'As' stem largely from irrational beliefs.

The fifth column from the left in Figure 4.1 outlines what we term the cognitive consequences of holding different beliefs. Whilst the inferences listed in column three give shape to your client's emotional experience (e.g. when the person faces a threat she will either experience anxiety or concern), the cognitive consequences listed in column five detail the kinds of thinking that your client engages in whilst holding different beliefs. As you will see if you inspect column five carefully, the type of thinking your client engages in as a result of holding rational beliefs is, in general, more realistic and balanced than the type of thinking she engages in as a result of holding irrational beliefs which tend to be skewed and distorted. While your client's inferences at 'A' are often distorted when she is disturbed, the inferences that she forms at 'C' (i.e. her cognitive consequences of irrational beliefs) will be even more distorted and skewed. The reason for this is that your client's inferences at 'A' trigger her irrational beliefs at 'B', while her inferences at 'C' are determined by these irrational beliefs.

The sixth column (i.e. the one on the far right) outlines the ways in which your client tends to act when he holds different beliefs. We term these 'action tendencies'. However, it is far from inevitable that your client will act in accordance with a particular action tendency. Let us give an example to illustrate these points. If your client holds an irrational, anxiety-creating belief, he will experience a strong tendency to withdraw from the situation in which he is anxious. However, he can go against his action tendency and remain in the situation until his feelings of anxiety dissipate. Indeed, the behavioural principle of exposure (Marks, 1978) requires your client to do just this. Encouraging your clients to act against their action tendencies is a core feature of REBT practice after you have helped them to dispute their irrational beliefs.

▶ Five approaches to teaching clients the distinction between healthy and unhealthy negative emotions

There are five approaches to helping yourself and your clients differentiate between healthy and unhealthy negative emotions. Before we list these, we do wish to stress that you can employ these approaches singly or together. As different approaches will be enlightening for different clients, we advise you to become familiar with all of them.

Using different terms

Because REBT theory distinguishes between unhealthy negative emotions and their healthy counterparts, in helping your clients to make this distinction in therapy it is important to use agreed terminology which reflects this important difference. There are two ways of doing this. First, you can use the REBT terminology as shown in Figure 4.2. This figure provides a brief reminder of these terms.

One problem that you may experience with taking this tack is that your client brings to therapy his own way of construing emotions and these constructions may be quite different to the REBT terms. It is quite common, for example, for your client to consider that unhealthy anger and guilt are constructive emotions and as such he would resist accepting your view that they are unhealthy. In order

Healthy negative emotions	Unhealthy negative emotions
Concern	Anxiety
Sadness	Depression
Remorse	Guilt
Sorrow	Hurt
Disappointment	Shame
Healthy anger	Unhealthy anger
Healthy jealousy	Unhealthy jealousy
Healthy envy	Unhealthy envy

Figure 4.2   Healthy and unhealthy negative emotions: REBT terminology

to clarify the REBT position here, you would need to make use of one or more of the four other approaches described in this section.

Another problem with relying solely on REBT terminology is that your client may well consider that healthy negative emotions are less intense than their unhealthy counterparts. For example, your client may consider remorse to be less intense than guilt. REBT's position on this issue is quite different – namely that this healthy negative emotion can be very intense and still be constructive. Thus, one can be intensely remorseful at breaking your own moral code without (i) demanding that you absolutely should not have acted in such a manner and (ii) condemning yourself as a person for your behaviour. REBT's theory of negative emotions posits qualitative rather than quantitative differences between healthy and unhealthy negative emotions, and thus one can be intensely remorseful without feeling guilty. A quantitative approach to negative emotions would place anxiety on a single continuum with differing levels of intensity of this emotion placed on this one continuum. In contrast a qualitative approach would employ two continua: one for anxiety, the other for concern with increasing levels of intensity of each emotion represented on each continuum. Thus, the quantitative approach does not keenly distinguish between anxiety and concern whilst the qualitative approach does. This crucial difference is shown in Figure 4.3.

In order to clarify these issues you will need to go beyond mere presentations of different terms and again use one or more of the four other approaches to distinguishing between healthy and unhealthy negative emotions to be described presently.

The second way of distinguishing between healthy and unhealthy negative emotions that employs different terms involves eliciting such distinctions from clients themselves. For example, one of your clients may use the terms 'helpful anxiety' and 'unhelpful anxiety' seemingly to differentiate between what in REBT terminology is known as concern and anxiety. Another of your clients may use the

Quantitative Model:

Increasing levels of anxiety (no clear distinction between anxiety and concern)

No Anxiety_____Intense Anxiety

Qualitative Model:

(i) Increasing levels of anxiety (clear distinction between anxiety and concern)

No Anxiety_____Intense Anxiety

(ii) Increasing levels of concern (clear distinction between anxiety and concern)

No Concern_____Intense Concern

Figure 4.3   Quantitative and qualitative models of negative emotions

terms 'furious' and 'pissed off' instead of REBT's unhealthy anger and healthy anger. As in the first example, many clients use a different qualifier to distinguish between a healthy negative emotion and its unhealthy counterpart. In the first example then, 'helpful' and 'unhelpful' were the different qualifiers used by this client seemingly to denote a distinction between REBT's anxiety and concern. We say 'seemingly' here because without exploring the matter further you will not know whether or not your client's terms match those used by REBT. Thus, in the example we are considering, in your client's mind 'helpful' anxiety may be much less intense than 'unhelpful' anxiety. As explained above and shown in Figure 4.3 this represents a quantitative model of negative emotions rather than the qualitative model advocated by REBT theory.

The other problem with accepting clients' emotional terms without exploring the meaning behind them is that these terms may reflect a different perspective on emotions than that put forward by REBT therapists. If you do not find out what your clients mean by their emotional terms then you have no way of discussing with them the problems that may be involved in their conceptualisations.

In conclusion, we hope you can see that relying solely on the 'using different terms' approach to helping clients distinguish between healthy and unhealthy negative emotions is fraught with problems. Consequently, you will need to employ one or more of the other four approaches to be discussed in this chapter to supplement this 'terms-based' approach.

Distinguishing between rational and irrational beliefs

As we have stated several times in this book, REBT theory holds that healthy negative emotions stem largely from rational beliefs and unhealthy negative emotions stem largely from irrational beliefs. It follows therefore that another approach to helping clients distinguish between healthy and unhealthy negative emotions involves referring to this part of theory.

For example, in helping your client distinguish between anxiety and concern you will want to point out that anxiety is based largely on irrational beliefs such as:

- This threat must not occur.

- It would be awful if this threat were to occur.

- I could not bear it if this threat were to occur

and in ego anxiety:

- If this threat were to materialise, it would prove that I would be worthless.

You will also want to point out that concern is based largely on rational beliefs such as:

- I would prefer it if this threat did not occur, but there is no reason why it must not happen.

- It would be bad if this threat occurred, but it would not be terrible.

- If this threat occurred, it would be difficult to tolerate, but I could bear it

and in ego concern:

- I would be a fallible human being if this threat were to occur. It would not prove that I am worthless.

Having presented the two different sets of beliefs in the context of the client's specific problem, you can then ask your client to use these different beliefs to judge whether he was experiencing anxiety or concern. If you use this beliefs-based approach to helping your client to distinguish between healthy and unhealthy negative emotions, then you can refer back to the example you used to teach him the 'ABCs' of REBT if you have already done so (see Chapter 3), or you can use this approach as a reminder when you do teach your client the 'ABCs'.

Distinguishing between different cognitive consequences of unhealthy and healthy negative emotions

Another approach to helping your client to distinguish between healthy and unhealthy negative emotions is to focus his attention on the different cognitive consequences that result from experiencing these different emotions. Here, then, the emphasis is on the utility of healthy and unhealthy negative emotions.

Continuing the example of teaching your client to distinguish between anxiety and concern, you will want to point out that anxiety has a number of cognitive consequences:

■ Your client will tend to overestimate the negative features of the threat.

■ He will tend to underestimate his ability to cope with the threat.

■ When facing the threat, he will tend to create an even more negative threat in his mind.

■ If he is carrying out a task while he is anxious, he will tend to have more task-irrelevant than task-relevant thoughts.

On the other hand, you will want to explain that concern has a different set of cognitive consequences:

■ Your client will not tend to overestimate the negative features of the threat.

■ He will tend to have a realistic view of his ability to cope with the threat.

■ When facing the threat, he will not tend to create an even more negative threat in his mind.

■ If he is carrying out a task while he is concerned, he will tend to have more task-relevant than task-irrelevant thoughts.

Having presented the two different sets of cognitive consequences in the context of the client's specific problem, you can then ask your client to use these different cognitive consequences to judge whether he was experiencing anxiety or concern.

Distinguishing between different action tendencies

As we explained in Chapter 2, when your client experiences an emotion she has a tendency to act in a number of ways. Because different emotions are associated with different sets of action tendencies, a fourth approach to teaching your client how to distinguish between healthy and unhealthy negative emotions is to focus her attention on these different sets of action tendencies.

Using the example of helping your client to distinguish between anxiety and concern, you will want to point out that when she is anxious, she will tend:

■ to withdraw physically from the threat (i.e. by leaving the situation);

■ to withdraw mentally from the threat (e.g. by changing the subject if she finds a topic of conversation threatening);

■ to ward off the threat (e.g. by using obsessive-compulsive or superstitious behaviour);

■ to tranquillise her feelings (e.g. by the use of alcohol, legal and illegal drugs, food, cigarettes, etc.); and

■ to seek reassurance so that the threat is neutralised, at least in her mind.

On the other hand, you will want to explain that concern is associated with a different set of action tendencies. When your client is feeling concern, she will tend:

- to face the threat; and

- to deal with the threat constructively without engaging in safety-seeking behaviour.

Once you have reviewed the two different sets of action tendencies in the context of your client's specific problem, you can then ask her once again to use these different action tendencies as a yardstick to judge whether she was experiencing anxiety or concern.

Distinguishing between different symptoms

The final approach to helping your client to distinguish between healthy and unhealthy negative emotions concerns focusing her attention on the difference in symptoms between the two different types of negative emotions. This is a somewhat problematic approach to use on its own as there is some overlap in symptoms associated with healthy and unhealthy negative emotions. For example, if you feel anxious you may well experience such symptoms as butterflies in your stomach, dry mouth and sweating. However, you may well experience these symptoms when you feel concerned and not anxious.

If you are going to use a 'symptoms-based' approach to differentiating between healthy and unhealthy negative emotions, the point to stress with your client is that when she has an unhealthy negative emotion (e.g. anxiety) she will experience more disabling symptoms and the degree of disability will be greater than when she has a healthy negative emotion (e.g. concern).

We made the point earlier that it is advisable to use a combination of the five approaches when helping your clients to distinguish between their healthy and unhealthy negative emotions. We will demonstrate this in an illustrative therapist–client dialogue. But first, let us summarise the five approaches in Figure 4.4.

Approach 1: Distinguishing between emotional terms (Terms-based approach)

Approach 2: Distinguishing between rational and irrational beliefs (Beliefs-based approach)

Approach 3: Distinguishing between cognitive consequences (Cognitive consequences-based approach)

Approach 4: Distinguishing between action tendencies (Action tendencies-based approach)

Approach 5: Distinguishing between symptoms (Symptoms-based approach)

Figure 4.4 Five approaches to distinguishing between healthy and unhealthy negative emotions

▶ **Teaching your client to distinguish between an unhealthy negative emotion (unhealthy anger) and a healthy negative emotion (healthy anger): an illustrative dialogue**

In this dialogue, I (WD) am counselling John who has been referred by his GP for 'anger management'. It is the second session and I am discussing a recent episode where he felt 'pissed off' at work. As will become clear, I am not clear at the outset whether by this he meant healthy anger or unhealthy anger. In the following part of the session I am attempting to clarify both for myself and for John whether his negative emotion was healthy or unhealthy. As you will discover, by 'pissed off' John meant unhealthy anger. As I will discuss later, it is important to help your client set goals which reflect healthy negative emotional responses to negative critical 'As' and this is particularly important when the emotion is anger. However, I will not discuss this issue here with John.

Windy: So, if I understand you correctly you felt 'pissed off' when your boss did not put you on the Gwilliam account. Is that right?

John: Yes, that's right.

Windy: Now in the therapy that I practice, we make an important distinction between what we call healthy and unhealthy negative emotions. The former are constructive responses to negative life events, whilst the latter are not so constructive. I'm not sure whether 'pissed off' is a healthy or an unhealthy response to the 'Gwilliam' episode. Will you bear with me while I ask you a few questions to help us both become clearer on this issue?

John: OK.

Windy: More specifically I want to discover whether you felt unhealthily angry or healthily angry. Does that distinction mean anything to you?

[This is an 'Approach 1' intervention]

John: Not really.

Windy: OK, let me explain. If you were healthily angry in this situation, you would have a set of beliefs similar to the following:

- I really want my boss to put me on the 'Gwilliam' account, but he doesn't have to do so.

- It's really unfortunate that my boss hasn't put me on to this account, but it isn't terrible.

- I can stand being deprived in this way, although it is difficult to tolerate.

- My boss isn't a bastard for depriving me of this opportunity, just a fallible human being who has done what I consider the wrong thing.

However, if you were unhealthily angry in this situation, you would believe something like the following:

- My boss absolutely should put me on the 'Gwilliam' account.

- It's terrible that he hasn't.

- I can't stand the deprivation.

- He is a bastard for depriving me of this opportunity.

Now which set of beliefs best accounted for your pissed off feeling at the time?

[This is an 'Approach 2' intervention]

John: Put like that I was unhealthily angry, because I believed that he was a bastard who shouldn't have treated me like that.

Windy: Right, but let's make doubly sure by looking at what you wanted to do in the situation.

Now, if you were unhealthily angry in the situation, you would have felt like attacking your boss physically or verbally; if not directly you would have felt drawn to getting back at him indirectly; or you would have felt like storming out. However, if you were healthily angry, your inclination would have been to assert yourself with him in an open and reasoned manner.

[This is an 'Approach 4' intervention]

John: Well, that clinches it then. I wanted to knock his block off.

Windy: So, it sounds as if you recognise that you were unhealthily angry rather than healthily angry. Do you generally refer to feeling 'pissed off' when you are angry?

John: I've never thought about it before... No, I use it quite loosely.

Windy: So, because it is important to distinguish between a healthy negative emotion like healthy anger and an unhealthy negative emotion like unhealthy anger, we need to use terms to reflect this distinction. Does it make sense to you to use the terms unhealthy anger and healthy anger as I have described them or can you think of more apt terms?

John: Yes, that sounds reasonable.

Windy: So we'll use this distinction throughout our work together.

In this segment, I (WD) used a combination of three approaches to ascertain that John was unhealthily angry rather than healthily angry when he said he was 'pissed off'. First, I used the 'terms-based' approach (Approach 1). Here, I introduced the REBT terms, unhealthy anger and healthy anger, to see if John could see the difference between them. When he said that he could not, I used the 'beliefs-based' approach (Approach 2) and outlined the likely irrational belief that underpinned his 'pissed off' feeling if this was unhealthy anger and the likely rational beliefs that underpinned this feeling if it turned out to be healthy anger. When John said that he related most to the irrational beliefs, thus confirming that he was unhealthily angry, I used the 'action tendencies-based approach' (Approach 4) to double-check. Finally, I returned to the 'terms-based' approach to agree on a shared language when discussing anger-related issues with John during counselling.

> How can you become more skilled at explaining the differences between healthy and unhealthy negative emotions to your clients? First, familiarise yourself with each of these different approaches. Second, pair up with a trainee colleague and, using a role-play format, practise explaining the differences between healthy and unhealthy negative emotions by employing arguments based on the five approaches. Record the role-play and play it to your REBT trainer or supervisor for feedback.

Becoming proficient at this skill will stand you in good stead when you come to assess your clients' problems using the 'ABC' framework, a subject to which we now turn.

Being specific in the assessment process

When your clients discuss their problems at the outset of therapy they often do so in general terms. It is difficult to assess clients' problems when they are couched in general terms. REBT theory states that people make themselves disturbed about specific events because they hold specific irrational beliefs about these events. These specific irrational beliefs may reflect more general, core irrational beliefs, but when your clients disturb themselves, it is in specific situations and because they hold specific irrational beliefs in those specific situations. Therefore, it is important for you to encourage your clients to provide specific examples of their emotional problems. Doing so will provide you both with the information you require to carry out an accurate assessment of these problems.

However, it is also important to give your client an opportunity to talk about his problems in his own way, at least until he considers that you have listened to him and shown that you have understood him from his own frame of reference. As you do this you can begin to construct an overall picture of the problems he is experiencing in his life. On more advanced courses in REBT, we devote quite a bit of time to the development of a problem list on which your client lists the problems he wishes to deal with during therapy. As such, this topic is beyond the scope of this introductory book (see Blackburn & Davidson, 1990).

► Select a target problem

After you have given your client an opportunity to talk about his problems in his own way, you will want to encourage him to discuss in greater depth the problem he wants to tackle first in therapy. This problem should be an emotional problem rather than a practical problem (Dryden, 1999a). Once you have agreed to tackle one of your client's emotional problems, you will be working on what is called, in REBT, a target problem.

> Target Problem = The problem that you have agreed to focus on with your client

You need to explain to your client that you are going to assess this target problem and thus you will need to stay focused on it until you have adequately assessed it and helped your client to deal with it. Guard against switching from problem to problem.

▶ Select and assess a specific example of your client's target problem

To help you keep focused and to gain the specific information you need in order to assess the problem thoroughly, encourage your client to provide a specific example of this target problem. This specific example might be:

- a recent example of the target problem;
- a typical example of the target problem; or
- a vivid example of the target problem.

What is important is that the problem is specific enough to provide you with a clear 'critical A' and a definite unhealthy negative emotion at 'C'. If you are successful in doing so, it makes assessing your client's irrational beliefs at 'B' relatively straightforward.

However, in all probability, your client will, in the course of the assessment of this specific example of his problem, move quite easily to a more general or abstract level of discourse. Guard against any tendency that you have to move to that general level of exploration. Don't hesitate to interrupt your client and encourage him to return to the specific example at hand. Explain the reason for your interruption and intervention. You may have to interrupt your client several times before he gets the point. Don't hesitate to do this, but do so politely and with tact.

You may also have to guard against your own tendency to move the client away from an assessment of the specific example of his problem to a more general assessment of the problem. Remember that when you assess a specific example of your client's problem this occurs at a specific time, in a specific setting and with specific people present.

As you may not realise that you are, in fact, moving your client away from the specific to the general, we recommend that you record assessment sessions with some of your fellow trainees in a peer counselling session. Identify occasions when you moved your 'client' from the specific to the general. Then, devise interventions that you could have made that would have helped you to stay specific.

You can do a similar exercise when your 'client' moved you away from the specific to the general and you did not bring her back to the specific example at hand.

CHAPTER SIX

Assessing 'C'

Once you have become skilled in REBT, you will be able to assess your clients' problems whether they supply you with emotional 'Cs', behavioural 'Cs' or cognitive 'Cs'. However, at this stage of your career as an REBT therapist, you will need to concentrate on being able to assess their emotional 'Cs' and as such in this chapter, we will show you how to assess these emotional 'Cs'. In doing so we will (a) encourage you to avoid 'A' → 'C' language in assessing 'C'; (b) tell you how to respond when your client believes that a healthy negative emotion is unhealthy; (c) help you to deal with vague 'Cs'; (d) advise you what to do when your client's 'C' is really an 'A'; and (e) suggest ways of intervening when your client gives you an extended statement when you ask for a specific 'C'.

► Avoid 'A' → 'C' language in assessing 'C'

When asking questions about how your client feels in a specific situation, be careful not to use what we call in REBT, 'A' → 'C' language. When you use 'A' → 'C' language you reinforce the idea in your client's mind that 'A' really does cause 'C'. As this is the antithesis to the REBT position and runs counter to what you may have taught your client if you have already introduced the 'ABC' model to him (see Chapter 3), by employing 'A' → 'C' language you will be giving your client conflicting and confusing messages. Here are some typical 'A' → 'C' questions that trainees ask at the beginning of their training in REBT:

- How did that make you feel?
- What feeling did that produce in you?
- Did that anger you?
- What feeling did that give you?
- What feeling did that provoke (or evoke) in you?
- What emotion did that give rise to?
- How did that lead you to feel?

We trust you can see that all these questions either explicitly state or strongly imply an 'A' causes 'C' theory of human emotion. For example, the question, 'How did that make you feel?' makes explicit that you think that 'that' (an unspecified event) can make your client feel something without recourse to any mediating variable (i.e. your client's beliefs). Therefore, 'A' ('that') is deemed to cause 'C' (your client's feelings).

How can you enquire about your client's feelings without explicitly stating or implying an 'A' → 'C' position? Let's examine two questions which avoid taking such a position.

When that happened, how did you feel?

In this question, you are putting forward a correlational relationship between 'A' (the event) 'When that happened' and 'C' (your client's feeling) 'how did you feel?' In doing so, you neither make explicit nor imply a causal relationship between 'A' and 'C'.

How did you feel about that?

In this question, you again advance a correlational relationship between 'C' ('How did you feel. . .') and 'A' (. . .about that?). However, the word 'about' makes it clear that your client's feeling is closely related to the event without implying that the former is caused by the latter. We recommend, therefore, that when you ask your clients about their feelings about 'A' that you include the word 'about' in your question. If you do, you will find it difficult to posit an 'A' → 'C' model of emotions and you will make it clear that your 'C' is closely related to the 'A' in question.

Here are a number of things that you can do to guard against asking 'A' → 'C' questions.

1. Become aware of 'A' → 'C' phrases in people's language. Watch soap operas on TV, for example and write down phrases that explicitly state or strongly imply an 'A' causes 'C' view of emotions.

2. Reformulate these 'A' → 'C' phrases into phrases that state a correlational view of human emotions.

3. Pair up with a trainee colleague and conduct a role-play of a counselling session. Have your colleague play the role of a client who makes numerous 'A' → 'C' statements. Correct your 'client' every time you identify an 'A' → 'C' statement.

    Record the session and in replay listen for any 'A' → 'C' client statements that you missed. Also, listen closely to your reformulations of these statements and evaluate your responses. Improve your phrasing as needed.

4. Get used to using 'A' → 'C' correlational statements and questions in your everyday speech. Correct yourself whenever you make an 'A' → 'C' connection in your speech. Notice 'A' → 'C' phrases in the speech patterns of others with whom you converse. Reformulate them in your mind, but don't correct others on this point. Some trainees become overenthusiastic and correct 'A' → 'C' language whenever they hear it. In our view, this is

an unwarranted intrusion into the social conventions of everyday conversation and we don't recommend that you do it.

5. Record your therapy sessions and listen to them carefully for instances of 'A' → 'C' thinking in your statements and questions. Correct these in your mind. Also listen to instances of 'A' → 'C' thinking in your clients' language. If you did not correct the most important of these, determine which were the most important to correct and think about how you could have done so. It is important to be circumspect. It is legitimately irritating for clients to be corrected every time they utter an 'A' → 'C' statement. You need to correct the most salient of these statements; you don't need to correct each and every one of them!

6. Take to supervision or training your ongoing difficulties in dealing with 'A' → 'C' statements, either your own or your clients'.

▶ When your client believes that a healthy negative emotion is unhealthy

In Chapter 4, we stressed the importance of helping your client to distinguish between a healthy negative emotion and an unhealthy negative emotion. This is very important to bear in mind while assessing 'C'. If your client has a healthy negative emotion about a negative 'critical A', then this is not targeted for change in REBT as it is regarded to be a constructive response to an aversive situation.

Explaining the above to your client is useful because it helps to reveal one of two related situations. First, it brings to light the idea held by some clients that calmness or the absence of feeling is a desirable and healthy response to a negative 'critical A'. At this point you can explain to your client that in order for him to be calm in the face of adversity, he would have to have an attitude of indifference about the adversity. Taking the example of John discussed in Chapter 4, he would have to believe: 'I don't care whether or not my boss puts me on the Gwilliam account' in order to feel calm about his boss's behaviour. Put like this, your client will generally understand the unrealistic nature of denying his healthy desires and no longer regard his healthy negative emotion as problematic.

Explaining the constructive nature of a healthy negative emotion may also reveal that your client has a second-order problem. Here, your client has an unhealthy negative emotion about what is a healthy negative response. For example, Dina was intensely, but healthily angry about being refused permission to go on leave. She was, however, unhealthily angry with herself for getting so healthily angry. Although her anger was healthy, Dina felt *unhealthily angry* about being *healthily angry*. Dina held the belief that she absolutely should not have strong feelings about being refused leave. She allowed herself to experience only mild or moderate negative feelings, but believed that strong feelings are not acceptable.

Explaining to clients like Dina that healthy negative emotions can be strong is sometimes sufficient here. When it is not, then the real emotional problem is your client's secondary problem which is then targeted for change.

> With a fellow trainee, role-play a scenario in which your client construes a healthy negative emotion as unhealthy. Help your partner to understand the functional cognitive consequences and action tendencies associated with the healthy negative emotion. Refer to Figure 4.1 (pp. 62–65) to help you.

▶ When your client's 'C' is vague

When you ask your client for her feelings about a negative 'critical A', she may well give you a vague feeling statement in reply. Here are some of the responses that clients may provide when you ask them how they felt about the negative 'critical As' in their lives:

- I felt upset
- I felt miserable
- I felt bad
- I felt tense
- I felt bothered
- I felt hot and bothered
- I felt jittery
- I felt down
- I felt devastated
- I felt pissed off
- I felt blue
- I felt jumpy
- I felt gutted

There are two problems with the feeling statements listed above. First, it is unclear whether they refer to healthy negative emotions or their paired unhealthy counterparts. You may think that 'devastated' may refer to an unhealthy negative emotion, but without further exploration, you cannot be certain. Second, it is unclear in many cases to which pair of emotions the feeling statement refers. Take the word 'upset' as an example. Leaving aside the issue concerning whether this refers to a healthy or an unhealthy negative emotion and assuming for the sake of discussion that it is an unhealthy emotion; what kind of emotion is it? Is it an anxious upset, a depressed upset or an angry upset? The answer is that we just don't know.

Whenever your client's feeling statement is vague, it is very important that you try to clarify it. In Chapter 4, I (WD) showed how I clarified John's vague feeling of being pissed off. If you recall from that chapter I mentioned that in addition to the terms you and your clients may use to refer to emotional states, you can utilise the following information in clarifying whether a negative emotion is healthy or unhealthy:

- the type of belief your client holds (rational or irrational);
- the cognitive consequences of holding the belief;
- her action tendencies; and
- her symptoms.

You can also use such information to clarify your client's vague negative emotion when you are unsure about its nature (e.g. whether it is anxiety/concern; depression/sadness; guilt/remorse etc). When you are unsure about the nature of your client's negative emotion, irrespective of its health, you can also refer to her inferences for clues. Thus, if your client is talking about a threat to her personal domain, she is likely to be anxious or concerned; if she is discussing hurting the feelings of a significant other, she is likely to feel guilt or remorse. Becoming very familiar with which pairs of negative emotions are associated with which inferences will be enormously useful in your quest to identify your client's specific unhealthy negative emotion. Having at your fingertips the knowledge outlined in Figure 4.1 is about the best preparation you can undertake for assessing your clients' 'Cs'.

▶ When your client's 'C' is really an 'A'

When you ask your client about her emotions about a negative 'critical A', she may reply with an inference rather an emotion. For example, your client may say the following:

- I felt rejected
- I felt punished
- I felt betrayed
- I felt abandoned
- I felt used
- I felt criticised
- I felt frustrated

If you inspect these statements carefully you will note that none of them represents actual emotions. We do not have an emotion called 'rejection' or one called 'used', for example. Rather we have emotions about the inference that we have been rejected or used at 'A'. Thus, your client expresses a 'C' that is really an inferred 'A', how can you best respond? The following is a constructed therapist–client dialogue showing one way that this can be done.

> Windy: How did you feel when Kevin said that to you?
>
> Karen: I felt rejected.
>
> Windy: Actually, Karen, rejection isn't a feeling. It is something that actually happened to you or something that you thought happened to you. Are you saying that you thought Kevin had rejected you?
>
> Karen: Yes.
>
> Windy: OK. Now, let's assume for the moment that Kevin did reject you, how did you feel about that rejection?
>
> Karen: When I thought that he had rejected me, I felt hurt.

Here it is important to note two things. First, I explained to Karen that rejection is not a 'C'; rather, it is an actual or inferred 'A'. Second, I said to Karen: '...let's assume for the moment that Kevin did reject you...' This is a typical REBT strategy. At this point, I did not challenge the validity of Karen's inference, i.e. that Kevin had rejected her. Rather, I encouraged her to assume temporarily that her inference was true so that in this case I could ascertain how she felt about this presumed rejection. REBT therapists tend to challenge the validity of their clients' inferences *after* they have identified, challenged and helped their clients to change the latter's irrational beliefs. REBT therapists argue that their clients are in a more objective (and therefore better) frame of mind to review the validity of their inferences once they are relatively free from the biasing effects of their irrational beliefs.

▶ When your client's 'C' is an extended statement

It is rare for your clients to have had any systematic psychological education. Consequently, your clients will usually be quite unclear about the nature of emotions, how to discriminate among different emotions and what mainly determines their feelings. We have already commented that your clients are likely to give you vague feeling statements when you ask them how they feel about the negative 'critical As' in their lives. Also, as we have just noted they may easily confuse their emotions with the inferences they make about 'A'.

There is one other problem that you will encounter when you attempt to assess 'C' that we wish to cover. This problem particularly occurs when you ask your clients questions about their emotions with the word 'feel' in it (e.g. 'How did you feel when that happened?'). Thus, when you ask your client how she felt about a given situation she may provide you with an extended statement of what she thought about the event in question. This extended statement usually begins with the words 'I felt...' followed by the extended thought. It may also commence with the phrase 'I felt that...'. The one thing that your client does not give you, however, is an accurate, clear account of her feelings.

Here are some examples of what we mean.

Example 1

Rhena: How did you feel when your mother interrupted you like that?

Client: I felt here she goes again, she never lets me finish a sentence.

Example 2

Rhena: How did you feel when your boss gave you that assignment to do?

Client: I felt that I would never be able to do it.

What can you do when your client gives an extended thought in reply to a question about her feelings? First, you can take the thought and find out what feeling was associated with it.

Rhena: How did you feel when your boss gave you that assignment to do?

Client: I felt that I would never be able to do it.

Rhena: And when you found yourself thinking that you would never be able to do it, what feeling did you experience in your gut?

Client: I felt very scared.

The points to note from this example are as follows.

- I (RB) formed a bridge between the client's extended thought and his feeling. I labelled his initial response as a thought without explanation and asked for the feeling associated with the newly relabelled thought.

- I added the words 'in your gut' to make it clearer that I was looking for a feeling not a thought.

The second thing you can do when your client gives you an extended thought instead of the feeling that you asked for is to explain what has happened. Tell your client that she has given you a thought rather than a feeling and then ask for the feeling again. When you do so, you might use the word 'emotion' rather than the word 'feeling', as for some people the word 'emotion' makes it clearer what you are looking for. For example:

Rhena: How did you feel when your mother interrupted you like that?

Client: I felt here she goes again, she never lets me finish a sentence.

Rhena: Actually, 'here she goes again, she never lets me finish a sentence' is a thought rather than a feeling. What emotion did you experience in your gut when she interrupted you?

Client: Oh, I see. I felt angry.

If your client still has trouble identifying an emotion, you might try giving him a list of emotions from which he is asked to select the closest one to his experience. It is also useful to limit your client to a one-word answer because this will curb his tendency to give you an extended answer. Dealing with clients who have an ongoing difficulty in identifying their emotions is beyond the scope of this book and, as such, you will need to take such issues to supervision. An important part of assessing 'C' is evaluating your client's motivation to change this unhealthy negative emotion. We will deal with this issue in Chapter 11.

As an exercise, pay attention to the words used by people to depict emotional states. You can do this by listening to people in your everyday life, on television and on radio. Make a note of examples of i) vague 'Cs', ii) feelings as extended statements and iii) 'As' described as 'Cs'. For each example, construct a response that would help clarify and specify the 'C'.

In the following chapter, we turn our attention to assessing the 'critical A'.

CHAPTER SEVEN

Assessing the 'critical A'

In order for you to get the most from this chapter, we advise you to re-read the section on inferences in Chapter 1. We also suggest that you review Figure 4.1, particularly the part of the figure which links each pair of negative emotions with the relevant inference. For, once you have identified your client's unhealthy negative emotion, you will know what type of inference is associated with it.

Your major task at this point is to identify your client's 'critical A', which you will recall is that part of the 'A' which triggers your client's irrational belief which is at the core of her unhealthy negative emotion. This 'critical A' can be an actual event, but more often than not it is an inference (which as you know may or may not be accurate). Accurately assessing the 'critical A' is a complex skill and since we do not want to confuse you or overload you with too many techniques of assessing 'critical As', we will only discuss two ways of so doing (see Chapter 7 of Neenan & Dryden, 1999 for additional methods of assessing the 'critical A'). As we do so, we want you to bear in mind one important point. Do not challenge your client's inferences. Assume that they are true until you have completed the assessment and disputing processes. There are, of course, one or two exceptions to this general rule but, at this point in your training, It is a sound rule to follow. This is such an important point that it bears repetition.

> While working to identify your client's 'critical A', assume temporarily that his inferences are correct. Do not challenge these inferences at this point.

▶ Identify the theme and its embodiment

When you use this technique you first identify which theme was present in the client's chosen specific example and then you discover which element embodied this theme. Once you have accurately done this you can drop the identified theme and continue with its embodiment which is the 'critical A'. Here is how I (WD) used this technique to identify John's 'critical A'. John felt unhealthy anger when he saw one of his colleagues, Peter, leave work early.

Windy: When you felt anger when you saw Peter leave work early, was he breaking one of your rules?

['Other transgresses my rule' is one of the major themes in unhealthy anger.]

John: Yes, I thought that Peter was showing disrespect to his colleagues by leaving early.

['Peter showing disrespect to his colleagues' is the embodiment of the 'transgression' theme.]

Windy: So what you were most angry about with respect to Peter leaving was that this meant that he was breaking your rule by showing disrespect to his colleagues. Is that right?

[Here I summarise by linking the identified theme – 'other breaking rule' – with its embodiment – 'by leaving early, Peter showed disrespect to his colleagues'.]

John: Exactly.

[As my assessment is correct I will drop the identified theme – 'other breaking your rule' – from my language from now on and just refer to its embodiment – 'by leaving early, Peter showed disrespect to his colleagues'.]

Review the emotions listed in Figure 4.1 in Chapter 4. Commit to memory the inferential themes associated with each emotional pairing. Doing so will assist you greatly when assessing your client's 'critical As' via the theme and it's embodiment method. You may find it useful to create an 'aide memoire' to which you can easily refer during therapy sessions until you know the inferential themes by heart.

▶ The 'magic question'

When you use the 'magic question' technique to identify your client's 'critical A', take the following steps:

Step 1. Ask your client to focus on the situation in which he disturbed himself (i.e. where he experienced his predominant unhealthy negative emotion).

Henry focused on the following situation in which he felt 'hurt': My friend Sophie was talking more to Jack than to me.

Step 2. Ask your client first to imagine that the situation cannot be changed. Then, ask him to identify the one factor that would get rid of or significantly reduce his unhealthy negative emotion in the situation.

> Henry identified the following factor which would have reduced his feelings of hurt: Knowing that Sophie likes me more than Jack.

Step 3. The opposite is probably the client's 'critical A'.

> Henry's critical A was: Sophie likes Jack more than me.

When using the magic question technique do not allow your client to change the actual 'A' at step 2. Doing so will not help you to identify the 'critical A'. Emphasize to your client that the situation at 'A' has happened, is happening or will happen. For example, Henry at step 2 may have said 'If Sophie had talked to me more than to Jack.' You may need to stress that the details of the situation should stay the same. Thus:

> Rhena: But, Sophie did in fact talk to Jack more. Given that is the case, can you decide on one factor that would stop you from feeling hurt about Sophie talking to Jack more than to you?
>
> Henry: If I knew for sure that Sophie likes me more than Jack.

In order to develop competence in these two methods, record their use in peer counselling and play the recording to your trainer for feedback. As you become more skilled in their use you may be able to use them conjointly, one as a validity check for the other.

Since identifying your client's 'critical A' is a difficult skill to learn, you will probably only learn to do so with competence by playing relevant portions of your recordings with clients to your supervisor for feedback. Our advice at this point of your career is don't be obsessive-compulsive about identifying your client's 'critical A'. Settling for a 'critical A' which is 'good enough', but not completely on target is better than delaying the process of assessment until you get the 'critical A' exactly right. If you do the latter, you may waste valuable therapy time and antagonise your client at the same time, thus placing strain on the therapeutic alliance. In the practice of REBT, as elsewhere in life it is important to adopt a non-perfectionist attitude.

You have now assessed your client's unhealthy negative emotion at C and his 'critical A'. You are now ready to identify the irrational beliefs at 'B' that mediate between 'A' and 'C'.

CHAPTER EIGHT

Assessing irrational beliefs

You have now identified your client's major unhealthy negative emotion and have discovered his 'critical A'. You are now in a position to assess his irrational beliefs. If you have taught your client the 'ABCs' of REBT (as discussed in Chapter 3) you will have taught him the role that demands play in emotional problems. In the money model you will also have alluded to the role that awfulising beliefs play in such problems.

If you have not previously gone over the 'ABCs' with your client, now would be a good time to do so and we refer you back to Chapter 3 for how to do this. If you have already gone over this material, you will still need to review it at this point. You will also need to expand your teaching to cover awfulising beliefs in more detail and to introduce low frustration tolerance beliefs and self-/other-/life-depreciation beliefs. The best way to do this is also to teach the rational alternatives at the same time. Let me (WD) demonstrate how to do this with Sue who was anxious about the prospect of the audience laughing at her when she gave a talk.

Windy: So to sum up, Sue, you were anxious about the prospect of the audience laughing at you.

Sue: Right.

Windy: Now your anxiety is what we call 'C', your emotional consequence. So let me write this up on this whiteboard under 'C'. Next, the prospect of the audience laughing at you is that part of the activating event that you were particularly anxious about. This is what I call the 'critical A', so I'll write this up on the whiteboard under 'critical A'.

'Critical A' = Prospect of audience laughing at me

'B' = ?

'C' = Anxiety

Now, do you remember when I taught you the 'ABCs' of REBT what 'B' stands for?

Sue: My beliefs.

Windy: Correct. As you see from the whiteboard we don't yet know what your beliefs are about the audience laughing at you that led to your anxiety. This is what we need to do now. OK?

Sue: OK.

Windy: Now do you recall from the money model what type of belief underpins people's emotional problems?

Sue: Their absolute demands.

Windy: That's right. And what were the healthy alternatives to these demands?

Sue: Non-dogmatic preferences.

Windy: Let me write these down under two main headings. Non-dogmatic preferences are the main type of rational beliefs; so I'll write that down under the heading 'rational beliefs' and demands are the main type of irrational beliefs. Now 'rational' basically means beliefs that will help you to achieve your basic goals and purposes, whereas 'irrational' means beliefs that will stop you from achieving these goals. I'll come back to the terms 'rational' and 'irrational' later.

Rational Beliefs	Irrational Beliefs
↓	↓
Non-dogmatic preferences	Demands

Any questions so far?

Sue: No that's quite clear. You've just summed up what you showed me earlier.

Windy: Right. What I want to do now is to show you the three other rational beliefs that stem from your non-dogmatic preferences and the three other irrational beliefs that stem from your rigid musts. Then we can apply this to determine which set of beliefs you were holding when you became anxious about being laughed at. OK?

Sue: Fine.

Windy: Now if you hold a non-dogmatic preference about something, you believe that you want it, but you don't insist that you must have it. If you believe that, then if you don't get what you want are you likely to believe (i) 'it's bad that I haven't got what I want, but it's not terrible' or (ii) 'it's awful that I don't have it'?

Sue: I'd believe that it's unfortunate.

Windy: Right, now if you believe that you absolutely have to have the object in question, which of those two beliefs that I have outlined will you hold?

Sue: I'd believe that it would be awful.

Windy: Right. Let me put that up on the board

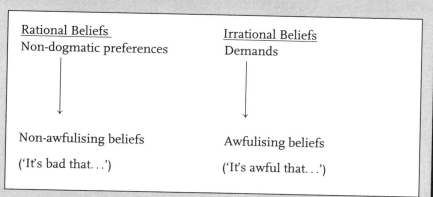

[I have drawn a line from non-dogmatic preferences to non-awfulising beliefs and a line from demands to awfulising beliefs to emphasise for the client that in both cases the latter are derived from the former. Not all REBT therapists hold that musts and non-dogmatic preferences are primary and that awfulising beliefs and non-awfulising beliefs and the other irrational and rational beliefs that I will describe presently are derived from these primary beliefs. Such REBT therapists would therefore omit the connecting lines.]

Windy: Any questions on awfulising beliefs?

Sue: Well, is that different from when I say 'It's awful weather.'

Windy: It is. When you are disturbed, 'awful' means that it is worse than 100% bad and it must not be as bad as it is. Whereas when you say that it is awful weather you really mean that it is bad weather and you aren't usually emotionally disturbed about it. Does that answer your question?

Sue: Yes, that's clear.

Windy: Now on to the next set of beliefs. When you hold a non-dogmatic preference and you don't get what you want, then will you tend to conclude that the resulting situation is tolerable, albeit difficult to bear or will you believe that you can't stand it when you don't get what you want?

Sue: I'd believe that it is tolerable.

Windy: Right, now if you believe that you absolutely must have the object in question, which of those two beliefs that I have outlined will you hold?

Sue: I'd believe that it would be intolerable.

Windy: That's right. Let me add that to the board.

Rational Beliefs	Irrational Beliefs
Non-dogmatic Preferences	Demands
↓	↓
Non-awfulising beliefs ('It's bad that...')	Awfulising beliefs ('It's awful that...')
HFT beliefs ('I can stand it')	LFT beliefs ('I can't stand it')

Any questions, Sue?

Sue: No. That's perfectly clear.

Windy: And do you go along with it or not?

Sue: It makes very good sense and I can already see how it applies to me.

Windy: I'm pleased about that; but I've got one other concept to go over before we see how it all applies to you. OK?

Sue: OK.

Windy: Now let's suppose that you believe that it would be preferable for you to do well in a forthcoming test, but that you don't have to do well. Now let's suppose that you fail the test. Would you believe (a) that you are a fallible human being for having failed or (b) that you are a thoroughgoing failure for having failed?

Sue: I'd believe that I was fallible.

Windy: But what if you believe that you absolutely have to do well in the test, which of those two attitudes towards yourself would you tend to hold?

Sue: I see what you're getting at. I'd believe that I was a failure.

Windy: This concept also applies to how you view other people, but we will get to that when it becomes relevant. Any questions or comments or should I put this concept up on the board?

Sue: Put it up on the board.

Windy: OK.

Rational Beliefs	Irrational Beliefs
Full Preferences	Demands
↓	↓
Non-awfulising beliefs ('It's bad that...')	Awfulising beliefs ('It's awful that...')
HFT beliefs ('I can stand it')	LFT beliefs ('I can't stand it')
Self-/Other-/Life-acceptance beliefs ('I'm a fallible human being')	Self-/Other-/Life-depreciation beliefs ('I'm a failure')

Now, let me give you a handout which is basically the same as I have on the board which you can use for future reference.

Sue, I've gone over the heart of the model that I use to help people to understand their emotional problems. Before we apply it to the problem that we have been focusing on, do you have any final questions or observations to make?

Sue: No. It seems to be a good model.

Windy: Any doubts or reservations?

Sue: Only about applying it.

Windy: Well, we'll come to that in due course. Now let's apply the model and see if we can determine the irrational beliefs that underpinned your anxiety about being laughed at by the audience.

[At this point I am going to use the four irrational beliefs that I have discussed with Sue as a guide to the assessment questions I am about to ask. My questions will therefore be theory-driven.]

Windy: Now, what demands, if any, were you making about being laughed at?

Sue: The audience must not laugh at me.

Windy: Did you have any awfulising beliefs about being laughed at?

Sue: It would be terrible if they laughed at me.

Windy: Any LFT beliefs? LFT stands for low frustration tolerance.

Sue: (looking up at the whiteboard)...That's the 'I can't stand it belief', isn't it?

Windy: Yes.

Sue: I wouldn't be able to stand it if they laughed at me.

Windy: Finally, were you depreciating yourself, the audience or the situation?

Sue: I was depreciating myself.

Windy: What did it sound like?

Sue: If they laugh at me it would prove that I was incompetent.

Windy: As a speaker or as a person?

Sue: Both.

Windy: So, let's complete the 'ABC' on this problem that we started earlier...(writing on the board)

'Critical A' = Prospect of audience laughing at me

'B' = (i) The audience must not laugh at me

(ii) It would be terrible if the audience laughed at me

(iii) I wouldn't be able to stand it if the audience laughed at me

(iv) If the audience laughed at me it would prove that I am an incompetent person

'C' = Anxiety

Now, Sue, is this an accurate assessment of your anxiety about being laughed at?

Sue: Very accurate.

The above is a theory-driven way of assessing your client's irrational beliefs. It involves two basic steps: first you teach your client the irrational beliefs that underpin emotional disturbance in general, dealing with any doubts, reservations and misunderstandings he may have along the way and second, you apply this viewpoint to the client's target problem. For a different, less theory-driven way of assessing clients' irrational beliefs see Dryden (1999a). We prefer the theory-driven method of assessing irrational beliefs because it has an educational as well as a therapeutic purpose. Here you actively teach your client which irrational beliefs to look for in both the target problem and in the other emotional problems he wishes to cover during therapy. As such, it tends to save therapeutic time and encourages the client to take responsibility for assessing their own problems.

In the next chapter, we deal with the important issue of assessing for the presence of your clients' emotional problems about their emotional problems or what is known in REBT as meta-emotional problems.

Assessing meta-emotional problems

Your clients will frequently make themselves emotionally disturbed about their emotional problems, thus unwittingly giving themselves a 'double dose' or 'two problems for the price of one'. We call these secondary emotional problems 'meta-emotional problems', a term which literally means emotional problems about emotional problems (Dryden, 2000). Like primary emotional problems, meta-emotional problems are characterised by unhealthy negative emotions.

There are two major issues that arise in REBT which pertain to meta-emotional problems. The first concerns assessment and the second relates to which emotional problem you target for change first: your client's primary emotional problem or her meta-emotional problem. We will deal with both these issues in this chapter.

Before showing you how to assess your clients' meta-emotional problems, let us first deal with a training issue. Some REBT therapists routinely determine whether or not their clients have meta-emotional problems, whereas others will enquire about their existence only when their clinical intuition leads them to suspect that meta-emotional problems may be present. At this stage of your career as an REBT therapist, you probably lack such intuition, so it might be advantageous for you to ask your clients routinely how they feel about their primary emotional problems. The drawback to doing this is that you may become confused. Many trainees find the REBT assessment process difficult enough when dealing with their clients' primary emotional problems. Introducing meta-emotional problems into the picture at a time when they are struggling with primary problems would prove too much for these trainees at this juncture. Whilst we will show you how to assess meta-emotional problems, we urge you to consider carefully your own skill and confidence level as an REBT practitioner when deciding whether or not you are going to deal with your clients' meta-emotional problems. Discuss this issue with your REBT trainer or supervisor.

There is no definite point in the assessment process to determine best whether or not your client has a meta-emotional problem. You can do so (i) as soon as your client has mentioned that he has a primary emotional problem; (ii) after you have assessed his primary problem; or (iii) after you have disputed the irrational beliefs that underpin his primary problem and he has started to effect some change on the problem. Another way of determining that your client has a meta-emotional problem is by investigating reasons why he is not making expected progress on his primary problem. One reason for this may be that he has a meta-emotional problem which is getting in the way of the work that he otherwise would be doing on the primary problem.

▶ (A) The 'ABCs' of meta-emotional problems

You carry out an assessment of your client's meta-emotional problem in the same way as you do his primary emotional problem. Here is an illustrative example.

Larry is anxious about giving presentations at work. I (WD) assessed the 'ABC' of his primary problem as follows:

'Critical A' = I won't get promotion if I don't give an excellent presentation

B = (i) I must get promoted

(ii) It would be awful not to get promoted

(iii) Not being promoted means that I'm totally incompetent

C = Anxiety

I then explored the possible presence of a meta-emotional problem as follows:

Windy: Now, Larry, some people have what I call secondary emotional problems about their primary problems...

[I usually refrain from using the term meta-emotional problems with clients as it can come over as psychological jargon.]

... What I mean by this is that if someone is angry, for example, then she may feel guilty about experiencing angry feelings. The anger is her primary problem and the guilt she feels about her anger is her secondary problem. Am I putting that clearly?

Larry: Yes, she has two problems; anger and the guilt she feels about her anger.

Windy: Right. Now let's see if you have a secondary problem about your primary anxiety. OK?

Larry: Yes.

Windy: Now when you are anxious about the prospect of not getting promotion, how do you feel about being anxious?

Larry: I'm ashamed of myself.

Windy: And what's the most shaming aspect about being anxious in that situation...?

[Note that I am not assuming that Larry's feelings of anxiety is his 'critical A'. As a result of my assessment, it seems that not coping is his 'critical A'.

Larry: Being anxious means I am not coping.

Windy: So, you are most ashamed about having anxious feelings in this situation. Let's see if we can figure out what beliefs you hold about your anxiety that are leading to secondary feelings of shame. We can use the sheet of irrational beliefs I've given you.

The 'ABC' of Larry's meta-emotional problem turned out thus:

Critical A = Not coping with the prospect of not being promoted

B = (i) I must cope with the possibility of not being promoted

   (ii) It is terrible not to cope

   (iii) Not coping means that I am a weak person

C = Shame

It is often helpful to your client to put both his primary emotional problem and his meta-emotional problem on the whiteboard so that he can see them clearly in diagrammatic form. Otherwise, your client might get lost in a welter of words. Figure 9.1 shows a diagrammatic form of Larry's two problems.

▶ Focusing on the meta-emotional problem as the target problem

When you have ascertained that your client has a meta-emotional problem, you are faced with a choice: (i) do you start to work on his primary emotional problem (or continue to work on this target problem if you have already started to work on it) or (ii) do you start to work on his meta-emotional problem (or switch to this target problem if you have started work on his primary problem)? First, let us reiterate what we said earlier. If you are unsure of your REBT skills and consider that working in therapy at both the level of your client's primary emotional problem and his meta-emotional problem is too daunting or confusing for you at this stage of your career as an REBT therapist, then just work at the level of your client's primary emotional problem.

<u>Larry's primary emotional problem</u>

'Critical A1' = Not getting promotion (if I don't give an excellent
                        presentation)

 'B1' = (i) I must get promoted

        (ii) It would be awful not to get promoted

        (iii) Not being promoted means that I'm totally incompetent

'C1' = Anxiety

<u>Larry's meta-emotional problem</u>

'Critical A2' = Not coping with the prospect of not being promoted

 'B2' = (i) I must cope with the possibility of missing a promotion

        (ii) It is terrible not to cope

        (iii) Not coping means that I am a weak person

'C2' = Shame

<u>Notes</u>

    a) The notation 'A1', 'B1', 'C1' represents Larry's primary emotional
       problem and 'A2', 'B2', 'C2' represents his meta-emotional problem

    b) The aspect that Larry is most ashamed about with respect to his
       anxiety is that he is not coping. So, in this example not coping,
       rather than the feelings of anxiety is Larry's 'Critical A'.

Figure 9.1 A diagrammatic representation of Larry's primary and meta-emotional problems

If you want to develop your skills at working with your clients' primary and meta-emotional problems then practise doing so in peer counselling. Pair up with a trainee colleague (with another trainee as observer) and have your 'client' choose a primary personal problem about which he has a meta-emotional problem. Assess both problems and choose which problem to start with; this then becomes the target problem. Record the interview and stop the recording when you become confused or lose your way. Review the recording at the place where you began to have difficulties and with the help of the observer and your 'client' get back on track. Do this whenever you become stuck until you can deal with primary and meta-emotional problems with confidence. This process should help you to develop competence at working productively at the level of primary and meta-emotional problems with your real clients.

Having made these points, here are four criteria for dealing with your client's meta-emotional problem before her primary emotional problem

1. When the presence of the meta-emotional problem interferes with the work that you are trying to do on your client's primary emotional problem in the session.

> For example, if while working with Larry on his unhealthy anxiety problem, I (WD) noticed that he seemed quite distracted, I would ask him what he was focusing on during our work. If Larry replied that he was riddled with shame over the weakness he exposed through his anxiety, I would encourage him to deal with his shame first then I would strive to help him feel disappointed about being anxious (rather than ashamed about it). After his shame was resolved and Larry felt healthily disappointed about his feelings of anxiety he could give his full attention whilst in session to working on overcoming his primary anxiety (about the possibility of missing a promotion).

2. When the presence of the meta-emotional problem interferes with the work that the client is trying to do on her primary emotional problem outside the session.

> For example, Larry may attempt to identify and challenge the irrational beliefs that underpin his anxiety about missing a promotion when he feels anxious prior to giving a presentation at work. However, he may fail to do so and be puzzled as to the reason why. In the next therapy session, it may become clear that Larry's feelings of shame about his anxiety (which he regards as a personal weakness and believes he absolutely should not have) are distracting him from confronting his primary anxiety problem between

sessions. Larry is more able to carry out the work he needs to do between therapy sessions in order to overcome his anxiety once he conquers his secondary emotional shame problem.

3. When the meta-emotional problem is clinically more important than the primary emotional problem.

There are certain client problems where the meta-emotional problem is clinically more important than the primary emotional problem. You will get to know these as you become clinically more experienced. However, two common client problems where the meta-emotional problem is more crucial are (i) generalised anxiety where your client's anxiety about anxiety is more of a feature than the primary anxiety and (ii) certain mild obsessive thought problems where your client's secondary intolerance of the original disturbing thought is the most salient feature of the problem. The final criterion for beginning with the meta-emotional problem is:

4. When your client sees the sense of addressing her meta-emotional problem before her primary emotional problem.

Even though the above three criteria for addressing your client's meta-emotional problem before her primary problem are sound, if your client does not see the sense in doing so, then proceeding with her meta-emotional problem will threaten the therapeutic alliance that you have developed with your client. Thus, it is useful to present your client with a plausible rationale for starting with her meta-emotional problem. Only begin this work when she sees the sense of so doing.

On this point, a good training exercise is for you to practise presenting such rationales in peer counselling to your fellow trainee 'client'. Record your rationales under each of the three conditions listed below:

1. When your 'client' is distracted by his meta-emotional problem when you are attempting to work on his primary emotional problem in the session.

2. When your 'client' is distracted by his meta-emotional problem when attempting to work on his primary problem outside the session.

3. When the meta-emotional problem is more clinically significant than his primary emotional problem.

Play your recordings to your REBT trainer or supervisor and get feedback on your performance.

In the next chapter, we will focus on goal-setting with your clients.

CHAPTER TEN

Goal-setting

It is easy sometimes to lose sight of the fact that the purpose of therapy is to help your clients achieve their goals. However, it should also not be forgotten that as a therapist you have goals in therapy as well. Thus, in a seminal book entitled *The Goals of Psychotherapy*, Mahrer (1967), the book's editor, concluded from his review of the contributions to the book that therapists have two major types of goals: (i) those concerned with the reduction of psychological disturbance and (ii) those concerned with the promotion of psychological health. As a therapist, the more you can encourage your client to be explicit about her goals and the more you can be explicit about your own goals, the better. Doing so will enable the two of you to work cooperatively toward agreed goals. Such cooperative striving towards the achievement of agreed goals is, as Bordin (1979) has argued, an important hallmark of effective therapy.

As we have already argued, REBT is an approach to psychotherapy that stresses the importance of explicit, open communication between you and your client. It also recommends that you set goals with your client. Thus, this therapeutic system encourages you to engage in the very activities that will help promote effective therapeutic change.

In this chapter, we will deal with goals at three levels. First, we will consider goals in relation to dealing with specific examples of your client's problems. Then, we will consider goals in relation to your client's problems as these are broadly conceptualised. Third, we will consider the issue of goals as they relate to the distinction between reducing disturbance and promoting growth.

► Setting a goal with respect to a specific example of your client's target problem

Let us outline the steps for effective goal-setting in REBT as these relate to specific examples of your client's target problem. As you will see, this is not the simple process it may appear at first sight.

Steps for effective goal-setting

In this section, we will outline the steps that you need to take in order to set therapeutic goals with your client with respect to specific examples of her target problems. Whilst your client may well have more than one problem, we will deal with the situation where you are working with a given client problem. We want to stress one point at the outset. Whilst we will outline a suggested sequence with respect to the steps you need to take to elicit your client's goals for change. it is important for you to note that you may well set goals at different times in the therapeutic process. For example, we make an important distinction between your client's defined problem and her assessed problem. The defined problem is the way your client sees or defines her focal concern, whereas the assessed problem is the same problem put into an ABC format. We argue below that it is important to elicit goals for both the defined problem and the assessed problem. However, please note that you may do this at different times in the REBT therapeutic process. The work you are likely to do on your client's goal as this relates to the assessed problem will occur later, and sometimes much later than the work you will do eliciting her goal as this relates to the defined problem. Remember this as we cover the following steps.

Step 1: Ask for a specific example of your client's target problem The first step in the goal-setting process is to encourage your client to give you a specific example of her more general problem. As we discussed in Chapter 5, you can best assess your client's target problem if she provides you with a specific example of it because this will help you to identify a specific 'critical A', a specific unhealthy negative emotion and specific irrational beliefs.

Step 2: Communicate your understanding of the problem from the client's point of view and come to an agreement with her on this defined problem The second step is for you to understand how your client sees the problem and to communicate this understanding to the client. This is important for two reasons. First, it helps your client to 'feel' understood. Second, knowing how your client sees the problem will help you to assess it using the ABC framework. It is at this point that your basic counselling skills come into play. As you need to convey understanding, we particularly recommend using the skills of clarification and reflection, In addition, you will need to phrase your attempts at understanding as just that – attempts. As such, there needs to be a tentative quality to your interventions which you need to put as hunches to be confirmed or denied rather than as incontrovertible facts.

For example, it is best for you to say: 'So, you seemed to find it difficult getting down to studying when you knew that your friends were out having a good time. Have I understood you correctly?', rather than 'You found it difficult getting down to studying when you knew that your friends were out having a good time.'

In the former statement, you phrase the statement in a tentative fashion and put your understanding as a hunch, which you are testing. This enables your client to correct you if you are off track. If you make the latter statement, however, you phrase the statement more definitely and do not check out your understanding of what your client has said. Rather, you proceed on the basis that you are right! This makes it more difficult for your client to correct you if you are off beam.

The purpose of being tentative and testing out your hunches is that it helps you to come to an agreed understanding with your client on the problem as she sees it.

We call this 'coming to an agreement with the client on the <u>defined problem</u>'. Later in the goal-setting process, you will need to arrive at an agreement with the client on the <u>assessed problem</u>.

Step 3. Elicit your client's goal with respect to the defined problem   It is important to elicit your client's goal in relation to the defined problem. Whilst this goal may change once you have assessed the problem, it is helpful, nonetheless, to learn what your client considers a satisfactory solution to her problem. Indeed, it is here that you will frequently discover that your client has unrealistic or unobtainable goals for change. If so, you will need to confront this issue. Whether you do so at the point when your client reveals her unrealistic or unobtainable goal or whether you choose to do so later, you do have to deal with the issue; otherwise, your client will think that you agree with her goal when, in fact, you don't. We will discuss how to deal with unrealistic and unobtainable goals in a moment, but first let us show you how you might usefully elicit your client's goal with respect to the defined problem.

Let us use the example that we introduced above. As a reminder the client (whose name is Clare) defined her problem with respect to a recent specific example as follows: 'I found it difficult getting down to studying when I knew that my friends were out having a good time.'

Here is how I (WD) would work with Clare to identify her goal as it relates to this defined problem.

Windy: So you found it difficult getting down to studying when you knew your friends were out having a good time. What would you like to achieve from counselling on this issue?

[Alternative questions might include:

  (i) What would you like to be able to do instead?

 (ii) How would you like to change?

(iii) What would be in your best interests to do?]

Clare: To be able to study even when I know my friends are out enjoying themselves.

If Clare replied that she didn't know, I would have employed other techniques such as:

- Imagery: This would involve asking Clare to imagine a preferred solution to her problem (e.g. 'Close your eyes and imagine a scene where you are doing what is productive for you even when your friends are out enjoying themselves. What would you be doing in that image?'). Having elicited this preferred scenario, I would ask Clare to give reasons for her choice.

- Time projection: This involves Clare projecting herself into the future and stating how she would like to have acted at the time in question (e.g. 'Imagine that we are a year in the future. Looking back would you rather have studied at the time we are discussing or not?'). Then, I would again ask her to give reasons for her answer.

- A best friend's suggestion: This involves asking Clare to imagine how her best friend would suggest she handle the problem. (e.g. 'Would your best friend suggest that you study even though you know that she and others might be out enjoying themselves? If so, why do think she would say that?'). If you use this technique you need to ensure that your client's best friend does, in fact, have her interests at heart.

- A worst enemy's suggestion: This is the opposite of the best friend's suggestion and is useful in that it would help Clare to see that an enemy might be quite happy to see her continue this self-defeating behaviour (e.g. 'What would your worst enemy suggest that you do when you know that your friends are out enjoying themselves and you need to study?'). I would again explore Clare's answer and ask her to set a suitable goal at the end of the exploration.

- Therapist suggested options: If none of the above techniques helped to elicit Clare's goals on her defined problem, then as therapist I might provide her with possible goal options. In doing so, I would give her an opportunity to discuss these options with me. [My role here is to encourage her to reflect on the advantages and disadvantages of all the provided options as a way of choosing a relevant goal.]

Step 4. Dealing with unrealistic and unobtainable goals It sometimes transpires when you are working with your client to identify her goals with respect to her defined problem that she will nominate goals that are unrealistic or unobtainable. As we pointed out earlier, when your client comes up with such a goal you do need to deal with it, but not necessarily at the precise time when your client discloses it. Thus, whilst making a mental or preferably a written note of this goal, you may choose to wait to deal with it until you have assessed your client's problem and determined her goal with regard to the assessed problem. When you decide to confront your client on her unrealistic or unobtainable goal is a matter of clinical judgment and we urge you to discuss such matters with your REBT supervisor. What we will do here is to detail the kinds of client goals that are unrealistic or unobtainable. Then, we will give an example of how to deal with the situation where your client nominates an unrealistic or unobtainable goal in relation to her defined problem.

What are unrealistic and unobtainable goals? It would be nice if your clients set goals for change that were achievable, realistic and involve them changing some aspect of themselves. Suffice it to say, this does not always occur! The following list contains the unrealistic or unobtainable goals that you will most frequently encounter in REBT.

1. <u>Changing impersonal negative events</u>. Here your client nominates a goal which involves a change in some aspect of the situation that he is disturbing himself about (in other words, 'A').

Let's suppose King Canute came to see you for counselling. His complaint is that he is unhealthily angry because the tide will not obey him and go back when he orders it to do so. You have accurately defined his problem and go on to ask him for his goal. He replies that he wants you to help him to change the tide so that it goes back at his command. Would you accept this as a legitimate therapeutic goal? Of course you wouldn't. You would explain to King Canute that influencing the tide is outside his control despite the fact that he is a king. You would encourage him instead to set as an achievable goal feeling healthily angry rather than unhealthily angry about the grim reality that the tide is not compliant with his wishes.

2. <u>Changing other people</u>. Some of your clients come to counselling convinced that their emotional problems are caused by the way other people treat them. They adhere to what we have called an 'A' → 'C' viewpoint. As such, when you ask them for their goals, they say that they want to change these people. This is not an obtainable goal since others' behaviour is outside the direct control of your clients.

One of your clients, Jill, is depressed because she claims that her boss made, from her perspective, an unreasonable demand on her at work. In response to your enquiry concerning her goal for change, she replies: 'I want my boss to stop making unreasonable demands on me.' If you consider this goal carefully, it points to a change in the other person's behaviour. Now, on the face of it, this may seem quite reasonable. If Jill's boss is making too many demands on your client what is wrong in Jill wanting him to change? The answer is both nothing and everything. There is nothing wrong with her goal if we treat it as a healthy desire, i.e. it is rational for her to want her boss to change. However, there is everything wrong with this statement as a therapeutic goal.

It is important for you to note and to encourage your client to appreciate that it is not within her power to change her boss. Jill can only realistically hope to change what is in her power to change – namely, her thoughts, behaviour, feelings, etc. Thus, as she cannot directly change her boss, you cannot, as her therapist, profitably accept this as a legitimate goal. Now, of course, Jill can influence her boss to change, and these influence attempts may be successful. This means that it is legitimate to accept as Jill's goal changes in her attempts to influence her boss because these new attempts are within her control. Accepting Jill's new influence attempts as a legitimate goal for change is very different from accepting a change in her boss's behaviour as a legitimate goal. The former is within Jill's control, the latter is not.

3. Feeling neutral about negative events. It sometimes occurs in REBT that clients indicate that they want to feel neutral about negative events. Consider Geraldine who was rejected by her boyfriend and felt very hurt about this. Here is an excerpt from my therapy with her that illustrates this unrealistic goal and how I responded to it.

> Windy: So, Geraldine, the problem as I understand it is that you feel very hurt about Keith ending the relationship. Have I understood you correctly?
>
> Geraldine: Yes you have.
>
> Windy: What would you like to achieve from counselling on this issue?
>
> Geraldine: I want not to feel anything about it.
>
> Windy: The only way I can help you do that is to help you to develop the belief. 'I don't care whether Keith ended the relationship or not. It is a matter of indifference to me.' How realistic is it for you to believe that?
>
> Geraldine: Put like that it isn't realistic at all. But it hurts so much I just want an end to the pain.
>
> Windy: I understand that you do feel very hurt about the ending of your relationship with Keith and I do want to help you deal with your hurt. But, I want to do so in a way that is realistic and lasting. The trouble with trying to convince yourself that you don't care when, in fact, you care too much is that it is a lie and you just can't sustain that lie. How about this as an alternative? What if I can help you to feel sorrowful about being rejected rather than very hurt about it? This would mean that you would still care about what happened to you, but you wouldn't care too much about it. How does that seem to you as a reasonable goal?

Geraldine: I see what you mean. That would be fine if I could achieve it.

[If Geraldine could not see the difference between hurt and sorrow, I would use a variety of teaching points to clarify this distinction (see Chapter 4).]

Windy: If you can see the sense of that then I'll do my best to help you achieve it.

4. Seeking goals which would perpetuate the client's irrational beliefs. Sometimes clients come up with goals with respect to their defined problems that are within their control, but pursuing these goals would serve to perpetuate their irrational beliefs. Let me give a few examples of what I mean from my (WD) practice.

Clare's defined problem (with respect to specific example): I found it difficult getting down to studying when I knew that my friends were out having a good time.

Goal: To leave my studies and join my friends whenever they go out without feeling guilty.

This would not be an unrealistic goal if Clare were studying for long hours and not taking any breaks from her work. However, in this case, Clare was procrastinating on her studies and was spending her time watching TV when she knew that her friends were out enjoying themselves. If I accepted her goal of joining her friends whenever they went out I would have been helping her, unwittingly, to perpetuate the irrational beliefs that underpinned her procrastination. Instead, I first established that studying was in Clare's best long-term interests and then helped her to plan her time so that she spent enough time studying and some time socialising with her friends.

Jill's defined problem: (with respect to specific example): I'm depressed because my boss made an unreasonable demand on me at work.

Goal: To tell my boss off whenever he makes unreasonable demands on me.

The problem with this goal is twofold. It does not deal with the issue of Jill's depression and it encourages her to develop a new emotional problem – unhealthy anger. Thus, if I accepted this goal I would have been leaving intact the irrational beliefs underpinning Jill's depression and encouraging the development of unhealthy anger-related irrational beliefs.

This is how I proceeded. First, I encouraged Jill to consider the benefits of healthy assertion over making unhealthy anger-based rebukes in the light of what she knows about her boss (review the material on healthy anger vs. unhealthy anger in Chapter 4 as an aid here). Second, I helped Jill to see that she would need to deal with her depression before she could assert herself adequately with her boss.

Geraldine's defined problem: I feel very hurt about Keith ending our relationship.

Goal: To beg Keith to take me back.

Once again this goal does not help the client to tackle her feelings of hurt about the rejection. Indeed, Geraldine is seeking to deal with the rejection by getting rid of it. In doing so, her begging behaviour indicates that she has another problem – a dire need either to have a relationship or a dire need for comfort. If I accepted her goal I would have bypassed her hurt-related irrational beliefs and legitimized whatever irrational beliefs underpin her begging.

Instead, I helped Geraldine to see that sorrow was a healthier alternative to rejection than hurt and instead of begging Keith to take her back, she planned instead to discuss his reasons for rejecting her and to learn from it if he pointed out to her things she did or failed to do that would impact negatively on her future relationships.

---

5. Seeking intellectual insight. Rational emotive behaviour therapy distinguishes between two types of insight: intellectual insight and emotional insight (Ellis, 1963). It defines intellectual insight as a light acknowledgment that your client's irrational beliefs are inconsistent with reality, illogical and self-defeating and that the rational alternatives to these beliefs are consistent with reality, logical and self-helping. However, such insight does not, by itself, change how your client feels and acts, but is seen as an important prelude to emotional insight. This form of insight is defined as a strong conviction that your client's irrational beliefs are inconsistent with reality, illogical and self-defeating and that the rational alternatives to these beliefs are consistent with reality, logical and self-helping. Here, though, this strong conviction does affect how your client feels and acts. In short, when your client has intellectual insight, he still experiences unhealthy negative emotions and acts in self-defeating ways when faced with negative 'critical As', whereas with emotional insight, he responds to these same 'As' with healthy negative emotions and self-enhancing behaviour.

When your client responds to your enquiry about goals by saying that he wants to understand the target problem, he or she often holds the implicit idea that gaining such insight is sufficient for change to occur. Unless this idea is identified and confronted, your client will only make limited gains from REBT. Whilst some clients do seek what may be called 'REBT intellectual insight' in that they are genuinely interested in what the approach has to say about the nature of their problems, most clients in my experience are looking for what may be called 'psychodynamic intellectual insight' in that they hope to identify childhood determinants of their problems which when discovered will lead to problem resolution. It follows from what we have said above that neither REBT nor psychodynamic intellectual insight is sufficient for psychological change to take place.

Explaining to your client that intellectual insight has its place, but is insufficient for change to occur, often helps him to set a more functional goal. It also helps the client to distinguish between insight as a therapeutic <u>means</u> and a change in psychological functioning as a therapeutic <u>goal</u>. This is demonstrated in the following interchange.

Windy: So you find it difficult getting down to studying when you know your friends are out having a good time. What would you like to achieve from counselling on this issue?

Clare: I'd like to understand why I have this problem.

Windy: What information are you looking for?

Clare: Well, there must be something in my childhood that would explain why I have so much difficulty studying when my friends are out.

Windy: Let's suppose there was. What would you hope having this information would do for you?

Clare: It would help me solve this problem.

Windy: And if your problem was solved what would be different?

Clare: I would be able to study even when I knew that my friends were out enjoying themselves.

[Note that this is Clare's real goal. She hopes that psychodynamic intellectual insight will provide the <u>means</u> whereby this <u>goal</u> can be achieved. It is important to distinguish between the means and the goal and this is what I address in my next response.]

Windy: Let me put what you've said a little differently. It sounds to me from what you've said that your goal is to be able to study even when you know that your friends are out enjoying themselves. You hope that the way to achieve this goal is by finding a reason in your childhood. Have I understood you correctly?

Clare: Yes.

Windy: Well, I'm happy to work with you towards your goal. However in REBT, we have a different view on the best way that people can achieve their therapeutic goals. Let me outline the REBT position on this issue...

[I would then discuss the REBT view of therapeutic change as it pertains to the role of intellectual and emotional insight. Namely, that in order to achieve emotional insight into rational beliefs it is necessary to dispute them and act on them repeatedly.]

Step 5: Assess the defined problem using the 'ABCs' of REBT and come to an agreement with him on this assessed problem As we have dealt fully with the issue of assessing your clients' problems in Chapters 5–9, we will make only a few points that are particularly relevant to the topic of goal-setting here. Remember that the emotional 'Cs' of your clients' problems will generally be unhealthy negative emotions (see Chapter 6). However, don't forget that 'Cs' can also be behavioural.

It is possible to treat behavioural 'Cs' in two ways. First, you can regard behavioural 'Cs' as actual expressions of action tendencies that stem from unhealthy negative emotions. In this case, you need to target these unhealthy negative emotions for change. Second, you can regard behavioural 'Cs' as stemming directly from your client's irrational beliefs and as such they can themselves be targeted for change.

As with the defined problem, it is important to agree with your client that your assessment of his problem is accurate. Doing so will help you to set a healthy goal with respect to the assessed problem. Conversely, failing to make such an agreement will lead to difficulties in goal-setting with respect to the inaccurately assessed target problem.

Step 6: Elicit the client's goal with respect to the assessed problem If you have accurately assessed the specific example of your client's problem, you will have identified an unhealthy negative emotion and, if relevant, a self-defeating behavioural response at 'C', a 'critical A' and a set of irrational beliefs at 'B'. The next step is for you to elicit your client's goal which is based on his assessed problem. This will be in relation to the 'critical A' and will usually involve a negative healthy emotion and a constructive behavioural response.

Let me discuss an example based on an assessment of Clare's defined problem as discussed above (see p. 105). If you recall, her defined problem with respect to the specific example she chose was: 'I found it difficult getting down to studying when I knew that my friends were out having a good time.'

My assessment of this problem revealed the following situational 'ABC':

> Situation: After planning to spend the evening studying, I heard that my friends had gone out.
>
> 'A' = The unfairness of being deprived of the company of my friends when I wanted it.
>
> 'B' = I must have fairness in my life at the moment. It's terrible to be deprived in this unfair way. I can't bear this unfair deprivation. Poor me!
>
> 'C' = Self-pitying depression and procrastination on studying.

Here is how I helped Clare set a realistic and functional goal with respect to the assessed problem. Note, in particular, that in keeping with REBT theory, I assume temporarily that Clare's inferred 'A' is true (see Chapter 7). Thus, I help her to set an emotional and behavioural goal in light of the 'unfairness' of the situation.

Windy: So, let's assume that you are in an unfair situation; how is your depression helping you to study?

[Note that here I am drawing on Clare's goal with respect to her defined problem, i.e. 'To be able to study even when I know my friends are out enjoying themselves.']

Clare: It's not. In fact, it's discouraging me.

Windy: Right, so what alternative negative emotion will help you to study?

[I deliberately phrased my question in this somewhat oblique way to encourage Clare to think hard about the issue.]

Clare: What <u>negative</u> emotion will help me study? I don't understand.

Windy: Well, think about it? You are never going to like the unfairness of the situation, are you?

Clare: No, I guess not.

Windy: Nor are you likely to be indifferent to it, are you?

Clare: No.

Windy: So, what's left?

Clare: To feel negative about it.

Windy: That's right, but there are two different types of negative emotions. There are what I call unhealthy negative emotions which generally inhibit people from adjusting to a negative life event or from taking constructive action to change it and there are healthy negative emotions which are constructive emotional responses to negative life events and do help people to change these events or make a constructive adjustment if the situation cannot be changed. Now, let's take your feelings of depression about the unfair situation where you need to study when your friends are out enjoying themselves. is your depression a healthy or unhealthy emotional response?

Clare: Clearly it's unhealthy.

Windy: Why?

Clare: Because it doesn't help me to study.

Windy: Right. Now, given that you are faced with what you consider to be an unfair situation, what would be a healthy negative emotional response?

Clare: To be disappointed or sad about it.

Windy: Right, now would that be a realistic feeling goal for you?

Clare: Yes, I think it would be.

Windy: And would it help you to get down to studying when you knew that your friends were out enjoying themselves?

Clare: Yes, I think it would.

Windy: So let me summarise. When you are faced with the unfairness of your friends going out to enjoy themselves, you want to strive to feel sad or disappointed, but not depressed about this and to get down to doing some studying. Is that right?

Clare: Yes.

Windy: OK, let's both make a note of that goal and let's move on to helping you to achieve that goal. . .

As mentioned above it is also possible to set a goal in respect of your client's assessed problem, where 'C' is just behavioural. This involves you encouraging your client to set a realistic and adaptive behavioural goal in the face of a negative 'critical A'. In Clare's case this would be: 'To get down to studying even when I am faced with the unfairness of staying in when I know that my friends are out enjoying themselves.'

Let us begin this section by distinguishing between a broad problem and a specific example of a broad problem. A broad problem tends to be general in nature and probably comprises several different examples. A specific example of a broad problem is just that – one concrete instance of a broad problem comprising several similar examples. For example, Clare's broad problem was 'procrastinating over my studies whenever there is something more attractive to do.' A specific example of Clare's broad problem was the one discussed at length above, namely: 'I found it difficult getting down to studying when I knew that my friends were out on Friday night having a good time.'

Many of the issues that we have just dealt with concerning setting goals with respect to specific examples of your clients' broad problems also emerge when you come to set goals in respect to these broad problems. As such we will not repeat ourselves. What we will do is to provide an example of one client's broad problems and the goals I (WD) set with her on the problems.

Problem 1: Feel anxious about approaching women, so don't do so

Goal 1: To feel concerned about approaching women, but not anxious about doing so. To approach them despite feeling concerned

Problem 2: Guilty about past wrongdoings and avoid those who I have wronged

Goal 2: To feel remorseful, but not guilty about past wrongdoings and make amends where relevant

Problem 3: Procrastinate over studies

Goal 3: To make a study timetable and keep to it

Problem 4: Feel anxious about hosting any kind of gathering in case something goes wrong and therefore avoid being a host

Goal 4: To arrange a gathering and feel concerned, but not anxious about something going wrong

Problem 5: Avoid going to shopping malls because I might feel anxious there

Goal 5: To go to shopping malls and feel concerned, but not anxious about the prospect of feeling anxious. Then to feel comfortable about going through repeated exposure

---

We want you to note five things about these goals.

1. All of the goals are within the client's sphere of influence, i.e. they are all achievable.

2. All of the goals indicate the presence of an emotional and behavioural state. It is important therefore to avoid setting goals with your clients that involve the diminution or absence of a state. Thus, instead of the goal 'to feel less anxious about...' encourage your client to strive 'to feel concerned, but not anxious about...' Similarly, instead of the goal 'not to feel guilty about...' encourage your client 'to feel remorseful, but not guilty about...'

3. Most of the goals contain a negative healthy emotion in response to a negative activating event. You will also note that whilst the presence of a healthy negative emotion is clearly stated, the absence of an unhealthy negative emotion is also made explicit.

4. All of the goals contain a piece of functional behaviour.

5. One of the goals (i.e. Goal 5) contains an initial healthy negative feeling which then becomes a comfortable feeling state as the result of repeated practice. This last point is important. Whilst it is functional for your client to have a healthy negative emotional response to a negative life event, as a counsellor concerned with your client's long-term well-being, you will want her to attempt to change this negative 'critical A' and increase the number of positive 'As' in her life. This brings us to the third issue concerning goal-setting in REBT.

▶ Moving from overcoming disturbance to promoting personal development

As we mentioned at the beginning of this chapter, it is possible to think of the goals of psychotherapy as falling into two categories: those to do with overcoming psychological disturbance and those which serve to promote psychological growth or personal development.

Overcoming disturbance goals (henceforth called OD goals) relates to the problems (i.e. disturbances) that clients bring to psychotherapy. Thus, when your clients have achieved their OD goals:

1. they experience healthy negative emotions when they confront the negative 'critical As' about which they previously disturbed themselves and

2. they are able to take constructive action to try and change these negative events.

Personal development goals (henceforth called PD goals), on the other hand, are related to a number of broad criteria of mental health which are not situation specific. PD goals, then, generally go well beyond OD goals. Although helping clients towards PD goals is beyond the scope of this book, it is important for you to realise that doing so is a legitimate task for REBT therapists. We outline REBT's view of some of the major criteria of mental health in Figure 10.1 to give you some idea of what helping your clients to pursue PD goals might involve for them (for a fuller discussion of REBT's position on these criteria consult Ellis & Dryden, 1997 and Dryden, 2000).

1. Enlightened self-interest

Here the person basically puts herself first and puts the interests of significant others a close second. Sometimes, however, she will put the interests of others before her own. Enlightened self-interest is therefore a flexible position and contrasts with selfishness (the dogmatic position where the person is only concerned with her own interests and is indifferent to the interests of others) and selflessness (the position where the person always puts the interests of others before her own).

2. Flexibility

Here the person is flexible in her thinking, open to change, free from bigotry and pluralistic in her view of other people. She does not make rigid, invariant rules for herself and others.

3. Acceptance of uncertainty

Here the person fully accepts that we live in a world of probability and chance where absolute certainties do not and probably will never exist.

4. Commitment to vital absorbing interests

Here the person is likely to be healthier and happier when she is vitally absorbed in personal projects outside herself than when she is not. These interests should be large enough to be involving and allow the person to express her talents and capacities.

5. Long-range hedonism

Here the person tends to seek a healthy balance between the pleasures of the moment and those of the future. She is prepared to put up with present pain if doing so is in her best interests and is likely to lead to future gain.

Figure 10.1   Examples of mental health criteria from an REBT perspective.

In general, you will help your client to work toward her OD goals before raising the issue of PD goals. In my experience most of your clients will wish to terminate therapy once they are have achieved their OD goals. In this respect, Maluccio (1979) found that clients were far more satisfied with what they achieved from therapy on termination than were their therapists. So don't be surprised if most of your clients are not interested in working towards personal development and don't regard this as a failure on your part if this is the case.

In the next chapter, we will discuss how you can capitalize on goal-setting by encouraging your client to commit herself to achieving her goals.

CHAPTER ELEVEN

Eliciting your client's commitment to change

▶ Introduction

It is not sufficient to elicit your client's goals. It is also important to elicit his commitment to change and work towards these goals. Therefore, in this chapter, we will discuss a method which you can use which is helpful in eliciting client commitment to change.

For your client to commit himself to change, it is important for him to see clearly that it is in his best interests to make the change. If your client does not see this, then he is hardly likely to commit himself to work towards his stated goal. You might ask, then, why your client might come up with a goal to which he is not committed. There may be a number of reasons for this. First, your client might identify a goal which others want him to achieve, but which he is either opposed to or ambivalent about. Thus, your client's parents may want him, for example, to become independent whereas he may wish to stay dependent or be in two minds about becoming independent. In order to help your client to commit himself to a goal, it is important to help him first evaluate fully the advantages and disadvantages of both the problem state and the alternative goal state. Over the years we have experimented with a number of ways of doing this. Having made several modifications to our approach of helping clients to weigh up the pros and cons of change, we now use a method that is quite comprehensive. I (WD) have devised a form called the 'Cost-Benefit Analysis Form' (CBAF) which I encourage clients to complete, especially when it is clear that a client is ambivalent about change.

▶ The 'Cost-Benefit Analysis Form' (CBAF): general principles

The 'Cost-Benefit Analysis Form' which appears in Figure 11.1 is easy to complete and is based on a number of principles.

1. There is an alternative to your client's problem and it is important for you to help him to put this in his own words.

2. The problem and the goal both have actual and perceived advantages and disadvantages.

COST-BENEFIT ANALYSIS
ADVANTAGES/BENEFITS OF
Option 1
SHORT TERM

For yourself	For other people
1: _____	1: _____
2: _____	2: _____
3: _____	3: _____
4: _____	4: _____
5: _____	5: _____
6: _____	6: _____

LONG TERM

For yourself	For other people
1: _____	1: _____
2: _____	2: _____
3: _____	3: _____
4: _____	4: _____
5: _____	5: _____
6: _____	6: _____

DISADVANTAGES/COSTS OF
Option 1
SHORT TERM

For yourself	For other people
1: _____	1: _____
2: _____	2: _____
3: _____	3: _____
4: _____	4: _____
5: _____	5: _____
6: _____	6: _____

LONG TERM

For yourself	For other people
1: _____	1: _____
2: _____	2: _____
3: _____	3: _____
4: _____	4: _____
5: _____	5: _____
6: _____	6: _____

Figure 11.1 The cost-benefit analysis form

COST-BENEFIT ANALYSIS
ADVANTAGES/BENEFITS OF
Option 2
SHORT TERM

For yourself	For other people
1: _____	1: _____
2: _____	2: _____
3: _____	3: _____
4: _____	4: _____
5: _____	5: _____
6: _____	6: _____

LONG TERM

For yourself	For other people
1: _____	1: _____
2: _____	2: _____
3: _____	3: _____
4: _____	4: _____
5: _____	5: _____
6: _____	6: _____

DISADVANTAGES/COSTS OF
Option 2
SHORT TERM

For yourself	For other people
1: _____	1: _____
2: _____	2: _____
3: _____	3: _____
4: _____	4: _____
5: _____	5: _____
6: _____	6: _____

LONG TERM

For yourself	For other people
1: _____	1: _____
2: _____	2: _____
3: _____	3: _____
4: _____	4: _____
5: _____	5: _____
6: _____	6: _____

Figure II.I   *(Continued)*

3. These advantages and disadvantages operate both in the short term and in the long term.

4. These advantages and disadvantages are relevant both for your client and for relevant others in his life. This relevance is at its most obvious when your client's problem is interpersonal in nature; however, even when the problem does not seem to involve anybody else, it is still worthwhile asking your client to consider the advantages and disadvantages for himself and for others.

It is important to ask your client to complete the CBAF when he is in an objective frame of mind. Otherwise, you will receive an analysis heavily influenced by his psychologically disturbed state. You may profitably help your client by encouraging him to fill in the form in a session until he understands how to complete it. Then he can finish the form as a homework assignment. For him to complete the form with you present in a therapy session is not a cost-effective use of session time. Suggest to your client that once he has completed the form, he puts it away until the next therapy session. Otherwise, he may ruminate on it in an unproductive way.

When you go over the form with your client in the following therapy session, first ask him to state what he learned from doing the task. If in his answer he states clearly that the goal is more attractive than the problem, you can then ask him to commit himself formally to the goal. This may involve him making a written commitment which you could both sign. It could also involve him making a public declaration of some kind indicating his commitment to achieving the goal. Whilst making one or both types of formal commitment is not a necessary part of the REBT change process, these procedures do bring home to your client that change is a serious business and one that is not to be entered into lightly.

You will note that we do not advocate going over the cost-benefit analysis form in detail with your client when he has stated that his goal is more desirable than the problem state and that he does wish to commit himself to achieving it. How-ever, if you study the form carefully you will frequently gain a lot of information, especially from the 'advantages of the problem' section and the 'disadvantages of the goal' section concerning likely obstacles to client progress. Therefore, it is im-portant that you retain a copy of the client's form and that you have it to hand when you are seeing him. It is also helpful if you encourage your client to keep a copy of the form to hand whenever he comes to therapy and at other times. Later, you will want to ask him to consult it for clues concerning obstacles to his continued progress.

When your client has completed the CBAF and is ambivalent about change or opts for the problem state over the goal state, then you need to go over the form with him in great detail. The purpose of doing this is to discover and deal with so-called advantages of the problem and perceived disadvantages of achieving the goal (we are assuming here that the goal is a healthy one, at least when taken at face value). Unless you deal with these sections of the form and correct the

```
COST-BENEFIT ANALYSIS
ADVANTAGES/BENEFITS OF SULKING
SHORT TERM
For yourself                          For other people
1. 'Safety valve' for anger          1. Lets people know I'm angry
2. Gives me time to think            2. Draws people's attention to a problem
                                        or mood
3. Release of frustration            3. Can jolt people into realising that their
                                        behaviour does have a negative effect
4. Shows dissatisfaction             4. _____
5. It's a sign of annoyance          5. _____
6.                                   6. _____
LONG TERM
For yourself                          For other people
1. None                              1. None
2. _____                        2. _____
3. _____                        3. _____
4. _____                        4. _____
5. _____                        5. _____
6. _____                        6. _____
DISADVANTAGES/COSTS OF
SULKING
SHORT TERM
For yourself                          For other people
1. It's a waste of energy            1. It causes an uncomfortable atmosphere
2. It's debilitating                 2. It creates tension in my relationships
3. It hides the real problem         3. _____
4. _____                        4. _____
5. _____                        5. _____
6. _____                        6. _____
LONG TERM
For yourself                          For other people
1. It puts me in a bad light with others  1. It causes a lot of misunderstandings
2. _____                        2. _____
3. _____                        3. _____
4. _____                        4. _____
5. _____                        5. _____
6. _____                        6. _____
```

Figure 11.2   Sandra's compleated cost-benefit analysis form

misconceptions you find there, it is not in the interests of either yourself or your client to ask him to commit himself to the goal. To do so under such circumstances is to get the change process off on the wrong foot. The following is an example of how to deal with such a situation. I (WD) will first present the client's cost-benefit analysis form (see Figure 11.2), then I will demonstrate how to challenge a client's misconceptions about the 'advantages' of the problem and the 'disadvantages' of achieving the goal. I will call the client in this example Sandra.

As you can see from Figure 11.2, Sandra is ambivalent about giving up 'sulking' (which is her general problem) and opting for the alternative 'communicating my

COST-BENEFIT ANALYSIS
ADVANTAGES/BENEFITS OF COMMUNICATING MY FEELINGS HONESTLY
TO OTHER PEOPLE
SHORT TERM

For yourself
1. Brings problems to a head
2. Releases pent-up anger
3. May help to resolve matters
4. _____
5. _____
6. _____

For other people
1. Brings problems to a head
2. Clarifies matters
3. May help to resolve matters
4. _____
5. _____
6. _____

LONG TERM

For yourself
1. Shows a determination to resolve matters
2. Represents more mature and positive action
3. _____
4. _____
5. _____
6. _____

For other people
1. Allows for compromise
2. _____
3. _____
4. _____
5. _____
6. _____

DISADVANTAGES/COSTS OF COMMUNICATING MY FEELINGS HONESTLY TO
OTHER PEOPLE
SHORT TERM

For yourself
1. May say things I may regret
2. I may lose relationships
3. _____
4. _____
5. _____
6. _____

For other people
1. Heightens excitability and emotionalism
2. They may feel hurt
3. _____
4. _____
5. _____
6. _____

LONG TERM

For yourself
1. May become unpopular
2. I may lose relationships
3. _____
4. _____
5. _____
6. _____

For other people
1. They may become wary of me
2. They may decide I'm too unpleasant to be around
3. _____
4. _____
5. _____
6. _____

Figure 11.2   *(Continued)*

feelings honestly to other people' which is Sandra's stated goal with respect to the general problem of sulking. Whilst you will most often use the cost-benefit analysis method with your client's general problems and goals, you can also use it with specific examples of general problems and related goals.

Responding to your client's perceived advantages of the problem and perceived disadvantages of achieving the goal

As Sandra is ambivalent about change it is important that I, as her therapist, review the form with her and respond in particular to the advantages she sees accompanying 'sulking' (her problem) and to the disadvantages that she sees

SHORT-TERM ADVANTAGES/BENEFITS OF SULKING	
For yourself	*Windy's response*
1. 'Safety valve' for anger	1. Controlled honest communication is a more effective way of channelling anger. It is even more effective if you first challenge your unhealthy anger-creating irrational beliefs leading to healthy anger.
2. Gives me time to think	2. You don't need to sulk to give you time to think. There is a difference between withdrawing for yourself in order to give yourself time to think and withdrawal 'against the other', which is what sulking is. In fact, the latter detracts from the quality of your thinking while the former promotes this.
3. Release of frustration	3. When you communicate honestly, you can release frustration, but in a way that is more likely to resolve problems than sulking.
4. Shows dissatisfaction	4. While you do show dissatisfaction when you sulk, you also show other things too, which are more likely to cause problems than solve them. When you communicate honestly you show dissatisfaction but again in a more constructive way than sulking.
5. It's a sign of annoyance	5. The above argument is also relevant here. Honest communication is a more reliable and healthy way of communicating annoyance than sulking. In keeping the channel of communication open you are more likely to resolve matters by talking them through than with sulking, which closes down the channel.
For other people	*Windy's response*
1. Lets them know I'm angry	1. Sulking may well let others know that you are angry, but it won't let them know what you're angry about. It is therefore liable to create more problems in this respect than it will solve.
2. Draws people's attention to a problem or mood	2. Again, sulking draws their attention to the fact that you have a problem, but it won't pinpoint the nature of the problem. By communicating honestly and openly you will let other people know exactly what your problem is.
3. Can jolt people into realising that their behaviour does have a negative effect	3. This may happen, but what is more likely to happen is that you will jolt them into realising that your behaviour has a negative effect on them.
LONG-TERM ADVANTAGES/BENEFITS OF SULKING	
None stated	

Figure 11.3 Responding to Sandra's misconceptions about the 'advantages' of her problem and the 'disadvantages' of her stated goal

SHORT-TERM DISADVANTAGES/COST OF COMMUNICATING MY FEELINGS HONESTLY TO OTHER PEOPLE	
For yourself	*Windy's response*
1. May say things I may regret	1. You are more likely to say things you may regret later when you are unhealthily angry. That is why I recommend that you change the irrational beliefs that underpin your unhealthy anger to rational beliefs. Doing so will enable you to be healthily angry instead. Healthy anger is directed at the other's behaviour, while unhealthy anger is directed at and puts down the other person.
2. I may lose relationships	2. You are more likely to lose relationships if you sulk angrily than if you honestly convey your healthy anger in a firm but caring manner.
For other people	
1. Heightens excitability and emotionalism	1. If this is a disadvantage for other people, then honest communication of healthy anger will reduce the intensity of the emotional atmosphere, whereas honest communication of unhealthy anger will increase excitability and emotionalism. That is another reason why I recommend that you first identify and challenge the irrational beliefs that underpin your unhealthy anger and replace it with a set of rational beliefs that will allow you to communicate honestly and firmly, but caringly, your feelings of healthy anger.
2. They may feel hurt	2. Yes, they may feel hurt when you honestly convey your annoyance, even if you choose your words carefully. However, they are less likely to feel hurt when you communicate your feelings of healthy anger than if you communicate your unhealthy angry feelings. Also, don't forget that other people may feel hurt when you sulk. There is no way of guaranteeing that others won't be hurt no matter what you do. The more important consideration is whether you want your relationships with others to be based on honest communication or uncommunicative sulking.
LONG-TERM DISADVANTAGES/COSTS OF COMMUNICATING MY FEELINGS HONESTLY TO OTHER PEOPLE	
For other people	*Windy's response*
1. May become unpopular	1. Yes, you may become unpopular if you honestly communicate your feelings of healthy anger. However, I would argue that

Figure 11.3 *(Continued)*

	in the long term you will be even more unpopular if you sulk or communicate your unhealthy anger. Don't forget, as well, that honest communication also involves expression of positive feelings. If you are open about your good feelings about others as well as your negative feelings about them, then you will in all probability increase your popularity.
2. May lose relationships	2. Again, you may lose relationships if you communicate honestly, but if you communicate feelings of healthy anger you will lose fewer relationships in the long term than if you sulk or honestly communicate your other-damning unhealthy angry feelings. This will especially be the case if you also communicate your positive feelings to other people.
For other people	
1. They may become wary of me	1. This is true, but they will probably become equally wary of you when they discover that you sulk. Also, expressions of unhealthy anger are more likely to lead to others being wary of you than expressions of healthy anger.
2. They may decide I'm too unpleasant to be around	2. This seems to be more a disadvantage for you than for others. Even if it is a disadvantage for them, I would argue, as I have done before, that this is more likely to happen if you sulk or show your unhealthy anger than if you show your healthy anger.

Figure 11.3   (*Continued*)

accompanying 'communicating my feelings honestly to other people' (her stated goal). In Figure 11.3 I (WD) outline a summary of the specific arguments I used with Sandra as I challenged the misconceptions on which these 'advantages' and 'disadvantages' appeared to be based. As we will demonstrate later in the chapter, the way I helped Sandra to question her reasoning on this issue was by asking Socratic-type questions. The summary nature of the arguments presented in Figure 11.3 makes it appear that I just told Sandra why she was in error. As you will soon see, this was far from the case.

Note that in my work with Sandra, she refers to unhealthy anger as 'anger' and to healthy anger as 'annoyance'.

Using Socratic questions to help your client rethink the perceived advantages of the problem and the perceived disadvantages of the stated goal

You will note that many of the arguments that I (WD) used with Sandra are directed at her distorted inferences. Thus, taking the short-term advantage of sulking providing a good way of showing dissatisfaction, I showed Sandra that whilst this may be so, there are better ways of doing so. I also show her that sulking may lead to greater problems that she has not considered. Once again, it is very important for you to realise that the arguments presented in Figure 11.3 are summaries. That is why they appear in didactic form. In actuality, I engaged Sandra in a Socratic dialogue on the issue as the following interchange shows.

> Windy: OK, Sandra. Now you say that a short-term advantage of sulking is that it helps you to show dissatisfaction. Do you see any way of showing dissatisfaction without sulking?
>
> Sandra: Well, letting people know honestly that I am dissatisfied will have the same effect.
>
> Windy: Right. Incidentally, if you sulk how do you know that in people's minds you are not showing other things too, like anger or being punitive?
>
> Sandra: I guess I don't.
>
> Windy: So which is a more reliable guide to showing dissatisfaction: sulking or honestly communicating your feelings?
>
> Sandra: Honest communication.
>
> Windy: Does that change your view that a short-term advantage of sulking is that it helps you to show dissatisfaction?
>
> Sandra: Yes. It helps me to see that sulking shows a number of things other than dissatisfaction and these other things like anger won't be beneficial to my relationships.

> In order to increase your understanding of how the 'Cost-Benefit Analysis Form' can be used, use it with yourself. Choose a personal goal you may be ambivalent about pursuing and use the form to increase your commitment achieving your goal.

Reconsidering the 'Cost-Benefit Analysis Form' and asking your client for a commitment to change

After you have helped your client to review the 'advantages' of his problem and the 'disadvantages' of the stated goal, it is important that you encourage him to reconsider his cost-benefit analysis of the problem and the goal. You can do this in two ways. First, you can have the client take his old 'Cost-Benefit Analysis

Form' and write in different colour ink reasons why the perceived advantages of his problems are, in fact, not benefits and the reasons why the perceived disadvantages of his goal are not, in fact, costs. Second, you can ask your client to complete a second CBAF which, if you have been successful in helping to correct the previous misconceptions that he made, should demonstrate a clear preference for his stated goal. If not, you need to proceed as above until a clear preference for one of the two options is demonstrated.

You will find, in conclusion, that the disputing process (which is the subject of the following chapters) will go more smoothly when your client has made a commitment to his stated goal than when he is still ambivalent about change. Trying to dispute your client's irrational beliefs without eliciting such a commitment is like running a race with a ball and chain around one leg. Encouraging your client to make this commitment is the key which removes such an impediment.

CHAPTER TWELVE

Preparing your client and yourself for the disputing process

It is important to prepare your client for the disputing process. Novice REBT therapists are sometimes so pleased to have identified an irrational belief that they launch into disputing it without helping their clients to understand what they are doing with predictable negative results. Assuming that you have taught your client the REBT's 'ABC' model, assessed her target problem, identified her goal for change and elicited her commitment to work to achieve this goal, what are the preparatory steps that you need to take before you dispute your client's irrational beliefs? There are two basic steps: (i) helping your client to see the relevance of disputing her irrational belief as a means of achieving her goal and (ii) helping your client to understand what disputing involves.

▶ Helping your client to see the relevance of disputing her irrational beliefs as a primary means of achieving her goal

After you have helped your client to see that her irrational beliefs underpin her target problem, it is equally important that you help her to see that changing these beliefs will help her to achieve her stated goal with respect to this problem. Here is an example of how to do this.

> Windy: So, recapping on the 'ABC' of your anxiety, 'C' is your feelings of anxiety, 'A' is the event in your mind that your boss will disapprove of you and 'B' is your irrational belief. 'My boss must not disapprove of me. I am less worthy if he does.' Is that accurate?
>
> Victor: Yes it is.
>
> Windy: From this assessment can you see what largely determines your feelings of anxiety?
>
> Victor: The belief that my boss must not disapprove of me.

Windy: Now let's recap on your goal. What would be a more healthy, but realistic response to receiving disapproval from your boss than anxiety?

Victor: As we said before, to feel concerned but not anxious about it.

Windy: So if your belief that your boss must not disapprove of you leads to your anxiety and your goal is to feel concerned, but not anxious about this possibility, what do we have to help you to change in order for you to achieve your goal?

Victor: We have to change my belief.

▶ Helping your client to understand what disputing involves

As we will discuss in greater detail in Chapter 13, disputing involves you asking your client a number of questions designed to encourage her to evaluate the rationality of her irrational beliefs and explaining any points about which she is not clear. As such it is useful to help your client understand what you will be doing and why you will be doing it. An example follows from my (WD) work with Victor.

Windy: Right, you need to change your irrational belief. The way I can best help you to do this is to encourage you to see why your irrational belief is, in fact, irrational. I will be doing this by asking you a number of questions designed to help you to understand this point. The reason why I will be asking you questions in the first instance is to help you to think about this issue for yourself. This is what Socrates, a famous Greek philosopher, did with his students. He didn't tell them the answers to various difficult philosophical questions. Rather, he asked them a series of questions, the purpose of which was to help them discover the answers for themselves. He helped them with his questions to be sure, but he didn't do the work for them. However, if my questioning doesn't help you to understand any given point, I will provide you with an explanation which will, I hope, clarify the point. I won't, in other words, leave you up in the air. Does what I say make sense to you?

Victor: Yes. What you're saying is that you will help me to re-evaluate my irrational belief by asking me questions about it. And you'll explain any points that I don't understand.

Windy: Shall we start?

Victor: Go ahead.

▶ How many of the four irrational beliefs should you dispute?

In our training courses on REBT, one of the most frequently asked questions about disputing is this: 'How many of my client's irrational beliefs should I dispute in an ABC?'. We have already shown you that your client can have up to four irrational beliefs in any one example of their problems: a demand, an awfulising belief, an LFT belief and a depreciation belief. Disputing them all is quite time-consuming and not always necessary. So here are some guidelines for choosing which irrational beliefs to dispute in any one example of your client's target problem:

Dispute your client's demand unless you have a good reason not to

Ellis (1994) has stressed that demands are at the very core of psychological disturbance. As such, if you follow Ellis's position, it is very important to dispute demands. If your client does not see that his demand has a central role in his disturbance and resists your disputing this irrational belief, dispute one (or more) of his three other irrational beliefs.

Dispute your client's demand and at least one of his three other irrational beliefs when it is not feasible to dispute all four

In my client workbook (Dryden, 2001) I (WD) recommend that clients work with a demand and *one* of their three other irrational beliefs, particularly when it is not feasible for them to dispute all four of their irrational beliefs. When it is not feasible for a client to dispute all four irrational beliefs (e.g. when her disputing skills are still developing), other than her demand we suggest that you encourage your client to chose whichever *one* remaining irrational belief best accounts for her disturbed reactions at 'C'. Having said this we have the following recommendations to make:

- Dispute your client's demand and self-depreciation belief where her problem is ego-related in nature.

- Dispute your client's demand and other-depreciation belief where she is unhealthily angry, this anger is non-ego-related in nature and is very much focused on the badness of the other person.

- Dispute your client's demand and either her awfulising belief or her LFT belief in other non-ego forms of disturbance.

- Dispute your client's demand and awfulising belief in non-ego anxiety where your client is preoccupied with the prospect of 'awful' things happening.

- Dispute your client's demand and LFT belief in non-ego anxiety where she is scared that she might not be able to tolerate various states and possible events.

- Dispute your client's demand and LFT belief in non-ego forms of self-discipline and in non-ego features of the addictions.

Dispute one of your client's irrational beliefs when session time is at a premium or that is all she can deal with

It sometimes transpires that you only have time to dispute one irrational belief or your client, for reason of level of disturbance or level of intelligence, can only process disputing work targeted at one of his irrational beliefs. When this is the case, dispute the one irrational belief with which the client most resonates or if he cannot choose select for him the one irrational belief he is most likely to change.

We hope we have shown in this chapter that while REBT has its preferred disputing strategies, it allows you a good deal of flexibility in choosing strategies in the light of your client's response and situation. However, with flexibility comes responsibility. So, become competent at all the disputing strategies to be discussed in the following chapters so that you can choose the most appropriate strategy for your client in a given situation and offer highly skilled disputing in executing this strategy.

You are now ready for the nuts and bolts of disputing irrational beliefs. We will begin by discussing the three major arguments that you need to use when disputing your client's irrational beliefs.

CHAPTER THIRTEEN

Disputing irrational beliefs: The three major arguments

The noted American REBT therapist, Raymond DiGiuseppe and his trainees once listened to numerous audiotapes of Albert Ellis conducting therapy in order to understand better the disputing process (DiGiuseppe, 1991b). As part of their analysis, DiGiuseppe and his trainees discovered that Ellis employed three major arguments while disputing his clients' irrational beliefs.

▶ What are the three major arguments?

The three arguments that Ellis used were as follows:

Empirical arguments

Empirical arguments are designed to encourage your client to look for empirical evidence that confirms or disconfirms the truth of her irrational beliefs. The basic question here is this: are her irrational beliefs realistic or consistent with reality?

Logical arguments

Logical arguments are designed to encourage your client to examine whether or not her irrational beliefs are logical. The basic question here is this: do the irrational belief components of her beliefs follow logically from the partial rational components of these beliefs?

Pragmatic arguments

Pragmatic arguments are designed to encourage your client to question the utilitarian nature of her irrational beliefs. The basic questions here are: (i) what are the immediate emotional, behavioural and cognitive consequences of your client's irrational beliefs and (ii): do your client's irrational beliefs help her or hinder her as she pursues her stated goals?

Now that we have described the three major arguments, we will outline the points you need to make as you apply these arguments while disputing the four irrational beliefs: demands; awfulising beliefs; low frustration tolerance beliefs and self-, other- or life-depreciation beliefs. As we do so please note that our focus is on the content of the arguments not on the way they are presented. We will deal with this latter point in the next chapter.

▶ Using the three major arguments with demands

You will recall from Chapter 1 that demands are rigid beliefs which, according to REBT theory, are at the core of psychological disturbance. From these demands or musts are derived three other irrational beliefs, i.e. awfulising beliefs, low frustration tolerance beliefs and self-, other- or life-depreciation beliefs. Demands are irrational for the following reasons.

Empirical argument – your client's demand is inconsistent with reality

Let's take Victor's demand: 'My boss must not disapprove of me.'

> If there were a law of the universe which stated that Victor's boss must not disapprove of him, then it would be impossible for the boss to do so no matter what Victor did. Such a law of the universe would forbid Victor's boss from ever disapproving of him. As it is always possible for his boss to disapprove of Victor, this proves that there is no empirical evidence to support Victor's demand that: 'My boss must not disapprove of me.'
>
> If Victor's demand belief were true it would mean that Victor's boss would lack free will. He would be deprived of his human right to form a negative opinion of Victor. As the boss does have the freedom to think negatively of Victor, this fact empirically disconfirms Victor's demand.
>
> If Victor's boss did ever disapprove of him, this would contradict Victor's belief. If, under these circumstances, Victor still believed that his boss absolutely should not have disapproved of him, then this would be tantamount to Victor believing: 'what just happened absolutely should not have happened', or 'reality must not be reality' which empirically is nonsense.

Logical argument – your client's demand component does not follow logically from his preference component

This argument is best made when we express Victor's demand in its full form: 'I would prefer it if my boss did not disapprove of me, therefore he must not disapprove of me.'

Victor's demand has two components: an 'asserted preference' component where he non-rigidly asserts what he wants ('I would prefer it if my boss did not disapprove of me') and an 'asserted demand' component where he transforms his non-rigid preference into a rigid must ('. . . therefore he must not disapprove of me). The latter component, being rigid, does not follow logically from the former component which is not rigid and thus taken as a whole Victor's demand is illogical (see Figure 13.1)

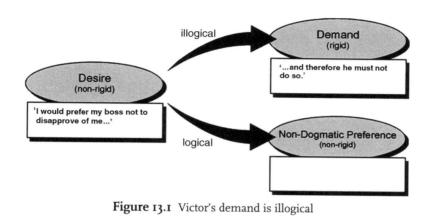

Figure 13.1 Victor's demand is illogical

Pragmatic argument – your client's demand leads to poor psychological results

Remember that Victor's demand is 'My boss must not disapprove of me.'

Victor's demand that his boss must not disapprove of him is likely to lead to poor emotional, cognitive and behavioural results. Thus, if Victor holds this belief in a situation where his boss approves of him, but there is a slight chance that he may incur such disapproval, then he will tend to get anxious and will tend to think and act in certain ways associated with anxiety (see Figure 4.1).

In addition, if Victor receives clear evidence that his boss does disapprove of him, then his 'must' will lead him to feel anxiety, depression or anger and again he will tend to think and act in self-defeating ways that relate to whichever unhealthy negative emotion predominates (see Figure 4.1).

Victor's demand that his boss must not disapprove of him will interfere with his stated goal. For example, if he wants to be healthily concerned about the prospect of being disapproved of by his boss, but not anxious about this, then his demand will constitute a major obstacle to Victor achieving this goal.

▶ Using the three major arguments with awfulising beliefs

According to REBT theory, an awfulising belief is an irrational derivative of a primary demand. It represents the tendency to evaluate events in grossly exaggerated, extreme ways. Awfulising beliefs are irrational for the following reasons.

Empirical argument – 'nothing is awful in the universe'

Ellis defines the term 'awful' when used in its disturbance-creating sense as more than 100 % bad and stems from the idea that it must not be as bad as it is. As such, you can never reach awful, because it empirically does not exist. As we have already noted, Smokey Robinson's mother's advice to her son aptly illustrates this idea: 'From the day you are born, 'til you ride in the hearse, there's nothing so bad that it couldn't be worse.' Thus, awful is not a property of the natural world; rather, it is a concept that constitutes a creation of the human mind.

> When Victor concludes: 'It would be awful if my boss disapproved of me', he is making an empirically unsupportable statement because he can presumably think of many occurrences that would be worse than being disapproved of by his boss.

Logical argument – 'it's awful that. . . ' does not logically follow from 'it's bad that. . . '

This argument is best made when we express Victor's awfulising belief in its full form: 'It's bad if my boss disapproves of me and therefore it's awful if he disapproves of me.'

> Victor's awfulising belief has two components: an 'asserted badness' component which is non-extreme ('It's bad if my boss disapproves of me) and an 'asserted awfulising' component which is extreme ('therefore it's awful if he disapproves of me). The latter component does not logically follow from the former since you cannot logically derive something extreme from something non-extreme. Thus, Victor's awfulising belief, taken as a whole is illogical. See Figure 13.2.

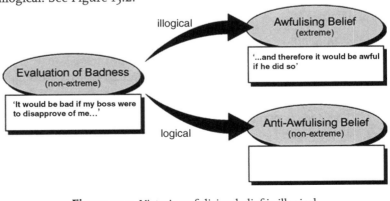

Figure 13.2 Victor's awfulising belief is illogical

Pragmatic argument – your client's awfulising belief leads to poor psychological results

Remember that Victor's awfulising belief is 'It is awful if my boss disapproves of me.'

> Victor's irrational belief that it would be awful if his boss disapproved of him is likely to lead to poor emotional, cognitive and behavioural results. Thus, if Victor holds this belief in a situation where his boss approves of him, but there is a slight chance that he may incur such disapproval, then he will again tend to get anxious and to think and act in ways associated with anxiety (see Figure 4.1).
>
> In addition, if Victor receives clear evidence that his boss does disapprove of him, then his awfulising belief will lead him to feel anxiety, depression or anger and again he will tend to think and act in self-defeating ways that relate to whichever unhealthy negative emotion predominates (see Figure 4.1).
>
> Victor's belief that it would be awful if his boss disapproved of him will interfere with his stated goal. Thus, if he wants to be healthily concerned about the prospect of being disapproved of by his boss, but not anxious about this, then his awfulising belief will constitute a major obstacle to Victor achieving this goal because it will lead to anxiety and not concern.

▶ Using the three major arguments with low frustration tolerance beliefs

According to REBT theory, a low frustration tolerance belief is another irrational derivative of a primary demand. It represents the position that one cannot tolerate frustrating or uncomfortable situations. This belief is irrational for the following reasons.

Empirical argument – your client can bear the so-called unbearable

If it were true that your client couldn't tolerate a frustrating or uncomfortable situation then she would literally die or would never experience any happiness for the rest of her life, no matter how she thought about the situation in question.

In this context, you can ask your client who believes she cannot stand something whether she could stand it if it meant saving the life of a loved one. She will invariably say 'yes'. This proves that the 'I can't stand it' statement is again anti-empirical because, if it were true that she couldn't stand the relevant situation, she would not be able to stand it under any circumstances.

If it were true that Victor couldn't tolerate being disapproved of by his boss, as he believes, then if this disapproval occurred Victor would have to die or forfeit any chance of future happiness. Obviously, neither of these two things would happen. The ironic thing about a philosophy of low frustration tolerance is that even when Victor tells himself that he can't stand his boss's disapproval he is standing it. Now, he could tolerate it better and be helped to do so. But the point is that he is tolerating it even when he is doing so poorly. Thus, it is completely anti-empirical for Victor to believe that he can't stand something even when it is very difficult to bear.

Logical argument – it makes no logical sense for your client to conclude that he can't stand something because it is difficult to tolerate

This argument is best made when we express Victor's LFT belief in its full form: 'It would be difficult to tolerate it if my boss were to disapprove of me and therefore I couldn't stand it if this happened.'

Victor's LFT belief is based on a non-extreme 'asserted struggle' component ('it would be difficult for me to tolerate it if my boss disapproved of me') and an extreme 'asserted unbearability' component ('therefore I couldn't stand it'). Once again since something extreme cannot follow logically from something non-extreme, Victor's LFT belief is illogical (see Figure 13.3).

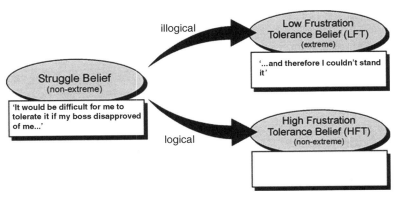

Figure 13.3 Victor's LFT belief is illogical

Pragmatic argument – your client's low frustration tolerance belief leads to poor psychological results

The points that we made with respect to the pragmatic consequences of holding demands and awfulising beliefs are also relevant to low frustration tolerance beliefs.

> Victor's LFT belief that he could not stand it if his boss disapproved of him is likely to lead to poor emotional, cognitive and behavioural results. Thus, again, if Victor holds this belief in a situation where his boss approves of him, but there is a slight chance that he may incur disapproval, then he will tend to get anxious and to think and act in ways associated with anxiety (see Figure 4.1).
>
> In addition, if Victor receives clear evidence that his boss does disapprove of him, then his LFT belief will lead him to feel anxiety, depression or anger and again he will tend to think and act in self-defeating ways that relate to whichever unhealthy negative emotion predominates (see Figure 4.1).
>
> Furthermore, Victor's belief that he could not stand it if his boss disapproved of him will interfere with his stated goal. Thus, if he wants to be healthily concerned about the prospect of being disapproved of by his boss, but not anxious about this, then his LFT belief will constitute a major obstacle to Victor achieving this goal because it will lead to anxiety and not concern.

▶ Using the three major arguments with depreciation beliefs

According to REBT theory, a self-, other- or life- depreciation belief is another irrational derivative of a primary demand. It represents the position that the worth or value of a person or life varies according to changing conditions. The common factor linking these three beliefs is the philosophy of depreciation. Here, we will concentrate our discussion on self-depreciation beliefs. However, similar points could be made for other-depreciation and life-depreciation beliefs. Your client's self-depreciation belief is irrational for the following reasons.

Empirical argument – it is empirically untenable for your client to rate his 'self'

Self-depreciation is known in common parlance as low self-esteem (LSE). If your client has LSE, the chances are that he wishes to have HSE (high self-esteem). However, both rest on the idea that it is possible for your client to rate (i.e. esteem) his 'self'. Is this in fact possible? To answer this question we need to define what we mean by the 'self'. Paul Hauck's (1991) definition of the self is as good as any (and better than most) so we will use it to construct our argument that it is empirically untenable for your client to rate his 'self'. Hauck (1991) defines the 'self' as 'every conceivable thing about you that can be rated' (p. 33). As such, your client's 'self' is too complex to be given a single rating.

Such an evaluation would be possible if your client was a single-cell amoeba; but he is a human organism who has millions of thoughts and feelings, has acted in countless ways and has very many traits and characteristics. Consequently, your client cannot give his 'self' a legitimate rating. Your client can and probably does give his 'self' an illegitimate rating, but this evaluation has nothing to do with the reality of who he is.

Even if it were possible for your client to give his 'self' a single rating with the help of a computer so powerful that it hasn't been invented yet, such an evaluation would be out of date as soon as it was made. Why? Because your client is not static, but constantly in flux. A rating, once made, is a static thing and thus cannot do justice to an ongoing, ever-changing organism such as your client.

> Thus, if Victor concluded that he was a bad person if his boss disapproved of him then he would be making an unempirical statement. If it were true that Victor were a bad person then everything about him would have to be bad now, in the past and in the future. This is hardly likely.

Logical argument – whilst your client can legitimately rate single aspects of his 'self' or what happens to him, it does not follow logically that he can rate his whole 'self'

It is sensible to for your client to rate given aspects of his 'self' because doing so helps him to determine whether or not these aspects aid him in the pursuit of his goals and purposes. It is also sensible for your client to rate what happens to him because doing so enables him to take constructive action to change what he can change and to adjust constructively to what he cannot change. Having rated a given aspect, however, it is illogical then for your client to proceed to rate his entire 'self'. Doing so would involve him making the logical error of over-generalisation or what is known as the part-whole error. Here, your client assigns a rating to his entire self on the basis of his evaluation of a part of his 'self' or of what happens to him. More formally a depreciation belief is made up of two components: a 'negatively evaluated aspect' component (i.e. 'part') and an 'asserted global negative evaluation' component (i.e. 'whole'). The latter is an illogical over-generalisation from the former. Another name for this illogicality is prejudice.

> Thus, if Victor concluded that he was a bad person if his boss disapproved of him then he would be making an illogical statement. He would take a negative situation (i.e. his boss's disapproval) and conclude on the basis of this that his whole 'self' was bad – a clear over-generalisation.

Pragmatic argument – self-depreciation leads to poor psychological results for your client

The points that we made with respect to the pragmatic consequences of holding demands, awfulising beliefs and low frustration tolerance beliefs also apply to self-depreciation beliefs.

> Victor's self-depreciation belief that he would be a bad person if his boss disapproved of him is likely to lead to poor emotional, cognitive and behavioural results. Thus, again, if Victor holds this belief in a situation where his boss approves of him, but there is a slight chance that he may incur such disapproval, then he will tend to get anxious and to think and act in ways associated with anxiety (see Figure 4.1).
>
> In addition, if Victor receives clear evidence that his boss does disapprove of him, then his self-depreciation belief will lead him to feel anxiety, depression, shame or ego-defensive anger and again he will tend to think and act in self-defeating ways that relate to whichever unhealthy negative emotion predominates (see Figure 4.1).
>
> Furthermore, Victor's belief that he is a bad person if his boss disapproved of him will interfere with his stated goal. Thus, if he wants to be healthily concerned about the prospect of being disapproved of by his boss, but not anxious about this, then his self-depreciation belief will constitute a major obstacle to Victor achieving his goal because it will lead to anxiety and not concern.

We made the point earlier that rating a specific aspect of one's self is useful in that doing so helps your client to determine whether or not this aspect aids him in the pursuit of his long-term goals and, thus, whether he needs to change that aspect. However, when your client rates his 'self' over and above the rating he assigns to that given aspect, doing so does not give him added benefit as he strives to determine whether or not the aspect is goal-enhancing. Indeed, rating his 'self' will hamper him in his deliberations about the usefulness of that specific aspect of himself. In this situation, doing two things at once – rating of the aspect and rating his 'self' will interfere with his major task – judging the utilitarian value of the aspect under consideration.

Once again, please remember that while we have concentrated in this section on the arguments you can use to dispute your client's self-depreciation beliefs, similar arguments can be made when disputing his other-depreciation and life-depreciation beliefs.

Having considered the three main arguments you can use while disputing your client's irrational beliefs and having applied these arguments to the four main irrational beliefs, we will now move on to consider the two major styles of disputing (consult Neenan & Dryden, 2002 for a compendium of additional disputing arguments). As a beginning practitioner of REBT, you need to develop competence in both major styles of disputing: Socratic and didactic. Your clients will differ in the value they derive from these different styles, so you may need to make predominant use of Socratic disputing with one client and didactic disputing with another. You will discover, though, that you frequently need to use both with a given client. Whichever style of disputing you use, the purpose of each style is the same – to help your client gain intellectual insight into the irrationality of her irrational beliefs and the rationality of her alternative rational beliefs, using the kind of arguments we discussed in this chapter.

CHAPTER FOURTEEN

Socratic and didactic disputing of irrational beliefs

In this chapter, we will consider the two major styles of disputing irrational beliefs: Socratic and didactic. We will begin by discussing Socratic disputing.

▶ Socratic disputing

As we briefly showed earlier, Socrates educated his students by asking them open-ended questions designed to encourage them to think critically about philosophical problems. He knew the answers to these problems, but he saw that there was little to be gained by telling his students the solutions. Rather, his goal was to help his pupils, through his questioning procedure, gain a way of thinking about philosophical problems which they could then apply to a broad range of questions and, most importantly, which they could use in his absence. This is similar to the sage who said that if you plant a crop for hungry people you help them now, but if you teach them how to plant crops you help them to help themselves now and in the future. Thus, when you employ Socratic-type questions while disputing your client's irrational beliefs, you are not only helping her to question the rationality of these beliefs in the present, you are also helping to develop a methodology for questioning the rationality of irrational beliefs in the future.

When you ask a Socratic-type question in disputing, it is important to take great care to evaluate your client's response. In particular, you need to monitor four likely responses: (i) your client has answered your question correctly; (ii) she has answered your question incorrectly; (iii) she has misunderstood your question and has provided an answer to a different question; (iv) she has changed the subject.

Let us deal with each of these situations in turn.

Socratic disputing when your client has answered your question correctly

When your client has answered your question correctly, it is important to assess the status of her answer. Has she given you the correct answer because she thinks it is what you want to hear? If so, does she also see the sense of it or is she looking for your approval? You need to examine these issues and deal with them (Socratically if possible) until your client sees for herself the correctness of her answer and provides it for no other reason than that it is the correct answer.

For example:

> Windy: So where is the evidence that you must pass your exams?
>
> Fiona: There isn't any.
>
> Windy: Why isn't there?
>
> Fiona: Because if there was such a law I could not fail.
>
> Windy: Do you believe that because you're convinced of it or because it is the answer you think I want to hear?
>
> Fiona: ... (pause)...Well, to be frank because it's the answer I think you want to hear.
>
> Windy: What if I wanted to hear the opposite answer?
>
> Fiona: Well ... I would still believe it.
>
> Windy: Even if I was disappointed?
>
> Fiona: Yes.
>
> Windy: Why?
>
> Fiona: Because it is true.
>
> Windy: So is it possible for you to believe that something is true even though I may be disappointed?
>
> Fiona: Yes it is.
>
> Windy: And is it desirable that you do so?
>
> Fiona: Yes it is.
>
> Windy: Why?
>
> Fiona: Because it will help me deal better with the concept of failing.

If your client's need for your approval is impeding her ability to think clearly about her target irrational belief, it is important that you change tack and, with her agreement, target her demand for your approval before disputing. Otherwise, her responses to you in any disputing sequence will be based on what she thinks you want to hear rather than her true considered opinion.

Socratic disputing when your client has answered your question incorrectly

When your client has answered your question incorrectly you need to use her answer to formulate another Socratic question. Keep doing this until your client has understood the rational point. For example:

Windy: So where is the evidence that you must pass your exams?

Fiona: Well, if I don't I'll find it harder to get a job.

[Here the client has provided evidence why not passing her exams would have disadvantages for her. She has not, though, provided evidence in support of the idea that she must do so.]

Windy: Is finding it harder to get a job evidence for the idea that you must pass your exams or for the idea that it is undesirable if you fail?

Fiona: Put like that, it's evidence for it being undesirable.

Windy: Do you have any other evidence in support of your belief that you must pass your exams?

Fiona: Well, my parents will be very upset if I fail.

Windy: Again, is that evidence in support of the idea that it is undesirable if you fail or that you absolutely must pass?

Fiona: It's undesirable.

Windy: Any other evidence in support of the idea that you must pass?

Fiona: I guess not.

Windy: What do you conclude from that?

Fiona: That I want to pass my exams, but there is no law that states that I have to do so.

Socratic disputing when your client has misunderstood your question and answers a different question

What do you do when your client thinks you have asked her a different question? If this is the case bring this to her attention as Socratically as you can, although you probably cannot avoid making an explanatory statement during this process. For example:

Windy: So, where is the evidence that you must pass your exams?

Fiona: I know exams are not a good way of assessing people, but they do need to be taken you know.

[Here it is clear that the client is responding to a very different question.]

Windy: Did you think I asked you why you consider exams to be a good way of assessing people or where is the evidence that you must pass yours?

Fiona: Oh. Did I hear you wrongly? Let me see ... Sorry, can you ask me the question again?

Windy: Where is the evidence that you absolutely must pass your exams?

Fiona: I guess there is none.

Socratic disputing when your client changes the subject

Finally, how do you respond when your client changes the subject? Here you have a number of options. First, you may consider that the client is following her train of thought rather than yours. In ordinary conversation, people do suddenly change the direction of a conversation because something the other person has said sparks off a thought in the person's mind which she then articulates. If you think this is the case, this is how you might respond:

Windy: So where is the evidence that you must pass your exams?

Fiona: You know my friend Jane is coming down this weekend.

Windy: Sorry, I'm a bit confused. Can you help me understand the connection between looking for evidence for the belief that you must pass your exams and your friend Jane visiting you this weekend?

Fiona: I'm sorry. You asking me that question reminded me that Jane's exams finish on Friday and she promised to come down when they were over.

Windy: So you are looking forward to seeing her. But do you think you will be able to concentrate on challenging your belief about having to pass your exams if we go back to it?

Fiona: I'm sure I will.

Windy: So where is the evidence that you must pass your exams?

At other times you will recognise that your client's change of topic while you are disputing her irrational belief is probably related to other, less benign factors. First, your client may have difficulty in keeping her attention on what you are both discussing. In this instance, ask your client for permission to interrupt her when she deviates from the issue and bring her back to the disputing sequence. If this doesn't work and you notice that it happens frequently no matter what you are discussing, it is probably a good idea to refer your client for a neuropsychological assessment or in cases of more profound attentional impairment for a neurological examination.

Second, you may suspect that your client finds your Socratic questions threatening in some way and thus she deals with the threat by avoiding the issue. If this is the case, it may be that your client finds the content of your questions threatening. For example, Fiona may change the subject because she does not want to face up to the issue that she has a problem with her exams or she does not want to confront the fact that she may be thinking irrationally about this issue. If correct, these constitute evidence that the client may have a meta-emotional problem that warrants exploration and intervention. You may need to switch focus to this meta-emotional problem if this is the case. Alternatively, your client may find the process of Socratic questioning difficult and she may change the subject to cope with her discomfort. If so, you may wish to be more didactic or, if you deem it important, you may wish to encourage her to tolerate her feelings of discomfort and persist with the Socratic questioning. Here is an example of dealing with one of these scenarios:

Windy: So where is the evidence that you must pass your exams?

Fiona: You know my friend Jane is coming down this weekend.

Windy: Fiona, you seemed to change the subject again when I asked you for evidence for your belief. Is there anything that you find uncomfortable about the question?

Fiona: Well...your question reminds me that I'm not handling this situation well.

[This is a clue that the client may have a hitherto undiscovered meta-emotional problem.]

Windy: And as you focus on the fact, and let's assume for the moment that it is a fact, that you aren't handling the situation well, how do you feel about that?

Fiona: Ashamed.

Windy: Given that you feel ashamed every time I question you about your demand that you must pass you exams, does that explain why you change the subject?

Fiona: Yes it does.

Windy: So shall we stick with challenging your demand to pass your exam or shall we deal with your feelings of shame first?

Fiona: I think we need to deal with the shame first.

This example demonstrates something interesting. Even though you may have worked carefully in the assessment phase of therapy to identify a meta-emotional problem, it may only be at the disputing phase that you discover that one exists and that it interferes with the work you are doing on your client's primary target problem. Sometimes you will only learn of the presence of a meta-emotional problem when your client acts to avoid discussing issues that he finds personally threatening (see Dryden, 2000).

Examples of socratic questions

In Chapter 15, we present disputing strategies carried out by Albert Ellis that illustrate the kind of Socratic questions that he used to ask. But, first, we will list some Socratic-type questions for each of the three major arguments discussed earlier; the target of the questions will be a demand.

Empirical

- Where is the evidence that you must...?
- Is there any evidence that you must. . . ?
- Where is the law of the universe that states that you must...?
- Is there a law of the universe which states that you must...?
- If there were a law of the universe that stated that you must...how do you account for the fact that you didn't do what the law dictated that you do?
- Would a scientist think that there was evidence in support of your must?

Logical

- Where is the logic that you must...?
- Is it logical to believe that you must...?
- Does it logically follow that because you want to...therefore you must...?
- Does that demand logically follow from your preference?
- Is it good logic to believe that because you want ... therefore you must...?
- Would a philosopher think that it was good logic to believe that because you want to...therefore you must...?

Pragmatic

- Where will it get you to believe that you must. . . ?
- What are the emotional and behavioural consequences of believing that you must...?
- Will that demand give you good results?
- Is it healthy for you to believe that you must...?
- How is believing that you must ... going to help you achieve your (long-term/healthy) goals?

- Is believing that you must... going to help or hinder you in the pursuit of your (long-term/healthy) goals?

▶ Didactic disputing

The term 'didactic disputing' is actually something of a misnomer because when you are being didactic in REBT you are teaching your client by telling him why irrational beliefs are irrational and why rational beliefs are rational. So the essence of didactic disputing is teaching rational principles by explanation, using the same three major arguments that have been reviewed earlier in this book, i.e. empirical, logical and pragmatic.

What we will do in this chapter is outline several criteria for good practice when disputing didactically. In doing so, we will also alert you to the most common problems that novice REBT therapists experience when using didactic disputing methods.

Keep your didactic explanations as short as possible

When you are challenging your client's irrational beliefs by providing her with information designed to cast doubt on the empirical, logical and pragmatic status of these beliefs, it is important that you keep your explanations as brief as possible. Otherwise you will provide your client with too much information to process adequately. Of course, your clients will vary quite considerably with respect to how much information they can process at a given time and you will want to take this issue into account when deciding how much information to provide a particular client with. If you are in doubt here, err on the side of caution and provide your client with less information than you believe she can digest.

> As a training exercise, record your therapy sessions and listen particularly to your didactic explanations. Write out ways in which you could have shortened your explanations and show these to your REBT trainer or supervisor. Also, play them the relevant recorded segment so that they can compare what you said to your client with the proposed shortened version.

Periodically check your client's level of understanding of the points you are didactically presenting to her

The purpose of presenting your client with information in a didactic manner is to help her to *learn* rational principles which she can later apply in her everyday life. We have emphasised the word *learn* here because many novice REBT therapists think that the goal of didactic disputing is to teach rather than to encourage the client to learn. As the emphasis here is on client learning rather than on therapist teaching, you need to ensure, in the first instance, that your client understands the points you are didactically presenting to her. You can best do this by periodically asking her questions like: 'I'm not sure that I'm making myself clear, can you put into your own words what you've heard me say?'

Note, in particular, two points about this question:

1. It puts the burden on you, as therapist, to make yourself clear in your communications rather than on your client to understand what you are communicating.

2. It encourages your client to be an active rather than a passive learner by asking her to put her understanding of what you have said into her own words. If your client still uses the same words as you employed, gently encourage her to reformulate her understanding of your points in her own words.

If your client makes errors of understanding in her responses, correct these prefacing your remarks by saying something like: 'I don't think that I phrased my explanation very well. Let me see if I can put it another way.'

This again shows that you are taking primary responsibility for your client understanding the rational message. If you don't do this your client may well blame herself for her failure to comprehend what you have been saying. Having prefaced your remarks in this way, make your point again and once more elicit your client's understanding. Proceed in this manner until your client has understood the point you have been making.

Once your client has understood a substantive rational point, ask her for her views on it

Just because your client has understood a rational point, it does not follow that she agrees with it. Thus, after your client has understood the substantive point you have been making, ask her for her views on it. Does she agree or disagree with it? Does she think that the point has some practical value for her? Don't be afraid to debate an issue with your client or to correct any misconceptions that she might reveal. However, do so in a non-defensive way and without attacking your client in any way.

▶ Using the socratic and didactic disputing conjointly

We have now introduced and discussed both the Socratic and didactic disputing styles and you should see clearly the differences between them. You may be thinking: 'How am I to know which style to use with which client?' Whilst this is a difficult and complex question to answer fully, let us provide you with this rule of thumb. Some clients will resonate to a predominantly Socratic style of disputing. Basically these will be intelligent clients who are accustomed to thinking for themselves. For other clients who are less intelligent and are less used to reflecting on their own cognitive processes, a more didactic style is indicated.

However, as we mentioned briefly earlier, you will probably need to use both disputing styles with most of your clients. What happens most often in REBT is that you will start with Socratic disputing and use didactic explanations to supplement your work. Here is a typical sequence of disputing that you will hear in the work of Albert Ellis, the founder of REBT (Yankura & Dryden, 1990).

Client: I must do well in my exams.

Therapist: Why do you have to do well?

[Socratic question]

Client: Because if I don't, my parents will feel let down.

Therapist: That's why it's unpreferable. But just because it is unpreferable if you don't do well, how does it follow that you must do well?

[A very brief didactic point followed by another Socratic question]

Client: Because I won't get a very good job later.

Therapist: But again that proves that it would be undesirable if you don't do well. You're saying, though, that you must do well. Now if there were a law of the universe that said that you had to do well, you would have to do well because you would have to follow that law of the universe. Now does that law of the universe exist?

[The therapist realises that the client isn't grasping the point when it is presented Socratically so he or she makes greater use of didactic explanation. However, note that at the end of the intervention, the therapist asks another Socratic question to encourage the client to reflect actively on the point that was presented didactically.]

We will consider Albert Ellis's disputing work more fully in the next chapter.

CHAPTER FIFTEEN

Examples of Albert Ellis's disputing work

In this chapter, we will provide and comment on therapeutic work carried out by Albert Ellis disputing the irrational beliefs of three of his clients. Each sequence focuses on a particular argument.

▶ Using empirical arguments

In this sequence Ellis is disputing the irrational belief of a client who insists that she absolutely must succeed in her career. Ellis is using primarily empirical arguments.

> Ellis: Why MUST you have a great career?
>
> Client: Because I very much want to have it.
>
> Ellis: Where is the evidence that you MUST fulfil this strong desire?
>
> Client: I'll feel much better if I do.
>
> Ellis: Yes, you probably will. But how does your feeling better prove that you must succeed?
>
> [So far, Ellis has been using Socratic-type questions. Note how he takes the client's answers to his questions which represent evidence in support of her rational belief (i.e. 'I want to have a great career, but I don't have to have one') and asks whether or not such evidence supports her irrational belief.]
>
> Client: But that's what I want more than anything else in the world.
>
> Ellis: I'm sure you do. But if we take 100 people like you, all of whom want a great career, want it more than anything else in the world, and would feel much better if they achieved it, do they all HAVE to succeed at it?
>
> [Here Ellis probably realises that he has to use a different type of argument

with this client. So he asks whether or not it is empirically true that 100 people who have the same strong preference as the client would all change this into a must.]

Client: If they are to have any joy in life, they have to do so.

[The client still does not get the point that Ellis is implying through his Socratic-type questions.]

Ellis: Really? Can't they have ANY pleasure if they fail to get a great career?

[Taking the lead from the client's last response, Ellis changes the focus of his argument again. If 100 people all must have a great career, none of them will have any pleasure if they don't achieve it. Ellis then questions whether this is empirically the case.]

Client: Well, yes. I guess they can have SOME pleasure.

[This is the first time that the client shows any sign that she can think rationally about the issue at hand. Note how Ellis capitalises on this.]

Ellis: And could some of them have a great deal of pleasure?

Client: Urm. Probably, yes?

Ellis: Probably?

Client: Well, highly probably.

Ellis: Right. So, no matter how much people greatly want success and would feel better about gaining it, they don't have to get it. Right?

[Here Ellis summarises the rational point and asks for agreement. I (WD) might have asked, 'What do you think of this idea?', in order to encourage the client to be more independent in her thinking.]

Client: Well, yes.

Ellis: Reality is that way – isn't it?

Client: It seems so.

Ellis: Back to you. Does YOUR great desire for a successful career mean that you ABSOLUTELY MUST achieve it – that the world HAS TO fulfil this desire?

[Having got the rational point over in an abstract way, Ellis then seeks to apply it to the client's own specific set of personal circumstances.]

Client: I see what you mean. Reality is the way it is, no matter how unpleasant I find it to be.

[The client shows signs of really understanding Ellis's point.]

Ellis: Exactly. Make a note of that Effective New Philosophy you just arrived at and keep thinking that way until you thoroughly believe it!

▶ Using logical arguments

In this segment Ellis is disputing the irrational beliefs of a client who insists that because he treated his friend very nicely and fairly, this friend ABSOLUTELY SHOULD treat him the same way. He does so using primarily logical arguments.

Ellis: Let's suppose that you're describing the situation with your friend accurately and that he treats you shabbily and unfairly after you consistently treat him well. How does it follow that because of your good behaviour he has to respond in kind?

Client: But he's unfair if he doesn't!

Ellis: Yes, we're agreeing on that. He IS unfair and you are fair. Can you jump from 'Because I'm very fair to him, he HAS TO BE fair to me?'

Client: But he's wrong if he isn't fair when I am.

[At this point Ellis and the client appear to be at cross-purposes. Ellis keeps asking the client why his friend MUST be fair to him and the client keeps replying that his friend is wrong and unfair which Ellis is not questioning.]

Ellis: Agreed. But because you are fair, and presumably right, and because he takes advantage of your fairness, does it STILL follow that he has to be right and to treat you fairly?

Client: It logically follows.

Ellis: Does it? It looks like a complete non sequitur to me.

Client: How so?

[This is a typical Ellis change of emphasis. He asserts that the client's belief is illogical and waits for the latter to ask why before expanding on his theme. He wants to get his client into an enquiring, 'Why do you say that?' mode.]

Ellis: Well, it's logical or consistent that he preferably should treat you fairly when you treat him well. But aren't you making an illogical – or 'magical' –

jump from 'Because he PREFERABLY should treat me fairly he ABSO-LUTELY HAS TO do so?' What 'logical' law of the universe leads to your 'He absolutely has to do so?'

Client: No law, I guess.

Ellis: No, in logic we get necessitous conclusions, such as 'If all men are human and John must be a man, John must be human.' But your 'logic' says, 'People who get treated fairly, often treat others fairly; I treat my friend fairly; therefore it is absolutely NECESSARY that he treat me similarly.' Is that a logical conclusion?

[This is another typical Ellis strategy. He begins by making a point in didactic fashion. As occurs here, this point illustrates a rational idea (in this case a logical idea). He then contrasts this with the client's irrational idea (in this case an illogical idea), but does not tell the client that his idea is illogical. Rather he encourages the client to think for himself by asking, 'Is that a logical conclusion?' It is worth studying this sequence in detail because it is so typical of Ellis's effective disputing work.]

Client: I guess not.

Ellis: Moreover, you seem to be claiming that because you act fairly and your friend behaves unfairly, his ACTS make him a ROTTEN PERSON. Is that logical thinking?

[Ellis infers other-depreciation from his client's must. He is probably correct; however, my (WD) practice would be to check my hunch with the client before proceeding.]

Client: Why not?

[As you will see, Ellis immediately answers the client's question. I would have encouraged the client to make a stab at answering his own question before going into didactic mode.]

Ellis: It's illogical because you're over-generalising. You're jumping from one of his rotten BEHAVIOURS – or even one of his TRAITS – to cate-gorising HIM, his totality as 'rotten.' How does that over-generalisation follow from a few of his behaviours?

[Here Ellis states the logical error that the client is making, shows him in what way the error is present in his belief about his friend and finally questions him about the logicality of that belief.]

Client: I can see now that it doesn't.

Ellis: So what could you more logically conclude instead?

[Here, Ellis encourages the client to be active in his thinking.]

Client: Well, I could think that he isn't one of his main behaviours. He is a person who often, but not always, acts rottenly.

Ellis: Good! Alfred Korzybski and his followers in General Semantics would approve of your new conclusion!

▶ Using pragmatic arguments

In the following piece of work, the client insists that if she believes that she must do well, she will succeed better at school and win others' approval. Ellis shows her that her irrational belief will in all probability produce poor results.

Client: If I am anxious about doing poorly at school because, as you say, I think that I must do well, won't my must and my anxiety motivate me to do better?

Ellis: Yes, in part. But won't they also defeat you?

[Here Ellis gives a straight answer to the client's straight question. But he then follows up by asking a question to encourage the client to think about the issue for herself. This is another typical Ellis disputing strategy.]

Client: How so?

Ellis: If you keep making yourself very anxious with 'I must do well! I must perform perfectly!' won't you preoccupy yourself so much that you DETRACT from the time and energy you can give to studying?

[Yet another typical Ellis intervention. Here Ellis is really making a statement in the guise of a question. The question format is to encourage the client's active participation, but the rational point that Ellis is making is clear.]

Client: Maybe. But I'll still feel quite motivated.

Ellis: Mainly motivated to obsess! You'll be DRIVEN to study and while you drive yourself, you'll keep thinking, 'But suppose I fail! Wouldn't that be AWFUL?' You'll worry about what your tests will be like, how you will handle them, how you will subsequently perform, etc. How will keeping the future so much in mind help you focus on the PRESENT studying?

[This intervention comprises a number of didactically made points with the question twist at the end.]

Client: It may not help.

Ellis: No, it's much more likely to sabotage. Moreover, even if you somehow succeed in your courses, do you want to be miserably anxious and depressed, WHILE you are succeeding?

Client: Frankly, no.

Ellis: And do you want to be SO absorbed in worrying about school that you have little time for relationships, sports, music and other enjoyments?

[Having succeeded in getting the point across to the client that her irrational belief will do her more harm than good, Ellis spends time – see his last two interventions and much of his following responses – emphasising this important point.]

Client: I don't think so. I passed my courses last term but was able to do little else.

Ellis: See! And what about the physical results of your constant worry and perfectionism?

Client: My physician thinks they are making my digestive tract hyperactive.

Ellis: I'm not surprised. And when you constantly worry, how do you feel about YOU for being such a worrier?

Client: Pretty shitty.

Ellis: Is THAT feeling worth it? But even if you felt bad about your anxiety and didn't put YOURSELF down for having it, you would still bring on endless frustration and disappointment by indulging in it.

Client: You may be right.

Ellis: Don't take my word for it. Look for yourself at the results you get from your perfectionist demands and figure out what you could say to yourself to replace them.

[Ellis often urges his clients not to take his word for it. However, his didactic style does encourage clients not used to thinking for themselves to do just that. Greater extended use of Socratic disputing would achieve this result more effectively.]

Client: Well, I could tell myself, 'It's great to do well at school, but I DON'T HAVE TO BE PERFECT. Even if my anxiety sometimes helps me to get good marks, it, too, has too many disadvantages and it isn't worth it.'

Ellis: Good! That's a much better way to think.

CHAPTER SIXTEEN

Helping your client to understand the rationality of his or her rational beliefs

In addition to helping your client understand the irrationality of his irrational beliefs, you need to encourage him to understand the rationality of his rational beliefs. First you need to help him to construct his rational belief which ideally should be the direct rational alternative to his irrational belief. In this chapter, we will first deal with the construction of each of the four major rational beliefs and then show you what you need to do to help your client understand the rationality of each rational belief which can be done by Socratic means, didactic means or a combination of the two.

▶ Non-dogmatic preferences

Construction of a non-dogmatic preference

When you help your client construct his rational belief, remember that a non-dogmatic preference has two components: (i) An 'asserted preference' component and (ii) a 'negated demand' component. As shown below:

> Demand: 'I must be liked by my new colleague.'
>
> 'Asserted preference' component: 'I want to be liked by my new colleague...'
> 'Negated demand' component: '...but she does not have to like me.'
>
> Non-dogmatic preference: 'I want to be liked by my new colleague, but she does not have to like me.'

Empirical argument for non-dogmatic preferences

Your client's non-dogmatic preferences are consistent with the internal reality of what she wants. To judge whether or not your client has a preference, look at what she says and how she acts. If a preference exists, for example, it will motivate her to approach certain things and to avoid others and this can be observed empirically. Holding a non-dogmatic preference is also consistent with reality because it does allow for the person not getting what she wants since the demand component is negated.

> Thus, Victor can provide evidence for his healthy preference: 'I would prefer my boss not to disapprove of me, but there is no reason why he must not do so.' It is consistent with the internal reality of what he wants and you can determine if this is the case by studying how he thinks, talks and acts. Also his rational belief is consistent with reality because it allows for the possibility that his boss may disapprove of him.

Logical argument for non-dogmatic preferences

Non-dogmatic preferences are logical in that they are made up of two components: (i) an 'asserted preference' component and (ii) a 'negated demand' component. Neither of these components is rigid and thus the latter follows logically from the former.

> Victor's non-dogmatic preference comprises two components: (i) an 'asserted preference' component 'I would prefer my boss not to disapprove of me...' and (ii) a 'negated demand' component '...but there is no reason why he must not do so.' Neither of these components is rigid and thus the latter follows logically from the former making Victor's full preference logical (see Figure 16.1).

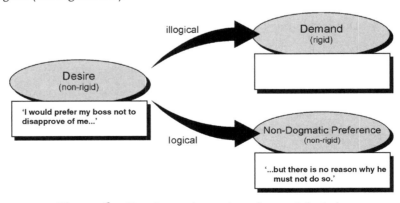

Figure 16.1 Victor's non-dogmatic preference is logical

Pragmatic argument for non-dogmatic preferences

Your client's non-dogmatic preferences are more likely to help her to achieve her goals and less likely to lead to psychological disturbance than her musts. In particular, her asserted preference will motivate her to do well and her negated demand will help inoculate her against self-disturbance.

> Thus, Victor's non-dogmatic preference about not having his boss's disapproval will more likely result in him achieving his goal of feeling concerned but not anxious about such disapproval than will his dogmatic demand.

▶ Non-awfulising beliefs

As mentioned in Chapter 1, a non-awfulising belief involves your client making non-extreme evaluations (from 0 %–99.99 %) on a continuum of badness.

Construction of a non-awfulising belief

When you help your client construct his non-awfulising belief, remember that it has two components: (i) an 'asserted badness' component and (ii) a 'negated awfulising' component. As shown below:

> Awfulising belief: 'It would be terrible if my new colleague did not like me.'
>
> 'Asserted badness' component: 'It would be bad if my new colleague did not like me...'
>
> 'Negated awfulising' component: '...but it wouldn't be terrible.'
>
> Non-awfulising belief: 'It would be bad if my new colleague did not like me, but it wouldn't be terrible.'

Empirical argument for non-awfulising beliefs

When making persuasive arguments in favour of non-awfulising beliefs, it is important to stress that they are consistent with reality. Thus, your client can prove that something is bad by looking at the actual or likely consequences for him. In addition, he can prove that something exists on a continuum of badness by discovering an event that can be worse.

> Thus, Victor can provide evidence for his non-awfulising belief. 'It is bad, but not terrible if my boss disapproves of me.' He could argue with justification that if his boss disapproves of him, he is more likely to dismiss Victor and less likely to promote him than if he approves of Victor. Also, Victor can prove his non-awfulising belief by pointing to situations that would be worse for him than being disapproved of by his boss.

Logical argument for non-awfulising beliefs

Non-awfulising beliefs are logical in that they are made up of two components: (i) an 'asserted badness' component and (ii) a 'negated awfulising' component. Both of these components are non-extreme and thus the latter follows logically from the former.

Victor's non-awfulising belief comprises two components: (i) an 'asserted badness' component 'It would be bad if my boss were to disapprove of me...' and (ii) a 'negated awfulising' component '...but it wouldn't be terrible if he did so.' Both of these components are non-extreme and thus the latter follows logically from the former (see Figure 16.2).

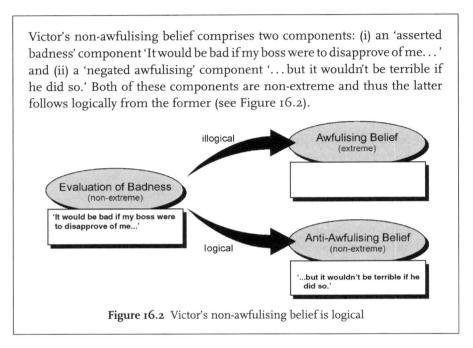

Figure 16.2 Victor's non-awfulising belief is logical

Pragmatic argument for non-awfulising beliefs

When making persuasive arguments in favour of non-awfulising beliefs, it is important to stress that they lead to immediate healthy functioning and aid longer-term goal achievement.

Thus, Victor's belief that it is bad, but not awful if his boss disapproves of him will help him to feel concerned, but not anxious about such disapproval. It will also help him to work effectively at his job, thus helping to minimise the chances that he will incur his boss's disapproval.

▶ High frustration tolerance (HFT) beliefs

HFT beliefs involve your client believing that she can tolerate difficult life situations and that it is in her interests to do so.

Construction of an HFT belief

When you help your client construct his HFT, note that it has three components: (i) an 'asserted struggle' component, (ii) a 'negated unbearability' component and (iii) a 'worth tolerating' component. As shown below:

LFT belief: 'I couldn't bear it if my new colleague did not like me.'

'Asserted struggle' component: 'It would be difficult for me to tolerate it if my new colleague did not like me...'

'Negated unbearability' component: '...but I could bear it...'

'Worth tolerating' component: '...and it would be in my interests to do so'

HFT belief: 'It would be difficult for me to tolerate it if my new colleague did not like me, but I could bear it and it would be in my interest to do so.'

Empirical argument for HFT beliefs

When making persuasive arguments in favour of HFT beliefs, it is important to stress that they are consistent with reality.

Thus, it is realistic for Victor to say that he can stand being disapproved of by his boss and that it is worth it for him to do so even though this situation would be difficult for him to tolerate. Indeed, empirically he can prove that he can stand his boss's disapproval even when he irrationally tells himself that he cannot do so. Because, even when he has such an LFT belief, he is standing the situation in that he has neither died nor has he forsaken the possibility of future happiness. He can also prove that it would be in his interest to tolerate such disapproval.

Logical argument for HFT beliefs

An HFT belief is logical in that two of its three components: (i) its 'asserted struggle' component and (ii) its 'negated unbearability' component are both non-extreme and thus the latter follows logically from the former.

Taking Victor's HFT belief, the two components that are relevant here: (i) his 'asserted struggle' component 'It would be difficult for me to tolerate it if my boss disapproved of me...' and (ii) his 'negated unbearability' component '...but I could bear it', are both non-extreme and thus the latter follows logically from the former (see Figure 16.3).

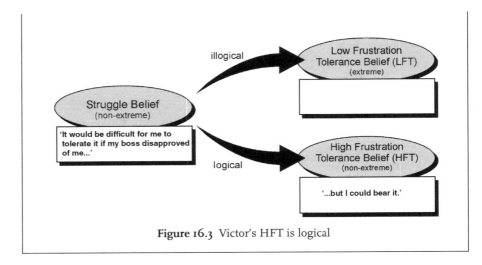

Figure 16.3 Victor's HFT is logical

Pragmatic argument for HFT beliefs

When making persuasive arguments in favour of HFT beliefs, it is important to stress that they lead to immediate healthy functioning and aid longer-term goal achievement.

> Thus, if Victor shows himself that he can stand his boss's disapproval even though it would be difficult for him to do so, this belief will help him to feel concerned but not anxious, which is his goal. In addition, his HFT belief will help him to concentrate on his job performance, thus decreasing the chances of him incurring his boss's disapproval.

▶ Self-/other-/life-acceptance beliefs

Accepting oneself and others as fallible human beings and life as a complex mixture of good, bad and neutral are the healthy alternatives to self-/other-/life-depreciation. We will outline the empirical, logical and pragmatic reasons for encouraging clients to endorse self-/other-/life-acceptance by taking the example of self-acceptance, although the same arguments can be applied to other-acceptance and life-acceptance.

Construction of a self-acceptance belief

When you encourage your client to construct his self-acceptance belief, help him to see that it has three components: (i) an evaluation of an aspect of self or of what happens to him (formally known as the 'negatively evaluated aspect' component), (ii) a negation of the view that his entire 'self' can be evaluated (formally known as the 'negated global negative evaluation' component) and (iii) an assertion of the fallibility, complexity and unrateability of his 'self' (known formally as the 'asserted complexity/fallibility/unrateability' component).

Self-depreciation belief: 'If my new colleague does not like me it proves that I am worthless.'

'Negatively evaluated aspect' component: 'It would be bad if my new colleague did not like me...'

'Negated global negative evaluation' component: '...but it wouldn't prove that I am worthless.'

'Asserted complexity/fallibility/unrateability' component: 'It proves that I am a complex, unrateable, fallible human being who is capable of being liked and disliked.'

Self-acceptance belief: It would be bad if my new colleague did not like me, but it wouldn't prove that I am worthless. It proves that I am a complex, unrateable, fallible human being who is capable of being liked and disliked.

Empirical argument for self-acceptance beliefs

When making persuasive arguments in favour of self-acceptance beliefs, it is important to stress that they are consistent with reality.

Thus, Victor can prove that he is human and fallible with positive, negative and neutral aspects. His essence does not change whether his boss approves or disapproves of him.

Logical argument for self-acceptance beliefs

Help your client to see that when he subscribes to a self-acceptance belief he avoids making the illogical part-whole error.

Thus, it makes sense for Victor to accept himself as a fallible human being even when his boss disapproves of him. It is perfectly logical, therefore, for him to evaluate this disapproval as negative whilst refraining from giving himself a single rating, as in doing so he is rating a part of his experience without rating his whole person. He does not, thus, make the part-whole error. Indeed, in self-acceptance beliefs the whole logically incorporates the part.

Pragmatic argument for self-acceptance beliefs

When making persuasive arguments in favour of self-acceptance beliefs, it is important to stress that they lead to immediate healthy functioning and aid longer-term goal achievement.

> Thus, if Victor accepts himself as a fallible human being even though his boss may disapprove of him he is likely to be concerned, rather than anxious about this disapproval. His self-accepting belief will also encourage him to focus on what he is doing at work rather than on what his boss is thinking of him. This will improve his chances of doing well at work which in turn will decrease the chances of his boss disapproving of him.

As we have already stated, similar arguments can be used in favour of other- and life-acceptance beliefs.

Once again please note that whilst we have presented didactically the arguments presented in this chapter, we do want to stress that you can help your client to understand these points Socratically as well as didactically.

> You can gain valuable practice by explaining the rationality of rational beliefs to willing friends and/or family members. Remember to practise using both didactic and Socratic arguments in your explanations. Make a note of any difficulties you encounter generating arguments and take these to your REBT supervisor or trainer for advice.
>
> You can also select a rational belief that you would personally like to strengthen and use the arguments in this chapter on yourself. By showing yourself why a rational belief is consistent with reality, logical and useful you will be better equipped to do so for your clients. Once again take to your REBT trainer or supervisor instances when you can't generate the appropriate arguments.

In conclusion, the purpose of disputing your client's irrational beliefs is to help her to gain intellectual insight into the fact that her irrational beliefs are inconsistent with reality, illogical and lead to poor psychological results as well as impede goal achievement, whereas rational beliefs are empirically based, logical and constructive. Don't expect that once your client sees this, she will also have corresponding emotional insight. She won't – yet. In order for her to integrate these concepts so that they make a significant difference to the way she feels and acts, she will need to put them into practice in her everyday life and do so repeatedly using a number of homework assignments. This is the subject of Chapters 17 and 18.

CHAPTER SEVENTEEN

Negotiating homework assignments

As we mentioned at the end of the previous chapter, it is important for your client to put into practice in her everyday life what she learns in therapy sessions. In this chapter, we will discuss several issues that need to be considered when encouraging your client to put her in-therapy insights into practice outside of sessions.

▶ What's in a name?

Traditionally, REBT therapists call the formal work that clients agree to do between therapy sessions 'homework assignments'. However, it is not envisioned that your client will only do this work 'at home'. Rather, your client will carry out such assignments in whatever extra-therapy context is deemed to be relevant. Thus, the term 'homework assignment' means work that your client agrees to do between therapy sessions. Whilst most of your clients will be happy to use the term 'homework assignment' when discussing with you the work they are prepared to do on themselves between sessions, it is important for you to appreciate that some clients will find this term off-putting.

The main reason for such antipathy concerns the associations that the term 'homework assignment' has with school. In our experience, such clients have negative memories of school in general or homework in particular. For example, one of my (WD) clients, Geraldine, associated homework assignments with being locked in her room by her tyrannical mother until she had finished her school homework before being allowed to eat her supper. Not surprisingly, Geraldine reacted negatively to the term 'homework assignment' the first time I used it in counselling. Indeed, she winced visibly at the very mention of the term.

Whilst there has been no research on the relationship between clients' reactions to the term 'homework assignments' and the extent to which they actually carry out such between-session tasks, our clinical experience has been that clients are more likely to carry out such tasks when they use positive (to them) terms to denote these tasks. Given that at least some of your clients will have negative reactions to the term 'homework assignment', it is important that you develop with them terms that have positive connotations.

As a training exercise, pair up with a trainee colleague and develop a list of terms, other than 'homework assignment', that describe the work that your clients need to do between therapy sessions if they are to get the most out of REBT. Do this task before you read the next paragraph.

Here is a brief list of terms that we have used with a sample of my clients who reacted negatively to the term 'homework assignment':

- between-session task;
- change work;
- improvement task;
- goal-achievement task;
- self-help assignment;
- progress assignment.

Having made the point that it is important to use a term that enables your client to construe between-session work positively, we will use the term 'homework assignment' in the remainder of this chapter for ease of communication.

▶ Discussing the purpose of homework assignments

Bordin (1979) has made the important point that therapeutic tasks need to be goal-directed if their therapeutic potency is to be realised. As discussed in Chapter 2, one of the most important tasks that your client has to perform in REBT is putting into practice outside therapy what she learns inside therapy. As we have shown above, the best way that she can do this is by carrying out homework assignments. However, as Bordin rightly notes, your client will be unlikely to carry out such assignments if (i) she does not clearly understand the point of doing so in general and (ii) if she does not clearly understand the specific purpose of specific assignments. As we have already dealt with the issue of helping clients understand the importance of carrying out homework assignments in general earlier in this book, we will concentrate here on the importance of helping your clients to understand the specific purpose of particular homework assignments.

The most obvious way of doing this is by keeping to the fore of the therapeutic discussion your client's goals. Here is an example of how to do this.

Windy: So, Barry, can you see that as long as you believe that you must never be rejected you will never ask a girl out for a date?

Barry: Yes, that's self-evident.

Windy: So what's the rational alternative to this belief?

Barry: That I'd rather not be rejected, but there's no reason to assume that I must not be rejected.

Windy: Right. Now, how can you strengthen this belief?

Barry: By asking women out for dates.

Windy: While practising which belief?

Barry: The rational belief that I've just mentioned.

Windy: So do you think it would be a good idea to ask a woman out for a date between now and next week to strengthen this belief?

Barry: OK.

Windy: Will you agree to do this?

Barry: Yes, I will.

Windy: What's the purpose of doing so?

Barry: To get over my anxiety about asking women out on dates and to get used to rejection if it happens.

Windy: That is in fact one of the goals that you mentioned when we discussed what you wanted to gain from counselling. Now, do you think that it would be a good idea to make a note of the homework assignment and the reason why you are going to do it?

Barry: Yes, I do.

▶ Different types of homework assignments

There are different types of homework assignments that you can suggest to your client. We will mention several here, but for a fuller discussion, consult Walen, DiGiuseppe and Dryden (1992) and Dryden *et al.* (1999).

Cognitive assignments

Cognitive assignments are primarily those which help your client to understand the REBT model and the role that beliefs play in human disturbance and health. They also provide your client with a means of identifying and changing irrational beliefs. Many cognitive assignments are thus structured in a way to help your client use the 'ABCs' of REBT to assess her own problems and use disputing techniques to challenge and change her irrational beliefs. Normally doing such assignments on their own helps your client to gain intellectual insight rather than emotional insight into rational principles. They, thus, serve a very important role in the initial and early-middle stages of therapy.

Much of the material that we have dealt with so far in this book can be adapted or tailored for client self-help use. Indeed, I (WD) have written an REBT client workbook based on this material (Dryden, 2001). Given this, we will illustrate only two types of cognitive technique here.

Reading assignments   Reading assignments are mainly cognitive in nature in that your client will gain cognitive understanding from such material. Such assignments are frequently known as bibliotherapy. There is a plethora of self-help books that cover different client problems from an REBT perspective. Initially, you will want to suggest that your client reads a text which introduces basic REBT principles. This may be best done after you have taught your client the 'ABCs' of REBT (see Chapter 3).

Howard Young (in Dryden, 1989) noted that clients are generally impressed if you suggest that they read a text or an article that you have written yourself and he thinks that doing so increases the chances that they will read the material. Whilst this awaits empirical investigation, it does make sense and for this reason I (WD) frequently suggest that my clients read *Ten Steps to Positive Living* (Dryden, 1994b) which outlines the basic principles of REBT. If my client expresses alarm at the thought of reading an entire book then I will suggest that he starts with the first chapter or I give them copies of the first two chapters of my client workbook *Reason to Change* (Dryden, 2001) which covers the basics of REBT theory and practice in a manner that is easily digested by most clients.

Of course, different clients will benefit from reading different introductory material and it is worthwhile becoming familiar with different introductory self-help REBT material so that you can suggest suitable reading material. These range from the simple, e.g. *A Rational Counseling* Primer by Howard Young (1974), to the more linguistically complex, e.g. *Feeling Better, Getting Better, Staying Better* (Ellis, 2001).

Later you might suggest that your client reads books or articles that are devoted to his specific emotional problems. I (WD) have written specific books on the major unhealthy negative emotions that clients seek help for including shame (Dryden, 1997), anger (Dryden, 1996) and envy (Dryden, 2002).

Another way of approaching REBT bibliotherapy is to suggest that your client reads a book on one or both of the two major forms of psychological disturbance (i.e. ego disturbance and discomfort disturbance). I (WD) have written a book on ego disturbance issues entitled *How to Accept Yourself* (Dryden, 1999b) and Jack Gordon and I have written a book devoted to discomfort disturbance issues entitled *Beating the Comfort Trap* (Dryden and Gordon, 1993).

Whichever books or articles you recommend to your client, it is important to note that the purpose of bibliotherapy is to encourage your client to develop intellectual insight into rational principles. Many clients believe that if they read and re-read articles and books on REBT then they will not only understand these principles but will automatically be able to internalise them into their behavioural and emotional repertoire. As we discussed in Chapter 2, it is very unlikely that this will happen, as internalisation of rational beliefs will usually only occur as a result of repeated cognitive, emotive *and* behavioural practice.

Here are three training exercises that will help you to make effective use of bibliotherapeutic materials.

1. Suggest to your trainee colleagues that you each review three different REBT self-help books. In doing so, briefly summarise the content of these books and develop a list of indications and contraindications for their use. This exercise will allow you and your colleagues (a) to compile a growing list of REBT reading resources and when they can best be used and (b) to develop your powers of criticism in relation to this material.

2. Begin to write your own REBT self-help material. This will enable you to increase your credibility with your clients as well as helping them to 'hear your voice' in the material that they read. I (WD) have found that when my clients say that they can 'hear my voice' in the books that I have written, then this helps to reinforce their within-therapy learning.

3. Pair up with a trainee colleague and as therapist help your 'client' to understand the purposes of reading assignments and, as importantly, the limits of bibliotherapy. As elsewhere, tape record the interchange and play it to your REBT trainer or supervisor for feedback.

Listening assignments

Reading assignments obviously involve your client using his or her visual mode of experience. Some clients, however, may not process information readily using this mode. Others may be blind or find reading the small print of self-help books or articles difficult because of failing eyesight. Given these points you will need to offer such clients a plausible and effective alternative mode of communication whereby important rational principles are conveyed.

Using the auditory mode of communication is the obvious alternative here and there are two major types of listening assignments that you can suggest your client does between sessions. First, you can suggest that your client listen to one or more of the numerous CDs that are put out by the Albert Ellis Institute (for a catalogue write c/o 45 East 65th Street, New York NY 10021, USA). Most of these CDs are in the form of lectures on client problems (such as anxiety, anger, depression and procrastination) and how these can be tackled using the principles of REBT.

Second, you can suggest that your client listens to a recording of her therapy sessions. Numerous clients report that they find listening to such recordings helpful. They frequently say that points that they did not quite understand during a therapy session became quite clear on later review.

There are three reasons why this might be the case. As a training exercise see if a small group of your trainee colleagues can identify them. You may well discover additional reasons. Do this exercise before reading further.

We hope that you were able to discover the three reasons which we will now discuss.

1. During therapy sessions, your client may be distracted by her own thoughts and feelings related to the problem that she is discussing with you. Such thoughts and feelings will interfere with her ability to process adequately the points you are trying to convey to her using Socratic or didactic means. On later review and freed from the distracting nature of these thoughts and feelings, your client may well be more able to focus on what you were saying than when you said it at the time.

2. During therapy sessions, your client may be reluctant to tell you that she does not understand what you are trying to convey to her. Even when you ask her for her understanding of the points you have been making, her correct response may belie her true understanding. On later review, and freed from the self-imposed pressure to understand what you are saying, she may, paradoxically, understand more fully than at the time the rational principles you were explaining.

3. When your client comes to listen to the recording of her therapy session, she can replay the entire session or segments of it as many times as she chooses. Unless she asks you to repeat points several times in the session (which the vast majority of clients will not do), your client only gets to hear once what you say in the therapy session. Repeated review of the entire session or salient segments of the session will often facilitate client understanding of rational principles.

Whenever we suggest that clients review recordings of therapy sessions, we suggest that they make written notes as this encourages them to be active in the reviewing process. We particularly ask them to note points that they found most salient and points that they could not understand even after repeated review. We stress that this is most probably attributable to our deficits as a communicator rather than their deficits in understanding what we were trying to convey.

Another benefit of encouraging your client to listen to recordings of her therapy sessions is that it helps her to re-orientate the therapy. Clients sometimes say, for example, that on reviewing the session they realised that they were not discussing what they really wanted to discuss or that they had omitted important information while discussing salient issues. In this way, your client may well help you to get therapy back on the most important track.

Of course, not all clients will find such listening assignments valuable. In particular, your client may well say that she felt worse after listening to a therapy session than before reviewing it. If this happens regularly, it may well be a sign that you need to suspend the use of this type of homework assignment. Common reasons for clients feeling worse after listening to recordings of therapy sessions usually centre on self-downing issues. Clients may say such things as:

- 'I hated the sound of my voice' (and implicitly – I put myself down for the way I sounded);
- 'I hated myself for sounding so pathetic';
- 'I couldn't believe how stupid I was for not understanding what you were saying.'

Whilst you may be able to encourage your client to practise self-acceptance while listening to facets of herself that she didn't like, most often you will find it more profitable to suspend 'audiotherapy' until your client has made more progress on her self-depreciation issues. Here as elsewhere in REBT it is important to be flexible.

Imagery assignments

When your client uses imagery assignments, she makes use of both her cognitive and affective modalities. Imagery assignments are obviously cognitive, although they draw on a different part of the brain to that which processes verbal information. They are also affective in nature because visual images, particularly clear images, are affect laden when they embody inferences that are central in the client's personal domain (see Dryden, 2000)

Imagery assignments can be used by your client between sessions as an assessment tool to identify irrational beliefs that are likely to underpin her predicted disturbed feelings in forthcoming situations. They can also be used by your client as a way of gaining practice in changing unhealthy negative feelings to their healthy counterparts by changing her irrational beliefs to rational beliefs. The important point that your client needs to bear in mind here is keeping the 'critical A' constant. Otherwise she may learn that she can change her feelings by changing the actual or inferred 'critical A'. As we showed in Chapter 2, belief-based change is regarded in REBT as more enduring than inference-based or environmental change.

A third way that your client can employ imagery assignments is as a form of mental rehearsal before carrying out behavioural assignments. Here, your client is advised to practise seeing herself in her mind's eye perform poorly as well as adequately. The purpose of encouraging your client to picture herself performing poorly is to help her to think rationally about such an eventuality. Preparing clients for failure as well as success is a typical REBT strategy.

While clients differ markedly in their ability to visualise clearly, a more important factor than image clarity in determining the employment of imagery assignments is the presence of client affect accompanying their use. In our view, such assignments are less useful with clients who experience no affect while picturing themselves in situations where they would in reality feel a lot of emotion than with clients who do experience affect while using imagery.

Behavioural assignments

Behavioural assignments involve your client doing something to counteract his irrational beliefs and to consolidate his rational beliefs. They are assignments which encourage your client to act on his non-dogmatic preferences and other related rational beliefs. Given this, behavioural assignments are often used simultaneously with cognitive assignments which provide your client with an opportunity to challenge and change his irrational beliefs. The main purpose of behavioural assignments, then, is to help your client to strengthen his conviction in his rational beliefs.

'Acting as-if' is a useful behavioural assignment that promotes emotional in-sight. It involves identifying specific opportunities for your client to behave 'as-if' he *already* strongly believes his rational preference. Through enacting the rational belief he wants to strengthen, your client will begin to see the benefits of holding rational beliefs. It is useful to base 'acting as-if' exercises on the action tendencies associated with the healthy negative emotion you and your client have identified as a goal (see Figure 4.1. **pp. 62–65**).

A discussion of the full range of behavioural assignments used in REBT is beyond the scope of this handbook, but can be found in Bernard and Wolfe (2000).

Emotive assignments

Emotive assignments are therapeutic tasks that fully engage your client's emotions. As such, as long as they meet this criterion, certain cognitive and behavioural techniques can be regarded as emotive assignments.

Thus, Ellis regarded certain cognitive techniques as emotive in nature when they are employed by clients with force and energy and he saw certain behavioural techniques such as 'shame-attacking exercises' as emotive because clients are en-couraged to do certain 'shameful' things and simultaneously 'attack' their shame by disputing the irrational beliefs that underpin this emotion. In addition, certain imagery methods, such as rational-emotive imagery, can be classified as emotive assignments because they attempt to engage fully your client's emotions.

As with behavioural assignments, the major purpose of emotive assignments is to help your client to turn his intellectual conviction in his rational beliefs into emotional conviction (see Chapter 2).

▶ The importance of negotiating homework assignments

The field of behavioural medicine has focused much attention on the factors associated with patient compliance with prescriptive medical treatment. How-ever, the term 'compliance' is an unfortunate one when used in counselling and psychotherapy as it conjures up the image of an all-knowing therapist telling the ignorant client what to do, with the client either complying or not complying with these instructions. Whilst it is debatable whether this image is even appropriate in the field of medicine, it is certainly unsuitable in the field of psychotherapy in general and REBT in particular.

On the other hand, the image of equal collaboration between therapist and client is also not appropriate in REBT. Whilst the egalitarian-collaborative model of the therapeutic relationship is appealing to therapists who view their main role as encouraging clients to use their own resources, it is viewed as dishonest by REBT therapists. It ignores, for example, the fact that as an REBT therapist you know more than your client about (i) the nature of psychological disturbance; (ii) how clients, in general, perpetuate their psychological problems and (iii) the processes of therapeutic change and how to facilitate it. Having this knowledge does not entitle you to view yourself as an all-knowing guru and act accordingly, but neither should it lead you to deny that you have such knowledge in the spirit of well-meaning, but ultimately misguided egalitarianism.

As we argued in Chapter 2, REBT theory holds that you and your client are equal in humanity, but unequal in knowledge and understanding of human disturbance and its remediation. This view of the therapeutic relationship in REBT underpins the importance of negotiating homework assignments with your client. This means that you neither unilaterally tell your client what he will do for homework, nor do you wait for him to tell you what he is going to do between sessions. It means that you will have an informed view concerning the best homework assignment for him at a given time, that you will express this view honestly with your client, but you will very much respect his opinion on the matter and will discuss with him your respective views with the purpose of agreeing a homework assignment to which he will commit himself.

Let us illustrate the differences between the three approaches to homework assignments that we have described. We will first set the scene and then vary the dialogue to highlight these differences.

Windy: So, Norman, you can now see that your anxiety about speaking up in class stems from two beliefs: first, the belief that you must know for certain that you won't say anything stupid and, second, that if you do say something stupid then other people will laugh at you which would prove that you would be stupid through and through. Right?

Norman: Right.

Windy: And the healthy rational alternatives to these two irrational beliefs are?

Norman: That I'd like to be certain that I don't say something stupid, but I don't need this certainty. And I can accept myself as a fallible human being in the event of saying something stupid and people laughing at me.

Windy: Now you also understand that if you want to really believe these two ideas, you need to … ?

Norman: Practise acting according to these two ideas.

1. *REBT therapist as unilateral expert: telling a client what he will do for homework*

Windy: OK, so what I want you to do between now and next week is to speak up five times in class, and practise your two rational ideas before, during and after doing this. Agreed?

Norman: … (pause) … (very hesitantly) … A-A-Agreed.

[As you can see, here I have unilaterally decided what is good for my client and I have told him what I want him to do. As the very hesitant response of my client shows, he is most unlikely to do this homework or, if he does, it will be out of fear.]

2. *REBT therapist as laissez-faire egalitarian: waiting for your client to tell you what he will do for homework*

Windy: So, Norman, what can you do between now and next week to practise and strengthen these two ideas?

Norman: Well, I suppose I can think about the ideas once a day.

Windy: OK, fine.

[Here, because I am overly keen to encourage my client to use his own resources, I do not query his own suggestion. Whilst the client may well carry out this assignment, he will not derive much benefit from it, primarily because it is not a behavioural task.]

3. *REBT therapist as authoritative egalitarian: negotiating a homework assignment with your client*

Windy: Now, Norman, let me make a suggestion about what you can do to strengthen these beliefs and then we can discuss it. OK?

Norman: Fine.

Windy: First of all, it is important to do something active to get over your fear. Can you see why?

Norman: Because if I don't, I won't overcome it.

Windy: Right, so how about speaking up in class while showing yourself before, during and after you do so that you'd like to be certain that you don't say something stupid, but you don't need this certainty. And that you can accept yourself as a fallible human being in the event of saying something stupid and people laughing at you?

Norman: OK, that sounds reasonable.

Windy: How about speaking up every college day between now and our next meeting?

Norman: That's five days! That seems a bit steep.

Windy: What would you suggest?

Norman: Twice?

Windy: How about a compromise of three or four?

Norman: Three it is then.

Note that here I have taken an authoritative stance by selecting for Norman a relevant behavioural task. However, I am egalitarian in that I ask him for feedback on my suggestion and I am prepared to negotiate a compromise. I thus show that I respect his opinion, but I also ask him to respect mine. My hypothesis is that the client is more likely to carry out this task than he would in the first scenario discussed above when I unilaterally told him what he was to do for homework.

▶ The 'challenging, but not overwhelming' principle of homework negotiation

Albert Ellis (1983) was openly critical of many popular behaviour therapy techniques that are based on the principle of gradual desensitisation. Ellis argued that the use of such techniques is inefficient in that it needlessly prolongs the length of therapy and that it tends to reinforce clients' philosophy of low frustration tolerance. By using gradual desensitisation methods it is as if the therapist is implicitly saying to the client: 'You really are a delicate flower who can tolerate virtually no anxiety or discomfort and that is why we will have to take things very gradually.'

Given this, Ellis argued that clients can help themselves best by doing homework assignments based on the principle of flooding or full exposure. Here, your client would practise strengthening his rational beliefs by seeking out situations in which he would be most anxious. He would then stay in these situations until he has strengthened his rational beliefs to the extent that he no longer feels anxiety. He would then do this frequently and repeatedly until he has overcome his problem. Ellis (1985) described a case where he helped a woman overcome her lift phobia by full exposure methods. The woman agreed to travel repeatedly in lifts in a short period of time until she could travel in them without anxiety. It goes without saying that the client needs to be very motivated to do this. Thus, Ellis's client had just been offered a desired job at the top of a New York skyscraper. Because it was impossible for her to take the stairs, she was faced with the choice of declining the position or travelling in the lift to her new office.

When your client has such motivation and is prepared to tolerate the high levels of discomfort to which flooding methods lead, you should encourage her to undertake homework assignments based on the principle of full exposure. However, in our experience, most clients will not agree to carry out such assignments. In such instances, is there a better alternative to homework assignments based on gradual desensitisation? The answer is yes and these are assignments based on the principle that I (WD) have called 'challenging, but not overwhelming.' Such assignments occupy a middle ground between flooding and gradual desensitisation methods. They constitute a challenge for your client, which if undertaken would lead to therapeutic progress, but would not be overwhelming for the client (in his judgment) at that particular time. Here is an example of how I (WD) introduce this concept to clients.

Windy: Now, Norman, how quickly do you want to overcome your fear of speaking up in class: very quickly, moderately quickly or slowly?

Norman: Very quickly.

Windy: And how much discomfort are you prepared to face in overcoming your problem: great discomfort, moderate discomfort or no discomfort?

Norman: Well, ideally no discomfort.

Windy: So you'd like to overcome your problem very quickly and without discomfort. Right?

Norman: Right.

Windy: Well, I'd really like to help you to do that but, unfortunately, I can't. Let me explain. If you want to overcome your problem very quickly, you will have to speak up in class very frequently and this will involve you tolerating much discomfort. Here you will have to do assignments based on the principle of full exposure. However, if you want to experience minimal levels of discomfort, then it follows that you will have to go very slowly. Here you will do assignments based on the principle of gradual desensitisation. A middle ground between these two positions is based on the principle that I call 'challenging, but not overwhelming'. Here you will choose to do homework assignments that are challenging, but not overwhelming for you at any point in time. This would involve you tolerating moderate levels of discomfort and would lead you to make progress moderately quickly. Is that clear?

Norman: Yes. You're saying that I can go slowly, moderately quickly or very quickly. The quicker I decide to go, the more discomfort I will have to tolerate.

Windy: That's exactly right. So, how would you like to proceed?

> Norman: According to the 'challenging, but not overwhelming' principle.
>
> Windy: Then let's see what you can do between now and next week that will allow you to practise strengthening your rational beliefs in a way that is challenging for you...

Let us make two concluding remarks on this issue.

1. We tend to dissuade any clients who say that they wish to follow the 'gradual desensitisation' route. We point out to them that doing so will be counter-productive in that taking this route will tend to reinforce their philosophy of low frustration tolerance. However, we do not insist that such clients begin with 'challenging, but not overwhelming' homework assignments. If the worst comes to the worst, we would start with the 'gradual desensitisation' route, hoping to 'transfer' them to the 'challenging, but not overwhelming' route as quickly as possible.

2. A number of clients who begin by carrying out 'challenging, but not overwhelming' homework assignments do switch to flooding-type assignments after they have made some progress and they get accustomed to tolerating moderate levels of discomfort.

▶ How to increase the chances that your client will do homework

In the following sections, we want to mention a number of principles that you can follow to increase the chances that your client will carry out his jointly negotiated homework assignment. Please note, however, that none of these methods will guarantee that he will actually do the assignment. Assuming that you have carried out the following steps, it is important not to lose sight of the fact that your client is ultimately responsible for whether or not he will do his homework. Thus, whether he does so or not, it is not a measure of your worth as a therapist (or even as a person!).

Teach your client the 'no-lose' concept of homework assignments

The 'no-lose' concept of homework assignments is designed to give your client additional encouragement to agree to carry out an assignment. While introducing the concept to your client you need to stress that there is no way that your client can lose if he agrees to undertake the homework task, and you need to emphasise three points as shown in the following dialogue.

Windy: So to recap, Norman, you have agreed to speak up in class on three occasions while showing yourself (i) that you don't need to be certain that you won't say anything stupid before you speak and (ii) that if you do say something stupid you can still accept yourself as a fallible human being even if people in your seminar group laugh at you. Is that right?

Norman: Well, I'm still a bit doubtful about it.

Windy: I can appreciate that, but let me put it this way. If you undertake to do the assignment, then there is no way you can lose. Do you know why?

Norman: No, why?

Windy: Well, let me put it like this. First, if you agree to do the assignment and you actually do it and it works out well, then that's good because you have made a big stride forward in meeting your goals. Right?

Norman: Yes, I can see that.

Windy: Second, if you agree to do the assignment and you actually do it, but it doesn't go well, then that's valuable because we can analyse what happened and you can learn from the experience. Do you see that?

Norman: Yes, I do.

Windy: And finally, if you undertake to do the homework assignment, but you don't do it, then that is also valuable. Do you know why?

Norman: ... Because we can find out how I stopped myself from doing it?

Windy: That's right. We can discover obstacles, which neither of us knew about, and then we can help you to overcome them. So, can you see why if you agree to do the assignment, you can't lose?

Norman: Very good. You should be a salesman!

Windy: I am. I'm trying to sell you on the concept of mental health and how you can achieve it!

Ensure that your client has sufficient skills to carry out the homework assignment

It is important that your client has the skills to carry out the negotiated homework assignment. For example, if you have suggested that he complete a written 'ABC' form, it is important that you first instruct him in its use. He is more likely to do the assignment if he knows what to do than if he doesn't.

Ensure that your client believes that he can do the homework assignment

Self-efficacy theory (Bandura, 1977) predicts that your client is more likely to carry out a homework assignment if he believes that he can actually do it than if he lacks what Bandura calls an 'efficacy expectation'. Given this, it is important to spend some time helping your client to see that he is able to carry out the homework task. One way to do this is to suggest that your client uses imagery techniques where he repeatedly pictures himself carrying out the assignment before he does so in reality.

It is important to distinguish between an efficacy expectation and the more objective question of whether or not your client has a particular skill in his repertoire. It is possible that your client has a skill in his repertoire but subjectively believes that he is unable to use this skill in a particular setting. Thus, it is insufficient to teach your client a skill such as filling in a written 'ABC' form. You also need to help him to develop the relevant efficacy expectation. Here is an example of how to do this.

Windy: So do you think you can speak up in class while showing yourself that you don't need to be certain that you won't say anything stupid and that you can accept yourself as a fallible human being if you do?

Norman: I'm not sure.

Windy: Well let's see. Close your eyes and picture yourself in class. Have you got that image in mind?

Norman: Yes, I have.

Windy: Good. Now see yourself showing yourself that you don't need to be certain that you won't say anything stupid and that you can accept yourself as a fallible human being if you do. Have you got that?

Norman: Yes.

Windy: Now keep those two beliefs in mind and see yourself speaking up in class. Can you do that?

Norman: Yes, I can picture that.

Windy: So does this show you that you can do this assignment in reality?

Norman: Yes, it does.

Give yourself sufficient time to negotiate a homework assignment

We have listened to many therapy sessions conducted by beginning REBT therapists over the years and have been struck by how little time such therapists allocate to negotiating homework assignments with their clients. They frequently leave the issue of homework to the very last minute with the result that they end up by telling their clients what they want them to do between sessions. Because negotiating a suitable assignment takes time, we suggest that you allocate 10 minutes to this activity. This will enable you to incorporate all of the issues that we have discussed in this chapter which, we argue, will increase the chances that your client will execute the homework task successfully.

If you have negotiated a suitable homework assignment in the early or middle part of a therapy session you will not need to devote 10 minutes to this task at the end of a session. However, it is still worthwhile allocating a few minutes to recap on the homework, otherwise your client may forget what his homework is. This latter point emerged from a book that my colleague, Joseph Yankura, and I (WD) produced on the therapy work of Albert Ellis entitled *Doing RET: Albert Ellis in Action* (Yankura and Dryden, 1990). We noted that Ellis did not consistently negotiate specific homework assignments with his clients at the end of a session. Ellis replied that he often makes homework suggestions during a therapy session. The important point here is not whether you did or did not negotiate a homework assignment, but whether your client remembers the homework. When we interviewed several of Ellis's clients for the book we came away with the impression that Ellis's clients did not recall that he consistently suggested specific homework tasks. One way to ensure that your client remembers that homework has been negotiated, particularly when this has been discussed in the main body of the session, is to review it at session's end.

Another way of encouraging your client to remember his homework is to suggest that he keeps a written record of the assignment. We will discuss this further in a later section.

Ensure that the homework assignment follows logically from the work you have done with your client in the therapy session

Much of the work you will do in a therapy session will be focused on one of your client's target problems. Towards the end of the session, you should negotiate a homework assignment with your client that logically follows from the work you have done with her on the target problem. The following is a rough guide of when to negotiate which type of homework assignment.

- Negotiate a reading assignment when the work you have done with your client has centred on helping your client to understand the relationship between her unhealthy negative emotion and her irrational beliefs.

- Negotiate a written homework assignment (e.g. an 'ABC' form) when the session work has centred on helping your client to identify and dispute her irrational beliefs and when you have trained your client in the use of the relevant written form.

- Negotiate an imagery assignment when the session work has focused on beginning to strengthen rational beliefs, but your client is not ready to undertake a behavioural assignment.

- Negotiate a behavioural assignment (along with a relevant cognitive disputing technique) when the session work has prepared your client to strengthen her rational beliefs by, for example, 'acting on her non-dogmatic preferences.'

■ Negotiate an emotive assignment when the session has been devoted to discussing how your client can deepen her conviction in her rational beliefs other than through the use of behavioural assignments.

To reiterate, whatever type of homework assignment you negotiate with your client, ensure that it is relevant to the work you have done with her in the session.

Ensure that your client understands the nature and purpose of the homework assignment

We mentioned this point earlier, but it is so important I wish to reiterate it here. At the end of the process of homework negotiation, it is useful to ask your client to summarise the homework assignment and its rationale. It is particularly important to ensure that your client has understood the reason why he has agreed to carry out the assignment. Our clinical experience has shown me that the more a client keeps the purpose of a negotiated homework assignment at the forefront of his mind, the more likely it is that he will do the agreed assignment. Here is an example.

> Windy: So let's recap. What are you going to do between now and next week?
>
> Norman: I'm going to speak up in class and practise my new rational beliefs.
>
> Windy: And what's the purpose of speaking up in class while showing yourself that you don't need to be certain that you won't say anything stupid and that you can accept yourself as a fallible human being if you do?
>
> Norman: Well, it will help me to be able to speak up in class whenever I want to say something without feeling anxious.

Help your client to specify when, where and how often she will do the homework task

If you can help your client to specify the number of times he will carry out the negotiated homework assignment, when he will do it and in what setting, then he is more likely to do it than if no such agreements are made. For example:

> Windy: Now, Norman, how many times between now and next week will you agree to speak up in class while practising your rational beliefs? I was thinking that four times might be a challenging number, but I don't want to suggest this if it is too overwhelming for you at this point.

Norman: Well, that sounds a bit steep. How about twice?

Windy: Shall we compromise on three?

Norman: OK then.

Windy: And where will you do this?

Norman: Well, I've got four seminars next week. I can do it in three of those.

Windy: Let's be really specific here.

Norman (looking in his diary): Well, I can do it in the Monday seminar at 3 pm, in the Wednesday seminar at noon and in the Friday seminar at 10 am.

Windy: Good, now let's talk about when in the seminars you will do this. In my experience it is better to do the homework early in the seminar rather than later. Does that make sense?

Norman: Yes, it does.

Windy: So would it make sense to speak up in the first 20 minutes of the seminar?

Norman: Yes, that makes sense.

Windy: Will you do it?

Norman: Yes.

Elicit a firm commitment that your client will carry out the homework assignment

It is important to get a firm commitment from your client to do the assignment rather than a vague commitment such as 'I think I can do that' or 'I'll try'. When your client makes a definite commitment to do the homework assignment, she is more likely to do it than if she makes a vague commitment. For example:

Windy: So would it make sense to speak up in the first 20 minutes of the seminar?

Norman: OK. I'll try to do that.

Windy: Let me show you the difference between 'do' and 'try'. Snap your fingers ... (Norman snaps his fingers) ... Now try to snap your fingers, but don't actually snap them ... (Norman makes the relevant movement but doesn't actually snap his fingers). Can you see the difference between 'try' and 'do'?

> Norman: When you do something you do it. But when you try, it doesn't mean that you will do it.
>
> Windy: So will you commit yourself to speak up in the first 20 minutes or will you commit yourself to trying?
>
> Norman: I'll do it.

Troubleshoot any obstacles to homework assignment completion

It has been our experience that when we have helped our clients to identify potential obstacles to homework completion and to find ways of dealing with these obstacles, then they are more likely to do the homework than when we have not instituted such troubleshooting. What may serve as potential obstacles to homework completion? Golden (1989) has provided a comprehensive list of such obstacles and we refer the reader to his excellent discussion of the subject. Given this, we will only consider here the most common obstacle which is a philosophy of low frustration tolerance (LFT). Clients often provide many rationalisations in their explanations of why they did not do their homework (e.g. 'I didn't have the time' or 'I forgot') when the real reason can be attributed to LFT (e.g. 'I didn't do the task because I thought I would feel too uncomfortable doing it'). It is thus worthwhile raising LFT as a potential obstacle to homework completion even though your client doesn't mention it. This is what I (WD) did with Norman.

> Windy: Now, Norman, it is often useful in therapy to troubleshoot any reasons why you might not do what you have agreed to do for homework. Can you think of any reason why you might not do yours?
>
> Norman: No, I'm pretty sure that I will do it.
>
> Windy: But what if you begin to feel very uncomfortable in the moments before you have decided to speak up?
>
> Norman: Good point. If that happened I might well duck out of doing it.
>
> Windy: What do you think you would need to tell yourself to speak up even though you are feeling uncomfortable?
>
> Norman: That I can speak up even though I am feeling very uncomfortable and that if I do speak up the discomfort will probably subside.
>
> Windy: Would that work?
>
> Norman: Yes, it would.
>
> Windy: So why not imagine yourself feeling very uncomfortable in the seminar situation and show yourself that you can speak up anyway.
>
> Norman: That's a good idea.

Encourage your client to keep a written note of his homework assignment and relevant details

Experienced General Practitioners know that one way of increasing the chances that patients will follow medical advice is to provide them with a written summary of that advice. There are several reasons why a patient may not remember medical advice. First, she may simply forget the advice. Second, the advice may be too complex to be processed properly at the time. Third, the patient may be anxious during the medical consultation and this anxiety may affect her cognitive functioning during and after that consultation.

The same factors may operate during the psychotherapeutic interview and having your client write down the homework assignment or providing her with a written summary of the assignment will increase the chances that she will carry out the assignment. Some REBT therapists keep a supply of 'No Carbon Required' (NCR) paper on which they write or have their clients write down the homework assignment. NCR paper provides an automatic copy for the therapist to keep in his or her files to be retrieved at the beginning of the next session when the therapist will check the client's assignment (see next chapter).

What information should be put on the written record? My (WD) practice is to have my client record the following information:

1. the nature of the assignment;

2. the purpose of the assignment;

3. how often the client will carry out the assignment;

4. where the client will carry out the assignment;

5. when the client will carry out the assignment;

6. possible obstacles to carrying out the assignment;

7. how these obstacles can be overcome.

The above seven sections can be completed by the client at the end of the therapy session in which the homework task has been negotiated. The following three sections are to be completed by the client between therapy sessions:

8. what the client actually did;

9. actual obstacles to carrying out the assignment;

10. what the client actually learned from carrying out the assignment.

Here is how Norman completed the first seven sections of the homework form at the end of the therapy session in which the assignment was negotiated.

1. *The nature of the assignment*

I will speak up in class while showing myself that I don't need to be certain that I won't say anything stupid and that I can accept myself as a fallible human being if I do.

2. *The purpose of the assignment*

Doing this will help me to be able to speak up in class whenever I want to say something, without feeling anxious.

3. *How often the client will carry out the assignment*

Three times.

4. *Where the client will carry out the assignment*

(i) Monday seminar at 3 pm; (ii) Wednesday seminar at noon; (iii) Friday seminar at 10 am.

5. *When the client will carry out the assignment*

During the first 20 minutes of each seminar.

6. *Possible obstacles to carrying out the assignment*

Feeling very uncomfortable.

7. *How these obstacles can be overcome*

I can show myself that I can speak up even though I am feeling very uncomfortable and that if I do speak up the discomfort will probably subside.

Rehearse the homework assignment in the therapy room

It is often a good idea to rehearse the assignment in the therapy session if this is practicable. If not you can use imagery rehearsal as a plausible substitute. Rehearsing your client's homework assignment in the session serves both to increase his sense that he will be able to do the assignment in reality and to identify potential obstacles to homework completion that haven't been identified through verbal discussion of this issue (see below).

Windy: Let's rehearse the assignment briefly. OK?

Norman: OK.

Windy: Shall I play your tutor and perhaps one other student and we can imagine that there are other students present too? Your task is to speak up while practising the two rational beliefs that we discussed. OK?

Norman: Fine.

Windy (as tutor): So this week we are discussing the role of Catholicism in Evelyn Waugh's novel *Brideshead Revisited*. Who would like to kick off?

[I first discovered that this was to be the topic for one of Norman's forthcoming seminars.]

Windy (as student): I think that Waugh shows his deep ambivalence about Catholicism in this novel because several of the characters are at one time scornful of it and at another time drawn towards it.

Norman: I would agree with that. For example, who would have thought that Sebastian would have ended up as he did, as a kind of unpaid caretaker in a religious order. And his father ended his life by making the sign of the cross, even though he spent most of his life being openly scornful of Catholicism....

Windy (as therapist): How did that go?

Norman: I did feel a bit anxious, but that went as I got into my stride.

Windy: Do you think this will help you to speak up in the seminar?

Norman: Well, I think I'll be more uncomfortable then, but I'm sure now that I'll be able to do it.

Use the principle of rewards and penalties to encourage your client to do the homework assignment

Sometimes it is helpful to suggest to your client that he can use the principle of rewards and penalties to encourage himself to do his homework assignment. Basically this involves your client rewarding himself when he does the assignment and penalising (but not condemning) himself if he fails to do it. This principle can be applied by your client particularly when he may not do the assignment owing to a philosophy of LFT, as in the following example.

Windy: So you still think that you might not do the assignment if you experience a lot of discomfort. Is that right?

Norman: I think so.

Windy: If that happens you can use the principle of rewards and penalties as an added incentive. Here is how it works. What do you like doing every day that you would be very reluctant to give up?

Norman: Reading the newspaper.

Windy: And what do you really dislike doing?

Norman: Cleaning the oven.

Windy: OK. If you speak up in class you can the read the newspaper and you won't have to clean the oven. However, if you don't speak up then you have to clean the oven and no reading the newspaper. Agreed?

Norman: Wow, that's tough.

Windy: That's right. Tough measures for tough problems.

Norman: OK. I doubt whether I'll need to use this principle, but I'll do it if I need what you call an added incentive.

[If your client is going to use the principle of rewards and penalties then have him write this agreement on his homework form.]

▶ Monitor your skills at negotiating homework assignments

We strongly encourage you to monitor your skills at negotiating homework assignments with the purpose of improving these skills. We suggest that you do the following:

Record your therapy sessions routinely and use the scale presented in Appendix 1 to evaluate your performance. Before you do so, please note that very few therapists will score highly on all of the scale's items. Indeed, some items will not be relevant and there is an opportunity to indicate this on the scale. However, if you do answer 'No' to any item (as opposed to 'Not Appropriate') then write down what you would have done differently given hindsight and what you would have needed to change in order to have answered 'Yes'.

As we have suggested throughout this book, take any enduring problems in negotiating homework assignments to your REBT supervisor or trainer.

Reviewing homework assignments

In this chapter, we will discuss the issues that arise when you come to review your client's homework. To give you an idea of the important role that reviewing homework assignments plays in the REBT therapeutic process consider the following view of the structure of REBT sessions put forward by Raymond DiGiuseppe (personal communication), the Director of Professional Education at the Albert Ellis Institute in New York:

> Review Homework
> Carry Out Session Work
> Negotiate Homework

Reviewing homework when therapy is under way, then, is often the first therapeutic task that you have to perform in a session as an REBT therapist and has a decided bearing on the rest of that session. Let us begin the discussion by outlining the most central principle of reviewing homework.

▶ Put reviewing your client's homework assignment on the session agenda

Reviewing your client's homework conveys to her two things. First it shows her that you consider homework assignments to be an integral part of the therapeutic process. If you, as a client, had agreed to carry out a homework assignment and had actually done so, how would you respond if your therapist did not ask for a report on what you did and what you learned from doing the assignment? My guess is that you would not be pleased. Being human, you would also be less likely to carry out future homework assignments than you would be if your therapist had reviewed the homework with you. For that is what we have found as REBT therapists and supervisors: clients are more likely to do homework assignments when their therapists initiate regular reviews of their previous assignments than when their therapists do not do so. Consequently, the first and perhaps the most important principle of reviewing your client's homework assignments is actually to review them!

The second thing that you convey to your client when you review her homework is that you are genuinely interested in her therapeutic progress. Earlier in the process of REBT, you will have helped your client to see that homework assignments are an important vehicle for stimulating therapeutic progress by helping her to deepen conviction in her rational beliefs. In other words, doing homework assignments helps your client to go from intellectual to emotional insight. Asking your client about her homework assignments shows that you are taking a regular interest in his or her progress on this issue. If you fail to review her assignments, you may convey the opposite: that you are indifferent to her therapeutic progress.

▶ When is it best to review homework assignments?

Having put reviewing homework assignments on the therapeutic agenda, when is the best time for you to initiate such a review? In our opinion, the best time to review your client's homework assignments is at the beginning of the next therapy session. If you set a formal, structured agenda for each therapy session with your client as many cognitive therapists do (see Beck *et al.*, 1979), you will put the item 'previous homework' on the agenda for every session. You will also want to suggest placing this item early on the agenda. The reason for this is that what your client did or did not do for homework and what she learned or did not learn from doing it will have an important influence on the content of the current session. On the other hand, if your practice is not to set a formal agenda at the beginning of every session, you will still want to initiate the homework review early in the session. Indeed, some REBT therapists routinely begin each therapy session with an enquiry about their client's previous week's homework. For example, Ed Garcia used to have a tape in the Albert Ellis Institute's professional tape library which begins with him asking his client, 'What did you do for homework?'

There are, of course, exceptions to this principle. For example, if your client comes into the therapy session in a very agitated or even suicidal state, we hope that you would deal with this crisis rather than attempt to review his last homework task! Here, as elsewhere, it is important to practise REBT in a humane, flexible manner.

▶ Important issues to consider when reviewing homework assignments

In the following sections, we will outline and discuss several points that you need to consider as you review your client's homework assignment.

When your client states that he did the homework assignment, check whether or not it was done as negotiated

When your client reports that he carried out the homework assignment, the first point to check when you review the homework assignment is whether or not he did it as negotiated. It may well happen that your client changed the nature of the assignment and in doing so lessened the therapeutic potency of the assignment.

You will recall that the homework assignment I (WD) negotiated with Norman was as follows:

> 'I will speak up in three different seminars while showing myself that I don't need to be certain that I won't say something stupid before I speak and that if I do say something stupid I can still accept myself as a fallible human being even if others laugh at me.'

There are a variety of ways in which Norman could have modified the assignment. Here is a selection of the large number of ways in which Norman might have changed the nature of his homework assignment:

1. Norman could have done the assignment as agreed, but only on one or two occasions rather than the three we negotiated.

2. He could have spoken up on three separate occasions, but without practising the new rational beliefs or without making any changes to his other distorted cognitions such as his inferences.

3. He could have spoken up on three separate occasions while changing his distorted inferences or other unrealistic thoughts rather than practising his new rational beliefs. For example, while speaking up he might have told himself that there was little chance of him saying anything stupid or, if he did, that people would be on his side rather than against him.

4. He could have spoken up on three separate occasions while thinking positive, Pollyanna-ish thoughts such as: 'Every time I speak up I'm getting better and better' or defensive thoughts such as 'It doesn't matter if I say something stupid' or 'It doesn't matter if the people in the seminar group laugh at me if I do something stupid.'

One common way in which your client may change the nature of his negotiated homework assignment is when he does not face the critical aspect of the situation that he has agreed to face. In REBT parlance, he has not faced the 'critical A'. For example let's suppose that your client has a fear of being rejected by women when he asks them to dance. In the session you work carefully to identify, challenge and help him to change the irrational belief that underpins his anxiety. Following on from this work you negotiate with him an assignment which involves him practising his new rational belief in the face of actual rejection by a woman. You stress to him that the important aspect of this assignment is not so much asking women to dance, but being rejected by them. Because the client is afraid of rejection, it is important that he faces rejection. At the next session, your client is pleased with the results of his homework. He asked a woman to dance, she accepted his invitation, they spent an enjoyable evening together and they have begun to date. The important point to note from a therapeutic point of view is that the client has not faced the 'critical A' that he agreed to face. As we will show you below, it is important that you help your client to see that whatever the outcome of his pleasant evening with the aforementioned woman, he has not confronted the source of his problem. How do you respond when it becomes clear that your client has changed the nature of his homework? We suggest that you do the following:

Step 1: Encourage your client by saying that you were pleased that he did the assignment.

Step 2: Explain how, in your opinion, he changed the assignment and remind him of the exact nature of the task as it was negotiated by the two of you in the previous session. In doing so, if indicated, remind your client of the purpose of the assignment which dictated its precise form.

Step 3: If your client made a genuine mistake in changing the nature of the assignment, invite him to re-do the assignment, but this time as it was previously negotiated. If he agrees, ensure that he keeps a written reminder of the assignment and ask him to guard against making further changes to it. Don't forget to review the assignment in the following session. If he doesn't agree to do the assignment, explore and deal with his reluctance.

Step 4: If it appears that the change that your client made to the assignment was motivated by the presence of an implicit irrational belief, identify and deal with this belief and again invite your client to re-do the assignment as it was previously negotiated, urging him once again to guard against making further changes to the assignment. Alternatively, modify the assignment in a way that takes into account the newly discovered obstacle.

Here is an example of how to put this into practice.

Windy: Let's begin by reviewing your homework. How did it go?

Norman: It went fairly well. I managed to speak up on two occasions.

Windy: I'm pleased to hear that. Did you practise the two rational beliefs at the same time?

[See step 1 above]

Norman: Yes, I made sure I did that.

Windy: Good. I'll check what you learned from doing the homework in a moment. But, first, are you aware that you didn't quite do all the homework?

[See Step 2 above]

Norman: You mean that I didn't speak up on three occasions?

Windy: Yes, it's important for me to understand what happened on the occasion that you didn't speak up. Can you help me to understand that?

Norman: Well, it was at the Friday morning seminar. I remember feeling quite uncomfortable ...but er ... I guess I thought that as I'd done quite well I would give myself a break and not speak up on that day.

Windy: I see. You said that you were feeling quite uncomfortable. What exactly was the nature of that feeling?

[Here I am seeking to clarify the client's 'C' (see Chapter 5). My hunch is that the client did not do the third part of his assignment because he was thinking irrationally at the time and this led to avoidance – see Step 4].

Norman: I was anxious...

I then proceeded to discover that Norman was anxious about saying something stupid in front of a female student whom he found attractive and who rarely attended seminars. I then identified and challenged Norman's new irrational belief: 'I must speak well in front of Joanna' and we negotiated a new homework assignment where he would seek out Joanna and have an intellectual discussion with her while practising his new rational belief. 'I'd like to speak well in front of Joanna, but I don't have to do so.' The second assignment that I negotiated with Norman concerned asking Joanna to attend the next seminar and, if she did, he would do the third part of his original homework task. I suggested that Norman ask Joanna to attend the next seminar because, left to her own devices, Joanna would probably not attend another seminar for quite a while.

Review what your client learned from doing the assignment

The next step in the homework-reviewing process concerns asking your client what he learned from doing the homework. If your client learned what you hoped he would learn, acknowledge that he did well and move on. If your client did not learn what you hoped he would learn, then you need to address this issue. Let me show how I dealt with this latter situation with Norman.

Windy: So, Norman, you managed to speak up on the three occasions as we agreed and you were also able to practise strengthening your new rational beliefs. Is that right?

Norman: Yes, that's right.

Windy: Good. Now what did you learn from doing the assignment?

Norman: I learned that it is very unlikely that I will say something stupid in a seminar setting.

Windy: Did you learn anything else?

Norman: No, that's about it.

[The purpose of the homework assignment was to help Norman over his anxiety about speaking up in class. The way Norman and I chose to do this was to have him challenge his irrational beliefs about being certain that he would not say anything stupid before he spoke and about how others viewed him and to have him practise the rational alternatives while speaking up.

Ideally, what I would have liked Norman to have learned was that he didn't need to be certain before he spoke and that if others laughed at him if he did say something stupid then he could accept himself as a fallible human being in this situation. However, he did not mention either of these two beliefs in what he learned. Rather, he said that he learned that it was now unlikely that he would say something stupid in class. Whilst this is an important learning, it is based on an inferential change which in REBT theory is considered to lead to less enduring results than belief change (see Chapter 2).

Consequently, my task is to explain this to Norman and encourage him to focus on making a change in belief, while not undermining what for him was likely to be a significant piece of learning.]

Windy: I think the fact that you learned that it is unlikely that you will say something stupid in class is important for you and by saying what I am about to say I do not mean to detract from this. OK?

Norman: OK.

Windy: Good. Now when you focused on the idea that you were unlikely to say something stupid how did this help you?

Norman: It got rid of the anxiety and helped me to speak up.

Windy: But how do you know for sure that you won't say something stupid?

Norman: I guess I don't.

Windy: Right, And let's suppose that you do say something stupid and people laugh at you, will the thought that you are unlikely to say something stupid help you to deal productively with that situation?

Norman: No, it won't.

Windy: Now, again, learning that you are unlikely to say something stupid in class is important and note that you did speak up without having a guarantee that you wouldn't say something stupid.

Norman: Right, but as we talk about it, I can see that I wasn't really telling myself that it was unlikely that I would say something stupid. I was telling myself that I definitely wouldn't say something stupid.

Windy: I see. Now that means that if you are to speak up without such guarantees and if you are to cope with people laughing at you then it would be really useful if you could speak up regularly in class and deliberately say something stupid on one or two occasions.

Norman: So that I introduce some uncertainty into the situation you mean?

Windy: Exactly. And so you can deal with the possibility or even actuality of people laughing at you.

Norman: Wow, that's a tough assignment.

Windy: Well, let's see if we can negotiate something challenging, but not overwhelming. The main thing though is for you to learn (i) that you can speak up even when there is the possibility that you may say something stupid and (ii) that you can accept yourself as a fallible human being when you do say something stupid and there is a chance that people will laugh at you.

[Norman and I then proceeded to negotiate an assignment using the guidelines discussed in the previous chapter.]

Capitalise on your client's success

How do you respond when your client has successfully done his homework and has learned what you hoped he would learn? We recommend that you reinforce him for achievement and suggest that he build on his success as I (WD) did with Norman.

Windy: So, Norman, you were able to speak up on three separate occasions while practising your rational beliefs. And you say that you are beginning to really believe that you don't need certainty that you won't say anything stupid before you speak up and that even if you do say something stupid and people laugh at you, you can accept yourself as a fallible human being in the face of ridicule. Is that right?

> Norman: Yes, that's right.
>
> Windy: How do you feel about what you have achieved and what you are learning?
>
> Norman: I feel really good about it.
>
> Windy: I'm pleased. I think you are doing really well ... (humorously) Of course that doesn't mean that you are a more worthwhile person!
>
> Norman: ... (laughs) Ha, Ha, Ha.
>
> Windy: Seriously though, you are doing well, so let's talk about how you can capitalise on your success. OK?
>
> Norman: OK.
>
> Windy: What do you think you can do between now and next week to extend this?
>
> Norman: Well, I guess I can undertake to speak up at every seminar.
>
> Windy: Good. How about undertaking to speak up at least twice at every seminar you attend?
>
> Norman: (humorously) You're a real taskmaster, aren't you?
>
> Windy: Does that mean yes or no?
>
> Norman: OK, I'll do it.
>
> Windy: Excellent. Let's make a written note of what you're going to do and where and when you are going to do it.

Responding to your client's homework 'failure'

Let's suppose that your client has done her homework, but it turned out poorly. When this happens, clients often say that they did the assignment, but 'it didn't work'. We have put the word 'failure' in inverted commas here because although clients regard the assignment as a 'failure', there is much to learn from this situation. So, when you encounter this so-called 'failure', remind your client of the 'no-lose' nature of homework assignments and begin to investigate the factors involved. But first ask for a factual account about what happened. Then, once you have identified the factors that accounted for the 'failure', help your client to deal with them and endeavour to re-negotiate the same or similar assignment. While you are investigating the factors which accounted for your client's homework 'failure', it is useful to keep in mind a number of such factors. Here is an illustrative list of some of the more common reasons for homework 'failure'.

- Your client implemented certain, but not all, of the elements of the negotiated assignment. For example, your client may have done the behavioural aspect of the assignment, but did not practise new rational beliefs with the result that he experienced the same unhealthy negative emotions associated with the target problem.

- The assignment was 'overwhelming, rather than challenging' for your client at this time.

- Your client began to do the assignment but stopped doing it because he began to experience discomfort which he believed he could not tolerate.

- Your client practised the wrong rational beliefs during the assignment.

- Your client practised the right rational beliefs, but did so in an overly weak manner with the result that his unhealthy negative emotions predominated.

- Your client began to do the assignment, but forgot what he was to do after he had begun.

- Your client began the assignment, but gave up because he did not experience immediate benefit from it.

- Your client began the assignment, but gave up soon after when he realised that he did not know what to do. This happens particularly with written 'ABC' homework assignments.

- Your client began the assignment, but encountered a 'critical A' which triggered a new undiscovered irrational belief which led him to abandon the assignment.

Let's look at how I (WD) responded to Norman when he reported a homework 'failure'.

Windy: Let's start by considering your homework. How did it go?

Norman: Not very well.

Windy: I'm sorry to hear that. Tell me what happened.

[Here, I begin by asking for a factual account of Norman's experience with the assignment.]

Norman: Well, before the first seminar, I practised the rational beliefs that we discussed and was all geared up to speak up. So after about 10 minutes I spoke up, but it didn't go too well. So I didn't do it again.

Windy: Now, do you remember the concept of the 'no-lose' homework assignment?

Norman: I think so. It means that if I do the assignment and it works out, that's fine. And it is also valuable if I do it and it doesn't work out well; that's also valuable because we can discover why.

Windy: Good. Now, let's see if we can discover why in your case. Let me start by asking you what rational beliefs you practised before speaking up at the first seminar.

[Norman's report indicated that he practised the correct rational beliefs and did so with sufficient force.]

Windy: Well that seems fine. Now let's look closely at what happened when you spoke up at the first seminar.

Norman: Well, there was a gap in the conversation so I went over the rational beliefs again and took the plunge and spoke up.

Windy: And what happened?

Norman: Well, I wasn't too anxious while I was speaking. But when I stopped I got a bit depressed.

Windy: What were you most depressed about?

[Here I am attempting to identify Norman's 'critical A'. It transpired that Norman was depressed about not saying something particularly noteworthy. His irrational belief was 'When I speak up in class, I must say something noteworthy and if I don't then I am something of a failure.' I then helped Norman to challenge and change this irrational belief]

Windy: So, Norman, can you now see why you got depressed about what you said and why you didn't speak up in the subsequent two seminars?

Norman: Yes, I can. That's really helpful. I can now really see what you meant by the 'no-lose' homework assignment.

Windy: That's really good. Now let me suggest that you do the same homework between now and next week, but this time how about practising the new rational belief as well, namely: 'I would like to say something noteworthy every time I speak up in class, but I don't have to do so. If I don't, I'm not a failure. Rather I am a fallible human being who says noteworthy and mundane things at times?'

Norman: That's a good idea.

[I then take Norman through an imagery assignment to give him some practice at the new rational belief, after which we both make a written note of his new assignment.]

Dealing with the situation when your client has not done the homework assignment

Despite the fact that you may have taken the utmost care in negotiating a homework assignment with your client and instituted all the safeguards that we discussed in Chapter 17, your client may still not carry it out. When this happens, we suggest that you follow a procedure similar to that we discussed in the previous section; that is, ask your client for a factual account of the situation where she contracted to do the assignment but didn't do it, remind her of the 'no-lose' concept of homework assignments, identify and deal with the factors that accounted for her not doing the assignment and then re-negotiate the same or similar assignment. As you investigate the aforementioned factors, be particularly aware of the fact that you may have failed to institute one or more of the safeguards reviewed in the previous chapter. If this is the case, and your failure to do so accounts for your client not carrying out the assignment, then take responsibility for this omission, disclose this to your client, institute the safeguard and re-negotiate the assignment.

On the other hand, if the reason why your client did not do the assignment can be attributed to a factor in the client that you could not have foreseen, help her to deal with it and again re-negotiate the same or similar assignment.

In investigating the reason why Norman did not carry out his homework, it transpired that he did not do so because he believed that he had to feel comfortable before speaking up.

> Team up with a trainee colleague, play the role of therapist and have him or her play Norman and see if you can help your 'client' over the obstacle and then re-negotiate the same homework assignment. Record the interchange and play the recording to your REBT trainer or supervisor for feedback.

Appendix II contains a form that we recommend you use with your clients when they consistently fail to initiate negotiated homework assignments. We suggest that you use this form in training as well.

> Again pair up with a trainee colleague and have him or her play the role of a client who doesn't do homework assignments for each of the reasons shown on the form in Appendix II and gain practice at helping your 'client' over the obstacle. Record the interchanges and once again seek feedback from your REBT trainer or supervisor.

In this book, we have concentrated on key aspects of REBT theory and practice. When dealing with the latter, we have shown you how to assess common client problems, dispute the irrational beliefs that underpin these problems and encourage your clients to act on their alternative and emerging rational beliefs in the pursuit of their goals. As this book's title makes clear, this book aims to teach you the fundamentals of REBT and as such we have deliberately omitted many of its elaborations. Having said that, we would not be happy that we have taught you the fundamentals of REBT without showing you how to respond constructively to the many doubts, reservations and objections that your clients may have to salient aspects of REBT theory and practice. As many of these are based on misconceptions of REBT, we have chosen to title the next chapter 'Dealing with your clients' misconceptions of REBT theory and practice'.

CHAPTER NINETEEN

Dealing with your clients' misconceptions of REBT theory and practice

As we noted at the end of the last chapter, you may find that your clients have a number of doubts, reservations and objections to the theory and practice of REBT. This is to be expected and you need to discuss these openly with them when their doubts, etc. are likely to interfere with the therapeutic process and with their progress. We have found in our clinical practice that clients present the same doubts, reservations and objections again and again. Consequently, we have decided to present these recurring doubts, etc. here and explain why they are misconceptions of REBT theory and practice. In presenting these doubts, reservations and objections that clients have about REBT, we will put them in the form of typical questions that clients ask. While our answers are each presented in the form of an extended didactic presentation, please note that in clinical practice, we engage our clients in a dialogue based on the content to be found in each response. We recommend that when you deal with your client's misconceptions about key aspects of the theory and practice of REBT, you engage her in such a dialogue and not talk at her. However, if you are going to use didactic explanations make sure that you check that your client understands the points that you are making and that you discuss her reactions to these points with her. Please note that in responding to these misconceptions we will write in the singular.

Question 1: REBT states that events don't cause emotions. I can see that this is the case when negative events are mild or moderate, but don't very negative events like being raped or losing a loved one cause disturbed emotions?

Answer: Your question directly impinges on the distinction that REBT makes between healthy and unhealthy negative emotions (see Chapter 4). Let me take the example of rape that you mentioned. There is no doubt that being raped is a tragic event for both women and men. As such, it is healthy for the person who has been raped to experience a lot of distress. However, REBT conceptualises this distress as healthy even though it is intense. Other approaches to therapy have as their goal the reduction of the intensity of negative emotions. They take this position because they do not keenly differentiate between healthy negative emotions (distress) and unhealthy negative emotions (disturbance).

Now, REBT keenly distinguishes between healthy distress and unhealthy disturbance. Healthy distress stems from your rational beliefs about a negative activating event, whilst disturbance stems from your irrational beliefs about the same event. I now have to introduce you to one of the complexities of REBT theory and as I do you will see that REBT is not always as simple as 'ABC'!

REBT theory holds that the intensity of your healthy distress increases in proportion to the negativity of the event that you face and the strength of your rational beliefs. Now, when a person has been raped, her intense distress stems from her strongly held rational beliefs about this very negative 'A'. As virtually everyone who has been raped will have strongly held rational beliefs about this event, we could almost say that being raped 'causes' intense healthy distress.

Now let me introduce irrational beliefs into the picture. REBT theory argues that you, being human, easily transmute your rational beliefs into irrational beliefs especially when the events you encounter are very negative. However, and this is a crucial and controversial point, the specific principle of emotional responsibility states that you are largely responsible for your emotional disturbance because you are responsible for transmuting your rational beliefs into irrational beliefs. You and others retain this responsibility even when you and they encounter tragic adversities such as rape. So REBT theory holds that when a person has been raped, she is responsible for transmuting her strongly held rational beliefs into irrational beliefs, even though it is very understandable that she should do this.

Actually, if we look at the typical irrational beliefs that people have about being raped, we will see that these beliefs are not an integral part of the rape experience, but reflect what people bring to the experience. Examples of irrational beliefs are:

- 'I absolutely should have stopped this from happening.'
- 'This has completely ruined my life.'
- 'Being raped means that I am a worthless person.'

Whilst it is understandable that people who have been raped should think this way, this does not detract from the fact that they are responsible for bringing these irrational beliefs to the experience. It is for this reason that REBT theory holds that very negative actual 'As' do not 'cause' emotional disturbance. This is actually an optimistic position. If very negative events did cause emotional disturbance then you would have a much harder time overcoming your disturbed feelings than you do now when we make the assumption that these feelings stem largely from your irrational beliefs. One more point. Some REBT therapists distinguish between disturbed emotions that are experienced when a very negative event occurs and disturbed feelings that persist well after the event has happened. These therapists would argue that being raped does 'cause' disturbed feelings when the event occurs and for a short period after it has happened, but if the person's disturbed feelings persist well after the event then the person who has been raped is responsible for the perpetuation of her disturbances via the creation and perpetuation of her irrational beliefs. These therapists argue that time-limited irrationalities in response to very negative activating events are not unhealthy reactions, but the perpetuation of these irrationalities is unhealthy. Thus, for these REBT therapists a very negative event like rape does 'cause' emotional disturbance in the short term, but not in the long term.

Question 2: I'm worried about the principle of emotional responsibility. Doesn't it lead to blaming the victim?

Answer: You have a major criticism of the principle of emotional responsibility which is so central to REBT theory. As I showed in my previous answer, when someone is raped, it is possible to argue that this very negative actual 'A' 'causes' the intense healthy distress that the person almost invariably experiences. However, if she experiences emotional disturbance, particularly well after the event happened, REBT theory holds that she is responsible for her disturbed feelings through the irrational beliefs that she brings to the event. However, there is a world of difference between being responsible for one's disturbance and being blamed for having these feelings. The concept of responsibility in this situation means that the person largely disturbs herself about the event because of the irrational beliefs she brings to that event. The concept of blame here means that someone believes that the person absolutely should not experience such disturbed feelings and is a bad person for having these feelings. This is obviously nonsense for two reasons. First, if the person disturbs herself about being raped then all the conditions are in place for her to do so. In other words, if she holds a set of irrational beliefs about the event, then empirically she should disturb herself about it. It is obviously inconsistent with reality for someone to demand that the person absolutely should not disturb herself in this way. Second, even if we say that it is bad for the person to have disturbed herself, there is no reason to conclude that she is a bad person for doing so. There is, of course, evidence that she is a fallible human being who understandably holds a set of irrational beliefs about a tragic event. Rather than being blamed for her disturbance, she should preferably be helped to overcome it. The concept of blame in this situation also tends to mean, at least in some people's eyes, that she is responsible for being raped and therefore should be blamed for it happening. This is again nonsense. Let me be quite clear about this. Rape inevitably involves coercion. Even if the woman is responsible for 'leading the man on', he is responsible for raping her. Nothing, including whether the woman experiences distressing or disturbed feelings, absolves him from this responsibility. So, if a woman has been raped nothing that she did or failed to do detracts from the fact that the rapist is solely responsible for committing the rape. As such, the woman cannot be held responsible for being raped. She can be held responsible for 'leading the man on' if this can be shown to be the case; but, I repeat, she cannot be held responsible for being raped. Thus, the principle of emotional responsibility means in this situation that the woman is responsible for her disturbed feelings only. She is not to be blamed for this, nor is she to be held responsible for being raped no matter how she behaved in the situation.

Question 3: But if you say that I disturb myself about your bad behaviour, for example, won't that lead you to say that my response has got nothing to do with your behaviour and isn't that a cop-out on your behalf?

Answer: The cop-out criticism of emotional responsibility can be stated thus. If a person is largely responsible for her own disturbed feelings, then if you act nastily towards her all you have to say is that because she largely disturbs herself about your bad behaviour then her feelings have nothing to do with you. In my answer to question 2, I pointed out that a rapist is responsible for carrying out a rape regardless of how the person who has been raped feels and regardless of any so-called mitigating circumstances. Now, if I act nastily towards you I am responsible for my behaviour regardless of how you feel about my behaviour. If my behaviour is nasty then I cannot be absolved of responsibility for my action just because you are largely responsible for your making yourself disturbed about the way I have treated you. Don't forget, if my behaviour is that bad, it is healthy for you to hold strongly a set of rational beliefs about it and, whereas I cannot be held responsible for your disturbance, I can be said to be responsible for your distress. Thus, I cannot 'cop out' of my responsibility for my own behaviour nor for 'distressing' you.

The cop-out criticism is also made of the REBT position on guilt. As I have shown in my (WD) book, *Overcoming Guilt* (Dryden, 1994c), guilt is an unhealthy emotion that stems from a set of irrational self-blaming beliefs about breaking one's moral code, for example. The healthy alternative to guilt is remorse which stems from a set of rational self-accepting beliefs about a moral code violation. The important point to note about remorse is that it does not absolve the person from taking responsibility for breaking his or her moral code. It does not, in short, encourage the person to 'cop out' of assuming responsibility for what he did. Now this is apparently a difficult point for people to grasp. For example, Marje Proops, a famous agony aunt, claimed to have read my book on guilt – in which I continually reiterate the non 'cop-out' position of remorse – but said in response to a letter from a reader who sought help to stop feeling guilty about sleeping with her best friend's husband that the reader SHOULD feel guilty. Proops feared that remorse and even guilt (which she clearly failed to differentiate) would provide the person with a 'cop-out' or an excuse for continuing to act immorally. The truth is, however, very different. Remorse is based on the rational belief, 'I wish I hadn't broken my moral code, but there is no reason why I absolutely should not have broken it. I broke it because of what I was telling myself at the time. Now let me accept myself and think how I can learn from my past behaviour so that I can act morally in the future.' As you see, in remorse the person takes responsibility for her behaviour, is motivated to act better next time by her rational belief which also enables her to learn from her moral code violation. By contrast, guilt is based on an irrational belief which will either encourage her to deny responsibility for her past action or interfere with her attempt to learn from it. So far from encouraging the person to 'cop out' of her responsibility, the principle of emotional responsibility encourages the person to take responsibility for her actions and for her disturbed guilt feelings. It further encourages the person to challenge her irrational, guilt-producing beliefs and adopt a rational, remorse-invoking philosophy so that she can learn from her past behaviour, make appropriate amends and take responsibility for her future behaviour.

Question 4: You have discussed the 'ABCs' of REBT, but I find this overly simplistic. Isn't the theory of REBT too simple?

Answer: First, let me say in answer to your question that I have presented enough of the theory of REBT to help you get started with its practice. If I presented the full complexity of the 'ABCs' of REBT, then I would run the risk of overwhelming you with too much information too soon. In reality, as Albert Ellis has argued, the 'ABCs' interact in often complex ways. Let me give you a few examples of this complexity. So far, as you have rightly observed, I have introduced the simple version of the 'ABCs' where 'A' occurs first and 'B' second to produce an emotional and/or behavioural consequence at 'C'. This is the version of the 'ABCs' that is usually taught to clients. Now let me introduce some complexity into the picture. If a person holds an irrational belief about an event, then he will tend to create further distorted inferences about this 'A'. For example, if you believe that you must be loved by your partner ('iB') and he shouts at you ('A1') then you will be more likely to think that he doesn't love you and is thinking of leaving you ('A2') than if you have an alternative rational belief ('rB'). So, instead of the usual formula: 'A' → 'B' → 'C', we have 'A1' → 'iB' → 'A2'. Second, if a person is already experiencing an unhealthy negative emotion then this will lead him to attend to certain aspects in a situation. Thus, if you are already anxious then you are more likely to focus on threatening aspects of a situation than if you are concerned, but not anxious. Putting this into a formula, we have 'C' → 'A'. I hope these two examples have given you a flavour of the complexity of the 'ABCs' of REBT and have helped you to see that whilst in its rudimentary form the 'ABC' model is simple, its full version is neither too simple nor simplistic.

Question 5: I get the impression that REBT neglects the past. Am I right?

Answer: As I have shown, REBT states that people disturb themselves ('C') by the beliefs ('B') that they hold about the negative activating events in their lives ('A'). Now 'As' can be present events, future events or past events. Thus, if a client is disturbed now about certain aspects of her past, then an REBT therapist would certainly deal with this using the ABC framework where 'A' is the past event (or events). What REBT questions, however, is the position that a client's past has MADE him disturbed now. This, you will recall is an example of 'A' causes 'C' thinking to which REBT objects. Now, even if we assume temporarily that the client was made disturbed as a child by a past event, or more usually by an ongoing series of events, REBT theory argues that the reason that the person is disturbed now about his past is because in the present he holds a set of irrational beliefs that he has actively kept alive or perpetuated from the past. Actually, the situation is more complex than this because REBT holds that we are not, as children, made disturbed by events; rather, we bring our tendencies to disturb ourselves to these events. Thus, REBT adheres to a constructivist position even about the origins of psychological disturbance. This means that you construct your disturbance rather than your past bringing it about. Your REBT therapist certainly works with the past, but does so mainly by looking at your presently-held irrational beliefs about your past. In addition, your therapist can consider your past disturbed feelings about specific or ongoing historical situations and help you to see what irrational beliefs you were holding then to create those disturbed feelings. I have also found it useful to make the past present by, for example, encouraging the client to have a two-chair dialogue with figures from the past to identify, challenge and change the client's present irrational beliefs about these figures. This technique has to be used sensitively as it often provokes strong emotion. To summarise, REBT does not ignore a client's past, but works with past material either by disputing currently held irrational beliefs about historical events or by challenging past irrational beliefs that the client may have held about these same events. However, REBT guards against 'A' → 'C' thinking by making it clear that it does not think that past events cause present disturbance.

Question 6: Doesn't the REBT concept of acceptance encourage complacency?

Answer: The REBT concept of acceptance certainly gives rise to a lot of confusion in people's minds. Some, like you, consider that it leads to complacency, others think it means indifference; yet others judge it to mean that we should condone negative events. Actually it means none of these things. Let me carefully spell out what REBT theory does mean by the term 'acceptance'. The first point to stress is that acceptance means acknowledging the existence of an event, for example, and that all the conditions were in place for an event to occur. However, it does not mean that it is good that the event happened, nor that there is nothing one can do to rectify the situation. Let's suppose that I betray your trust. By accepting this event, you would acknowledge that I did in fact betray you, that unfortunately all the conditions were in place for this betrayal to occur, namely that I had a set of thoughts which led me to act in the way that I did. Accepting my betrayal also means that you actively dislike my betrayal (i.e. you don't condone the way I treated you), but that you do not condemn me as a person. Furthermore, acceptance certainly does not preclude you from taking constructive action to rectify the situation. Acceptance, in short, is based on a set of rational beliefs that leads you to feel healthily negative about my behaviour, rather than emotionally disturbed about what I did. The same argument applies to the concept of self-acceptance. When I accept myself for breaking my moral code, I regard myself as a fallible human being for my wrongdoing. I do not condone my behaviour;

rather, I take responsibility for it, strive to understand why I acted in the way that I did, learn from the experience, make appropriate amends and resolve to apply my learning so that, in similar circumstances, I can act morally. So rather than encouraging complacency, acceptance is the springboard for constructive change.

Question 7: Doesn't REBT neglect my emotions?

Answer: The short answer to this question is no. Your question focuses on the meaning of the term 'rational'. Many people think that the term 'rational' means devoid of emotion. They think that the model of psychological health advocated by REBT is epitomised by Mr Spock in *Star Trek* or the android, Data, in *Star Trek: The Next Generation*, who were both seemingly incapable of experiencing human emotion. This is far from the case. The term 'rational' in REBT means, amongst other things, experiencing healthy emotions, i.e. emotions which aid and abet you as you strive to pursue your basic constructive goals and purposes. Your REBT therapist is particularly interested in helping you identify your unhealthy negative emotions about negative activating events as a prelude to identifying your irrational beliefs which are deemed to underpin these emotions. As a first step in therapy, your therapist helps you to challenge and change these irrational beliefs so that you can think rationally about these events and feel healthily negative about them. In addition, unlike other therapists, your REBT therapist encourages you to feel intense healthy negative emotions about very negative events. As your REBT therapist keenly differentiates between healthy and unhealthy negative emotions, a distinction that other therapists tend not to make, she will be able on theoretical grounds to help you feel healthily distressed without feeling emotionally disturbed.

On the other hand, your REBT therapist does not believe that emotional catharsis is therapeutic per se, nor will she encourage you to explore the subtle nuances of your emotions. Rather, she will encourage you to acknowledge your feelings, to feel your feelings, but thence to detect and dispute the irrational beliefs that underlie these feelings when they are unhealthily negative. So whereas REBT therapists certainly do not neglect their clients' emotions, they do adopt a particular stance towards these emotions as outlined above.

Question 8: With its emphasis on techniques, doesn't REBT neglect the therapeutic relationship?

Answer: The famous American psychologist, Carl Rogers, wrote a seminal paper in 1957 on the therapeutic relationship which for many set the standard against which other approaches should be judged. Rogers argued that there were a set of necessary and sufficient 'core conditions' that the therapist had to provide and the client had to perceive the therapist as having provided these conditions for therapeutic change to occur. Two years later Albert Ellis, the founder of REBT, published a reply in which he acknowledged that these conditions were important and frequently desirable, but they were hardly necessary and sufficient. This has been the REBT position ever since. Thus, REBT therapists do not neglect the therapeutic relationship. However, they do not regard the relationship as the *sine qua non* of therapeutic change. Some REBT therapists regard the development of a good therapeutic relationship as setting the ground for the 'real therapy' to take place, i.e. the application of REBT techniques. My own position is somewhat different. I regard the application of REBT techniques and so-called relationship factors as interdependent therapeutic variables. The one set of variables depend for their therapeutic effect on the presence of the other set. Finally, research has shown that REBT therapists scored as highly as therapists from other schools on measures of the 'core conditions' provided by clients. If REBT therapists are neglecting the therapeutic relationship, their clients don't seem to think so!

Question 9: REBT therapists may not neglect the therapeutic relationship with their clients, but isn't this relationship unequal?

Answer: It depends on what you mean by unequal. Your REBT therapist considers herself to be equal to you as humans. She is neither more worthy than you, nor vice versa. However, on different aspects of your respective selves, there are likely to be inequalities. You may know more about gardening or be more sociable than your therapist, for example. You are equal in humanity, but unequal in certain areas. Now, the purpose of therapy is to help you to overcome your psychological problems and live more resourcefully. In this area, your REBT therapist claims to know more about the dynamics of emotional problems and facilitating personal change than you, at least from an REBT perspective, and this does constitute an inequality as do the ones mentioned earlier that are in your favour. REBT therapists openly acknowledge this real inequality, but stress that it needs to be placed in the context of a relationship between two equally fallible human beings.

Question 10: How do you respond to the criticism that REBT therapists brainwash their clients?

Answer: First, let me be clear what I mean by brainwashing. Brainwashing is a process where the person to be brainwashed is isolated from her normal environment and from people whom she knows, is deprived of food, water and sleep and when judged to be in a susceptible state is provided with information and beliefs which are usually counter to the information and beliefs she would normally hold. Obviously, by this definition REBT therapists do not brainwash their clients. However, I think you mean something more subtle than this. I think you mean that REBT therapists tell their clients what to think without due regard to their current views and press them hard to believe the REBT 'line'. If this is what you mean then I would deny that well-trained, ethical REBT therapists would do this (I cannot speak for untrained individuals who pass themselves off as REBT practitioners). REBT holds that one of the hallmarks of mental health is the ability to think for oneself and to be sceptical of new ideas. It regards gullibility, suggestibility and uncriticalness as breeding grounds for emotional disturbance. So, in presenting rational principles, skilled REBT therapists elicit both their clients' understanding of these concepts and their views of these ideas. There usually follows a healthy debate between client and therapist where the therapist aims to correct the client's misconceptions of these rational principles in a respectful manner (as I hope I am demonstrating with you now). At no time does the therapist insist that the client must believe the rational concepts he is being taught. If a therapist does so insist, this is evidence of the therapist's irrationality such as: 'I have to get my client to think rationally and if I fail in this respect this proves that I am a lousy therapist and a less worthy person as a result.' Also, you will recall from the previous module that I stressed that REBT therapists encourage their clients to voice their doubts, reservations and objections about REBT and take these seriously. This is almost the antithesis of brainwashing. Now, it is true that REBT therapists do have a definite viewpoint concerning the nature of psychological disturbance and which conditions best facilitate therapeutic change. It is also true that REBT therapists are open with their clients concerning these views and strive to present them as clearly as they can. However, just because REBT therapists teach REBT principles to their clients, it does not follow that they are attempting to brainwash their clients or impose their views on them.

My own practice is to make clear that (i) I will be offering a specific approach to therapy based on a particular framework; (ii) there are other approaches to therapy that offer different frameworks; and (iii) I am happy to make a referral if it transpires that the client is better served by a different therapeutic approach. I believe that many REBT therapists act similarly with their clients. This, I hope you will agree, is a long way from brainwashing. REBT therapists have preferred therapeutic goals, but are prepared to negotiate and make compromises if it becomes clear that the client is unwilling or unable to work towards philosophic change. I have yet to hear of a brainwasher who is prepared to negotiate and make compromises!

Question 11: But don't REBT therapists tell their clients what to feel and what to do?

Answer: My answer to this question is similar to my reply above. REBT therapists keenly discriminate between healthy and unhealthy negative emotions. Their initial goal is to help clients minimise their disturbance about negative 'As', while encouraging them to acknowledge, experience and channel their healthy distress about these 'As'. However, you REBT therapist will make clear that you have a choice concerning your feelings and behaviour. Just because REBT theory advocates that you minimise your disturbed feelings, but not your distressed feelings, it does not follow that you have to agree with this view. The same is true of behaviour. Your REBT therapist may well point out to you the self-defeating nature of your behaviour, but she does not insist that you follow her lead. As with the issue of beliefs, your REBT therapist has preferences concerning how her clients feel and behave in relation to the issue of psychological health and disturbance and they may well articulate these preferences during therapy. After all, your REBT therapist genuinely wants to help her clients live psychologically healthy lives and she believes that she has a good theory to help her clients do this. However, your REBT therapist respects her clients' freedom and does not transmute her preferences into musts on this issue, even if this means that a particular client may continue to perpetuate his psychological problems. That person's REBT therapist will, of course, explore the reasons for this, but will not in the final analysis insist that the client do the healthy thing. Incidentally, in areas not related to the issue of psychological health and disturbance, REBT therapists are quite *laissez-faire* about their clients' feelings and behaviour. For example, whether you pursue stamp-collecting or body building is not the therapist's concern assuming that both of these activities are based on preferences and are not harmful to others or to the environment.

Question 12: From what you have been saying, it seems to me that REBT therapists prevent clients from finding their own solutions to their problems. Am I right about this?

Answer: In answering this question, I need to distinguish between two types of solutions: psychological solutions and practical solutions. In REBT, a psychological solution to your problems in the main involves you identifying, challenging and changing your irrational beliefs. Whereas a practical solution involves, amongst other things, responding behaviourally to negative 'As' in functional ways. In this analysis, achieving a psychological solution facilitates the client applying the practical solution and, therefore, preferably should be achieved first.

Now, your REBT therapist assumes that you as client will not achieve a philosophically-based psychological change on your own. She further assumes that she needs to help you in active ways to understand what this psychological solution involves and how you can apply it. Once she has helped you to do this then you are generally able to choose the best practical solution to your problem. If not, your REBT therapist will help you to specify different practical solutions to your problem, will encourage you to list the advantages and disadvantages of each course of action and to select and implement the best practical solution. So, in summary, REBT therapists actively encourage their clients to understand and implement REBT orientated psychological solutions to their problems and assume that once this has been done then clients will often be able to see for themselves which practical solutions to implement. When the therapist does intervene in the practical problem-solving phase of therapy, it is to help the client weigh up the pros and cons of his own generated solutions and to select the most effective course of action.

Question 13: Isn't REBT too confrontational?

Answer: REBT is basically an active-directive approach to psychotherapy where your therapist intervenes actively and directs you to the attitudinal core of your problems and helps you to develop a plan to challenge your self-defeating beliefs which constitute this core. In disputing your irrational beliefs, the therapist does take the lead in questioning you concerning the empirical, logical and pragmatic nature of these beliefs. The disputing techniques of the therapist often seem overly confrontational to therapists who advocate less directive counselling methods. It is the contrast between these methods and the active-directive methods of REBT that lead these therapists to conclude that REBT is TOO confrontational. If your REBT therapist prepares you adequately for her active-directive methods, particularly her challenging disputing techniques, then in general you will not consider the therapist to be TOO confrontational, although the observing less directive therapist who does not fully understand what the REBT therapist is trying to do might consider this therapist to be overly confrontational. However, if your therapist fails to give a satisfactory rationale for her challenging behaviour then she may well be experienced by you as TOO confrontational.

Question 14: You say that REBT is a structured therapy, but doesn't it 'straitjacket' clients?

Answer: Whilst it is true that REBT is a structured approach to psychotherapy, it is also the case that skilled REBT therapists vary the amount of structure according to what is happening in the session. Thus, at times your REBT therapist may be quite unstructured, for example when you have started to talk about a newly discovered problem or she may use session structure rather loosely, for example in the ending phase when prompting the client to assess a problem using the 'ABC' framework. Of course, at other times your REBT therapist will be quite structured, particularly when disputing your irrational beliefs. Again, if the therapist provides a rationale for the use of a tight structure and the client understands and assents to this, then the client won't consider that he has been 'straitjacketed' by the therapist although the observer might make such a conclusion.

Question 15: Isn't it the case that REBT is only concerned with changing beliefs?

Answer: REBT therapists are primarily concerned with helping their clients to pursue their basic goals and purposes. In order to facilitate this process, the therapist encourages you to experience healthy rather than unhealthy negative emotions about negative 'As' and to act functionally in the face of these negative events. Now, REBT therapists do hold the view that a central way of helping clients to achieve all this is to encourage them to change their irrational beliefs, but this is not their sole goal. So, REBT therapists are interested in helping clients to change their beliefs, their feelings, their behaviour, their images, their interpersonal relationships and the aversive events in their lives. As such REBT is a multimodal rather than a unimodal approach to therapy. A similar issue relates to how REBT is often portrayed in therapeutic outcome studies. In some of these studies REBT is deemed to be synonymous with its cognitive restructuring methods rather than a multimodal approach which also employs emotive, behavioural, imaginal and relationship-enhancement techniques. As such, psychotherapy researchers have also wrongly concluded that REBT therapists are ONLY interested in helping their clients to change the latter's beliefs.

Question 16: REBT relies heavily on verbal interchange between therapist and client. It also advocates concepts that are difficult to grasp. Doesn't this mean that REBT only works with highly verbal, intelligent clients?

Answer: This is a common criticism of REBT and I can understand why you have made it. I have presented REBT to you in its complex sophisticated form. I have used a lot of words and explained its concepts in a way that reflects this complexity. However, skilled REBT therapists can also tailor the way they explain REBT concepts to match the verbal and intellectual capacities of their clients. Rest assured that REBT has been used with clients who are not particularly verbal nor intelligent. By all accounts, it works well with these client groups as long as appropriate modifications are made.

We have now reached the end of this training handbook. We hope that you have enjoyed it and let us close by hoping that the book has encouraged you to pursue further training in REBT (see Appendix III).

Homework skills monitoring form

Listen to the recording of your therapy session and circle 'Yes', 'No' or 'N/A' (Not Appropriate) for each item. For every item circled 'No', write down in the space provided what you would have done differently given hindsight and what you would have needed to change in order to have circled the item 'Yes'.

1. Did I use a term for homework assignments that was acceptable to the client?

   Yes   No   N/A

2. Did I properly negotiate the homework assignment with the client (as opposed to telling him/her what to do or accepting uncritically his/her suggestion)?

   Yes   No   N/A

3. Was the homework assignment expressed clearly?

   Yes   No   N/A

4. Did I ensure that the client understood the homework assignment?

   Yes   No   N/A

5. Was the homework assignment relevant to my client's therapy goals?

   Yes   No   N/A

6. Did I help the client understand the relevance of the homework assignment to his/her therapy goals?

   Yes   No   N/A

7. Did the homework assignment follow logically from the work I did with the client in the session?

   Yes   No   N/A

8. Was the type of homework assignment I negotiated with the client relevant to the stage reached by the two of us on his/her target problem?

   Yes   No   N/A

9. Did I employ the 'challenging, but not overwhelming' principle in negotiating the homework assignment?

   Yes   No   N/A

10. Did I introduce and explain the 'no-lose' concept of homework assignments?

    Yes   No   N/A

11. Did I ensure that the client had the necessary skills to carry out the homework assignment?

   Yes   No   N/A

12. Did I ensure that the client believed that he/she could do the homework assignment?

   Yes   No   N/A

13. Did I allow sufficient time in the session to negotiate the homework assignment properly?

   Yes   No   N/A

14. Did I elicit a firm commitment from the client that he/she would carry out the homework assignment?

   Yes   No   N/A

15. Did I help the client to specify when, where and how often he/she would carry out the homework assignment?

   Yes   No   N/A

16. Did I encourage my client to make a written note of the homework assignment and its relevant details?

   Yes   No   N/A

17. Did the client and I both retain a copy of this written note?

Yes   No   N/A

18. Did I elicit from the client potential obstacles to homework completion?

Yes   No   N/A

19. Did I help the client to deal in advance with any potential obstacles that he/she disclosed?

Yes   No   N/A

20. Did I help the client to rehearse the homework assignment in the session?

Yes   No   N/A

21. Did I use the principle of rewards and penalties with the client?

Yes   No   N/A

Possible reasons for not completing self-help assignments

▶ (To be completed by client)

The following is a list of reasons that various clients have given for not doing their self-help assignments during the course of counselling. Because the speed of improvement depends primarily on the amount of self-help assignments that you are willing to do, it is of great importance to pinpoint any reasons that you may have for not doing this work. It is important to look for these reasons at the time that you feel a reluctance to do your assignment or a desire to put off doing it. Hence, it is best to fill out this questionnaire at that time. If you have any difficulty filling out this form and returning it to the counsellor, it might be best to do it together during a counselling session. (Rate each statement by ringing 'T' (True) 'F' (False). 'T' indicates that you agree with it; 'F' means the statement does not apply at this time.)

1. It seems that nothing can help me so there is no point in trying.   T/F

2. It wasn't clear, I didn't understand what I had to do.   T/F

3. I thought that the particular method the counsellor had suggested would not be helpful. I didn't really see the value of it.   T/F

4. It seemed too hard.   T/F

5. I am willing to do self-help assignments, but I keep forgetting.   T/F

6. I did not have enough time. I was too busy.   T/F

7. If I do something the counsellor suggests I do it's not as good as if I come up with my own ideas.   T/F

8. I don't really believe I can do anything to help myself.   T/F

9. I have the impression that the counsellor is trying to boss me around or control me.   T/F

10. I worry about the counsellor's disapproval. I believe that what I do just won't be good enough for him/her.   T/F

11. I felt too bad, sad, nervous, upset (underline the appropriate word(s)) to do it.   T/F

12. It would have upset me to do the homework.   T/F

13. It was too much to do.   T/F

14. It's too much like going back to school again.   T/F

15. It seemed to be mainly for the counsellor's benefit.   T/F

16. Self-help assignments have no place in counselling.   T/F

17. Because of the progress I've made, these assignments are likely to be of no further benefit to me.   T/F

18. Because these assignments have not been helpful in the past, I couldn't see the point of doing this one.   T/F

19. I don't agree with this particular approach to counselling.   T/F

20. OTHER REASONS (please write them in).

Training in rational emotive behaviour therapy

1. For further details of training courses in REBT in Britain, contact:

   (a) UK Centre for Rational Emotive Behaviour Therapy
       Broadway House, 3 High Street,
       Bromley BR1 1LF

       Tel: 020 8228 1185
       Fax: 020 8228 1186
       Course bookings: 020 8318 4448

       www.managingstress.com
       admin@ukrebt.com

   (b) Postgraduate Admissions Office
       Goldsmiths College
       New Cross
       London SE14 6NW

       020 7919 7171 (ask for Postgraduate Admissions)

       admissions@gold.ac.uk

   (c) The Centre for REBT at The University of Birmingham
       UK Affiliate of the Albert Ellis Institute
       School of Psychology
       University of Birmingham
       Edgbaston
       Birmingham B15 2TT

       Tel: 0121 678 3115
       Fax: 0121 678 3163

       www.rebt.bham.ac.uk

2. For further details of training courses in REBT worldwide, contact:

Training Co-ordinator
Albert Ellis Institute
45 East 65th Street
New York
NY 10021
USA

Tel: 001 212 535 0822

www.albertellisinstitute.org

References

Bandura, A. (1977) *Social Learning Theory*. Englewood Cliffs, NJ: Prentice-Hall.

Beck, A.T. (1976) *Cognitive Therapy and the Emotional Disorders*. New York: International Universities Press.

Beck, A.T., Rush, A.J., Shaw, B.F., & Emery, G. (1979) *Cognitive Therapy of Depression*. New York: Guilford.

Bernard, M.E., & Wolfe, J. (Eds) (2000) *Rational Emotive Behavior Therapy: A Resource Guide for Practitioners*. 2nd Edition. New York: Albert Ellis Institute

Blackburn, I., & Davidson, K. (1990) *Cognitive Therapy for Depression and Anxiety: A Practitioner's Guide*. Oxford: Blackwell Scientific.

Bordin, E. (1979) The generalizability of the concept of the working alliance. *Psychotherapy: Theory, Research and Practice,* **16**, 252–260.

DiGiuseppe, R. (1991a) A rational–emotive model of assessment. In: M.E. Bernard (Ed.), *Using Rational–Emotive Therapy Effectively*. New York: Plenum.

DiGiuseppe, R. (1991b) Comprehensive cognitive disputing in rational-emotive therapy. In: M.E. Bernard (Ed.), *Using Rational-Emotive Therapy Effectively*. New York: Plenum.

DiGiuseppe, R., Leaf, R., & Linscott, J. (1993) The therapeutic relationship in rational–emotive therapy: Some preliminary data. *Journal of Rational–Emotive and Cognitive-Behavior Therapy,* **11**, 223–233.

Dryden, W. (1985) Dilemmas in giving warmth or love to clients: An interview with Albert Ellis. In: W. Dryden, *Therapists' Dilemmas*. London: Harper & Row.

Dryden, W. (1986) Vivid RET. In: A. Ellis & R. Grieger (Eds), *Handbook of Rational–Emotive Therapy, Volume 2*. New York: Springer.

Dryden, W. (1987) *Current Issues in Rational-Emotive Therapy*. Beckenham, Kent: Croom Helm.

Dryden, W. (1988) Language and meaning in rational-emotive therapy. In: W. Dryden & P. Trower (Eds), *Developments in Rational-Emotive Therapy*. Milton Keynes: Open University Press.

Dryden, W. (Ed.) (1989) *Howard Young – Rational Therapist: Seminal Papers in Rational-Emotive Therapy*. Loughton, Essex: Gale Centre Publications.

Dryden, W. (Ed.) (1990) *The Essential Albert Ellis*. New York: Springer.

Dryden, W. (1991) *Reason and Therapeutic Change*. London: Whurr.

Dryden, W. (1994a) *Progress in Rational Emotive Behaviour Therapy*. London: Whurr.

Dryden, W. (1994b) *Ten Steps to Positive Living*. London: Sheldon.

Dryden, W. (1994c) *Overcoming Guilt*. London: Whurr.

Dryden, W. (1996) *Overcoming Anger*. London: Sheldon.

Dryden, W. (1997) *Overcoming Shame*. London: Sheldon.

Dryden, W. (1999a) *Rational Emotive Behavioural Counselling in Action*. 2nd edition. London: Sage.

Dryden, W. (1999b) *How to Accept Yourself*. London: Sheldon.

Dryden, W. (2000) *Invitation to Rational Emotive Behavioural Psychology*. 2nd edition. London: Whurr.

Dryden, W. (2001) *Reason to Change: A Rational Emotive Behaviour Therapy (REBT) Workbook*. Hove, East Sussex: Brunner-Routledge.

Dryden, W. (2002) *Overcoming Envy*. London: Sheldon.

Dryden, W., Ferguson, J., & Clark, A. (1989) Beliefs and inferences – a test of a rational–emotive hypothesis: 2. On the prospect of seeing a spider. *Psychological Reports*, **64**, 115–123.

Dryden, W., & Gordon, J. (1993) *Beating the Comfort Trap*. London: Sheldon.

Dryden, W., & Trower, P. (Eds) (1989) *Cognitive Psychotherapy: Stasis and Change*. London: Cassell.

Ellis, A. (1963) Toward a more precise definition of 'emotional' and 'intellectual' insight. *Psychological Reports*, **23**, 538–540.

Ellis, A. (1976) The biological basis of human irrationality. *Journal of Individual Psychology*, **32**, 145–168.

Ellis, A. (1983) The philosophic implications and dangers of some popular behavior therapy techniques. In: M. Rosenbaum, C.M. Franks & Y. Jaffe (Eds), *Perspectives in Behavior Therapy in the Eighties*. New York: Springer.

Ellis, A. (1994) *Reason and Emotion in Psychotherapy*. Revised and Expanded Edition. New York: Birch Lane Press.

Ellis, A (2001) *Feeling Better, Getting Better, Staying Better*. Atascadero, CA: Impact.

Ellis, A. (2002) *Overcoming Resistance: A Rational Emotive Behavior Therapy Integrated Approach*. 2nd Edition. New York: Springer.

Ellis, A., & Dryden, W. (1997) *The Practice of Rational Emotive Behavior Therapy*. 2nd edition. New York: Springer.

Gilmore, I. (1986) An exposition and development of the debate on the nature of the distinction between appropriate and inappropriate beliefs in rational-emotive therapy. *Journal of Rational-Emotive Therapy*, **4**(2), 155–165.

Golden, W.L. (1989) Resistance and change in cognitive-behaviour therapy. In: W. Dryden & P. Trower (Eds), *Cognitive Psychotherapy: Stasis and Change*. London: Cassell.

Hauck, P. (1991) *Hold Your Head Up High*. London: Sheldon.

Mahrer, A.R. (Ed.) (1967) *The Goals of Psychotherapy*. New York: Appleton–Century–Crofts.

Maluccio, A.N. (1979) *Learning from Clients: Interpersonal Helping as Viewed by Clients and Social Workers*. New York: Free Press.

Neenan, M., & Dryden, W. (1999) *Rational Emotive Behaviour Therapy: Advances in Theory and Practice*. London: Whurr.

Neenan, M., & Dryden, W. (2002) *Cognitive Behaviour Therapy: An A–Z of Persuasive Arguments*. London: Whurr.

Rogers, C.R. (1957) The necessary and sufficient conditions of therapeutic personality change. *Journal of Consulting Psychology*, **21**, 95–103.

Sacco, W.P. (1981) Cognitive therapy in vivo. In: G. Emery, S.D. Hollon & R.C. Bedrosian (Eds), *New Directions in Cognitive Therapy*. New York: Guilford.

Segal, J. (1993) Against self-disclosure. In: W. Dryden (Ed.), *Questions and Answers on Counselling in Action*. London: Sage.

Walen, S.R., DiGiuseppe, R., & Dryden, W. (1992) *A Practitioner's Guide to Rational-Emotive Therapy*. 2nd edition. New York: Oxford University Press.

Yankura. J., & Dryden, W. (1990) *Doing RET: Albert Ellis in Action*. New York: Springer.

Young, H.S. (1974) *A Rational Counseling Primer*. New York: Albert Ellis Institute.

Index

Note: The abbreviation REBT is used for Rational Emotive Behaviour Therapy